The Emergence of the Neo-Satanist Church

A Comparison with the Theology of the Prosperity, Hillsong, Word-of-Faith, and New Apostolic Reformation Movements

By Anthony Uyl MTS

Devoted Publshing
Ingersoll, Ontario, Canada 2025

The Emergence of the Neo-Satanist Church
A Comparison with the Theology of the Prosperity, Hillsong, Word-of-Faith, and New Apostolic Reformation Movements
By Anthony Uyl _{MTS}

The text of The Emergence of the Neo-*Satanist Church*: *A Comparison with the Theology of the Prosperity, Hillsong, Word-of-Faith, and New Apostolic Reformation Movements* is all protected under Copyright ©2025 Devoted Publishing. The covers, background, layout and Devoted Publishing logo are Copyright ©2025 Devoted Publishing. This edition is published by Devoted Publishing a division of 2165467 Ontario Inc.

For details on CC-BY of Chapter One: go to http://creativecommons.org/licenses/by/4.0/.

All quoted material has been kept within Fair Use in the United States, and Fair Dealing within the United Kingdom and Australia. Other quoted material is kept within the copyright restrictions of the country of origin or as indicated by the publisher on the publisher's website. Any believed infringement of these policies is not a challenge to the copyright status of the author or publisher in question.

Unless written permission is given for any material, all use of this material to be reproduced, stored in a retrieval system, or transmitted in any form by any means, electronic, mechanical, photocopying, recording or otherwise is forbidden. All rights reserved.

Unless otherwise noted, all scriptures are from The Holy Bible, English Standard Version®, Copyright© 2001 by Crossway, a publishing ministry of Good News Publishers. Used by permission.

Scripture quotations marked (NIV) are taken from The Holy Bible, New International Version®. Copyright© 1973, 1978, 1984, 2011 by Biblica, Inc.™. Used by permission of Zondervan

Scripture quotations taken from the (NASB®) New American Standard Bible®, Copyright © 1960, 1971, 1977, 1995, 2020 by The Lockman Foundation. Used by permission. All rights reserved. lockman.org

Scripture quotations marked (KJV) are taken from the King James Version, public domain.

Scripture quotations taken from the (LSB®) Legacy Standard Bible®, Copyright © 2021 by The Lockman Foundation. Used by permission. All rights reserved. Managed in partnership with Three Sixteen Publishing Inc. LSBible.org and 316publishing.com.

Scripture quotations marked (CLV) are taken from the Clementine Latin Vulgate, public domain.

Scripture quotations marked MSG are taken from The Message, copyright © 1993, 2002, 2018 by Eugene H. Peterson. Used by permission of NavPress, represented by Tyndale House Publishers. All rights reserved.

Drop Cap and Table of Contents fonts are AnglicanText by Typographer Mediengestaltung and used under a Free For Commercial Use License (FFC).

ISBN: 978-1-77356-527-9

Contact Us Online:
Email: devotedpub@hotmail.com.com
Authors' X (Formerly Twitter): @AnthonyDevPub
Authors' Instagram: @uylanthony

Table of Contents

Dedication – 5
Introduction – 7
Chapter I: An Academic Article to Read First – 11
    1 James and the Path toward Heterodoxy – 11
    2 James and Royal Occultism – 19
    3 The Devil and the King – 23
Chapter II: Analysis – 27
Chapter III: Defining Esotericism – 33
    Ideology of Merkavah Mysticism – 35
    Ideology of the Right-Hand Path – 39
Chapter IV: Defining Satanism – 47
    The Gnostic Roots – 47
    The Biblical Truth – 49
    Back to Defining Satanism – 49
Chapter V: This is Spiritual Warfare. They Are Not People. They Are Demons. – 63
    The New Inquisition – 66
Chapter VI: An Example of Hillsong's Music Coming from the Occult – 69
    Brian Houston and the Occult – 71
    Andrew Denton and the Occult – 79
    Darlene Zschech and the Occult – 87
    Chris Tomlin and the Occult – 97
Chapter VII: Defining Necromancy – 101
    Zschech and Tomlin Teaching As Above, So Below and Necromancy – 101
    Exegeting Leviticus 19:31 – 104
    Exegeting Deuteronomy 18:9–14 – 105
    Exegesis of Isaiah 8:16-22 – 108
    Exegeting Isaiah 19:1–4 – 109
    Conclusion – 112
Chapter VIII: Lilith – 113
Chapter IX: The Age of Aquarius, Klaus Schwab, the Order of Nine Angles, and the Eschatology of Prosperity, Word of Faith, and the New Apostolic Reformation Movements – 131
    The Age of Aquarius – 131
    Klaus Schwab – 137
    The Order of Nine Angles – 140
    The Neo-Satanist Eschatological Beliefs Revealed – 148
        Back to the Statements of the Satanist Churches – 165
        Kabbalistic Children by Sexual Rites – 169

    Bringing this Entire Chapter Together – 174
Chapter X: The Flawed Argument of the "Doctrinal Smell Test" – 177
    Do These Pass the Doctrinal Smell Test? – 178
    Why Do Churches Use This Stuff Then? – 182
    Conclusion – 183
Conclusion: Call Your Leaders to Repent – 187
Bibliography – 191

Dedication

I dedicate this book to Evelyn, when I was going through my own personal "tribulation" in 2022, you offered support in the small way that you did and I thank you. At the same time, getting to know you during that time, like you, I realized that God's truth and his church are worth fighting for. Without getting to know you, this fight may not have continued and this book would not have happened. Thank you.

My message to anyone, like Evelyn taught me: When it comes to God's truth and his church, keep fighting, even if you are no longer able to stand, keep fighting. Never willingly let the demonic win.

INTRODUCTION

Back in 1999, a movie was released that shook most of the Western world. While the overall philosophy of the movie is not important, there are two related scenes in particular I want to draw attention to.

In the movie, after living in a hell-like apocalypse world, an ally of the protagonists of the movie turns to the main villain to make a deal. In the first scene of the betrayal, this former ally is holding up a piece of steak in a fancy restaurant and comments that he knows the steak is not real. This former ally is commenting that everything about it is a fake simulation, and he knows that. Suddenly, the former ally puts that piece of steak in his mouth and says, "Ignorance is bliss."

Suddenly, the scene shifts to the main antagonist of the movie. The former ally promises that he will give the antagonist anything he wants if the villain will put the former ally back into this fake world and not remember anything about the apocalyptic world he comes from. After some negotiating, the former ally, a man codenamed, "Cypher", agrees to deliver the leader of his group to the villain.

In a later scene, where the main hero of the story is taken to another person inside the fake world for guidance, the team is attacked by enemies and Cypher manages to escape. Once he is back into the apocalyptic world, the rest of the team stuck in a computer simulation, Cypher starts to murder the other members of the team, in order to hand the leader of the group over the to villain.

Some of you may have guessed that the movie was the box-office hit The Matrix starring Keanu Reeves. The character, Cypher, was willing to do whatever it took to get back to a state of ignorance where reality is not an issue. The facts did not matter to him, he wanted to live in an illusion where he was not responsible for his own ignorance of the truth.

Unfortunately, the church, even "biblical" churches are much in the same situation today. While they will argue that they in no way agree with Hillsong, Bethel, Elevation, Tomlin or any of the other Word-of-Faith (WoF), New Apostolic Reformation (NAR), or prosperity churches and their affiliated artists, the problem is that these same churches have absolutely no problem playing their music on Sunday mornings. Some churches will have no restriction whatever and play whatever songs they want. Some churches will put it through some kind of review board to see which ones have "good words" otherwise known at the Doctrinal Smell Test.

While I have written articles that have proven the Doctrinal Smell Test to be faulty, that the music cannot be redeemed, and that the music is all intended for extremely occultic purposes since all the churches and artists in these movements have a theological view that is the same as theistic-Satanism, still many people are resisting the truth.

They are ready to do anything to remain ignorant even to the point of telling people not to come back to their churches until they are willing to submit to that music.

There are two arguments that are used despite the "words are good" argument. That, like the government, they are not responsible for the way the money is spent. Unfortunately, taxes to the government are required, paying the money to Faithlife's "Proclaim" or other Christian Copyright distributors is not.

These churches will also use the argument that "they did not know." Unfortunately, that is a ridiculous argument. Why? Under no worldly government is ignorance of the law an excuse. So, no surprise that Romans 1 makes it clear that no one can claim to be ignorant of God, or sin. We as humans, have the responsibility, to study the Bible and know what is true and what is not, what is sin and what is not. Since these churches, since even before the internet was like it is today, the resources that allowed us to see what these churches believe have always been out, yet, we have chosen to continue to be ignorant and use that as an excuse.

However, ignorance is no longer an option.

After reading through Elle Hardy's *Beyond Belief: How Pentecostal Christianity is Taking Over the World* I have come to realize there is a much bigger problem here. Looking through the documents and books that Hardy references, the problem is unfortunate to a degree that we can no longer turn a blind, emotional, eye to the problem.

To be quite honest: the reality behind what that money is being used for, that using that music in church generates, and the causes that are being supported by these same churches pretty much amount to things such as being an accomplice to terrorism and war crimes. Seriously. If you do not believe me wait, I will provide the evidence for what I am saying. Just a warning, it is grim and does not speak well of the church in the future if things do not change immediately.

Honestly, it is so abhorrent, that church leaders and music teams that have actively promoted and enforced the use of this music in that they have enacted church discipline on those that refuse to be involved in this occultic, and murderous, music, need to stand up and publicly repent of what they have done and what they have been supporting. Like Cypher, some church leaders, elders, and music team leaders are willing to do quite literally anything to preserve their fake ignorance and moral superiority in using this garbage.

Chapter I: An Academic Article to Read First

So, here is a lengthy academic article to read about King James I, the same King James that commissioned the King James Bible. He argues for his divine right to rule as he wills and that he is above the law. James argues that he is even above laws that he put in place. To understand why this is important I have included the entire article. Note that I have chosen to keep the footnote formatting the same as it was in the original article.

The original article was published by De Gruyter in *Pólemos* 2022; 16(1): 9–23 and is CC-BY. The original document can be found at:

https://doi.org/10.1515/pol-2022-2002

Political Theology from Satan to Legitimacy

By Pier Giuseppe Monateri[1]

Abstract: Political theology is often the subject of debate. In this contribution we will trace an alternative declination of this concept in modern political thought. Starting from James I's thought, the article will show the most arcane and heterodox sides of sovereignty and the multiple configurations of the political body. Keywords: political theology, heterodoxy, royal occultism, demonology, sovereignty

1 James and the Path toward Heterodoxy

Along with the classic tradition of political theology, a very different synthesis with direct reference to Eusebius of Caesarea (265–340), can be found in the works of the intellectual King James I (1566–1625), who composed *The True Law of Free Monarchies*, and circu-

---

1. Corresponding author: Pier Giuseppe Monateri, University of Torino, Torino, Italy, E-mail: pier.monateri@unito.it

lated it as an anonymous work in 1598.² Identifying the two targets of James as King of Scotland is rather simple. On one side, he would hit John Knox (1505–1572) and the Presbyterians for their theory that the king was bound in his actions by an original covenant with the people. On the other side, he would combat the Catholics submitting the sovereign to the direct or indirect control of the Roman pontiff.³

As King of England, he endeavored to fight against the Puritans and the common lawyers. This last point must be strictly scrutinized, since the common lawyers, in contrast to the Catholics, the Presbyterians and the Puritans, were not a sect or a religious group, but their tenets were, rather obviously, the most dangerous of all for a monarch of his kind. Indeed, the definition of English law as the "law of the land", which today goes practically unnoticed, implies that it is not the king's law.

In his cited book as well as in his speech in Parliament of March 21, 1609, James I designed a sketch of a royal sovereignty of supernatural origin, otherwise known as the divine right of kings. He described it as a form of perfect government because it was the closest to the divine archetype that could not be limited by any other earthly power.⁴ Three are the pillars of this royal authority: divine revelation, the laws of nature, and the laws of the *realm*.

The first pillar is based on Ps. 82.6 "*ego dixi dii estis*" (I say that you are gods), where according to His Majesty's interpretation, God is affirming that the kings are divine, and that, as in Luther, they can respond only to Him for their actions. The king's duty is that of administering justice (Ps. 101) and to give just laws to the people (2 Kings 18 and 22–23; 2 Chor. 29 and 34–35), to keep the peace (Ps. 72) and to be a good shepherd procuring abundance to his realm (1 Sam. 8; Ger. 29). As a minister, he is a servant of God for the good of all the righteous (Rm. 13, 1–7).

The second pillar is legal and historical and pertains particularly to the origins of the Scottish monarchy. In theory, we could imagine that the flock of the feeble convened to entrust their protection to the strongest under certain specified conditions. Until then the law would have preceded the institution of the monarchy. But story has it that King Fergus left Ireland to conquer a Scotland inhabited by barbar-

---

2. King James I was the author of works such as *Daemonologie* (1597), *The True Law of Free Monarchies* (1598) and *Basilikon Doron* (1599). See Charles McIlwain (ed), *The Political Works of James I* (Cambridge: Harvard University Press, 1918).

3. Francis Oakley, *The Watershed of Modern Politics. Law, Virtue, Kingship and Consent (1300–1650)* (New Haven: Yale University Press, 2015) 254.

4. James I, "Basilikon Doron", in Charles McIlwain (ed), *The Political Works of James I* 1–52.

ians to whom, after their defeat and submission, he gave his laws. It follows that it is the king who precedes the law and not vice versa, and that is why he has precedence over all other classes, the parliament and its laws. As a necessary consequence, the kings make the laws, and it is not the laws that make the kings.[5] A sovereign will always try to remain faithful to his laws, but in no way is he bound by them. He can act as he wishes without being questioned by any jurisdiction.

A third argument advanced in the name of the law of nature is as follows: a king is like a father to his people, or like a head to the body; in both cases he is leading the subordinate parts of the whole. Just as a father can punish a son for the sake of the family, so can the head cut an arm off for the salvation of the whole body. It is understood that the body could not reciprocally cut the head off, even if sick, for it would immediately perish.[6]

His conclusion is almost apparent. Obedience is always due to a sovereign king as he has been enthroned by God. He is also owed guardianship of the faith in accord with the Act of Supremacy of Henry VIII (1534). He is the rightful and legitimate head of the Church of England, and has full power to reprise, punish, reform, rule, correct and amend all the mistakes, heresies and abuses for the glory of the Christian religion and for the keeping of the union and peace of the realm.

As has been noted, the political theology of James I seems to be based on two apparently inconsistent premises.[7] On one hand, the king is clearly bound to realize the good of the kingdom, and he is responsible for it. Then there would be a divine order establishing what is right or wrong on Earth and would sanction every deviation, even those of a king. Right and wrong, good and evil have been laid down by God, *before* the institution of civil governments and the elevation of monarchs so that justice does not depend on the king's will. An arbitrary monarch becomes a tyrant and an enemy of God's justice. We could well say that for James a monarch is free because 'he does not recognize any other power on Earth above himself' (Job 41:25). No one on Earth has jurisdiction over him. This contradiction leads to an inescapable conclusion: the sovereign must obey God's laws, but on Earth, his laws are God's laws. There is no *residue* left from the heavenly order to the worldly political one. The latter is perfectly mirroring the former, and the former is completely transfused in the latter. The world order is a hierarchy of jurisdictions and obedience

---

5. James I, "The True Law of Free Monarchies", in Charles McIlwain (ed), *The Political Works of James I* 53–70.

6. James I, "The True Law of Free Monarchies" 64–66.

7. Merio Scattola, *Teologia politica* (Bologna: Il Mulino, 2007) 82.

designed by God. There is no disjuncture, nor discontinuity between the temporal and the spiritual. Only the king knows what is good and evil and when and how to act. The only duty of the subjects is to obey.

At this point, we can certainly trace an important parallel with the work of Jean Bodin (1530–1596), and especially his reception in Germany, even if we may find in these matters an obviously much more complex and baroque evolution toward the metaphysics of metaphors applied to political theory.[8] The world political order described by these authors becomes indeed a *representation* of the divine order of the universe. This point is rather important from an ontological perspective. The Roman Emperor was the Lord of the World. The Byzantine Emperor was the *ikon*, the true image of God on Earth, participating in His essence. German emperors became figures of the Christ or the Anti-Christ. Now the world could start to be seen as a theatre, the physical space of a representation of invisible characters and forces. The king re-presents God, making Him present again.

As Walter Benjamin has noted, there is an ontological side in a metaphor as a metaphor is an experience.[9] We can read the original passage on the *Dominus Mundi* in the Digest either in the sense that the Roman emperor is the master of the world or in the sense that he is like the Lord of it. But what does it really mean that he is a *representation* of the Lord?

Here we touch upon the existence of invisible entities that become visible even if they are not *incarnated* by someone. A king is not an incarnation of some invisible entity; rather, he is a representation, no less than parliaments are representations of the people. We turn toward a world theatre that is essentially an aesthetic world, where aesthetics is to be thought of as the dimension in which something invisible becomes visible. The matter is then, as we think James likely understood, that of the *residue* that can separate that which is represented and that which is representing. For his theory of sovereignty, it was essential that no residue could be left in the king's performance of God's role on Earth. Any possible residue would operate politically and legally in the very possibility of a jurisdiction over the king's acts, if not finally in the possibility of his execution for high treason.

James's theological reflections can be seen in the context of strongly alternative and competing political and constitutional theories. This is especially so against the background of those murky discussions

---

8. Michael Stolleis, 'La reception de Bodin en Allemagne' *Quaderni fiorentini* 24 (1995) 141.

9. Walter Benjamin, *The Origin of German Tragic Drama* (London: Verso, 2009). See also Bainard Cowan, "Benjamin's Theory of Allegory" *New German Critique* 22 (1981) 109.

which have characterized the definition of emergency powers and of the king's different *personae*. This debate bypasses the problem of the Stuarts' presumed despotism,[10] and must be fully appreciated in relation to the revival of the imperial mysticism grounded upon the notion of *dominium mundi*.

From our perspective, the judgment delivered in 1606 by Chief Baron Fleming in the *Bate's Case* is of critical importance.[11] At its heart lies the crucial remark that Fleming made about the "absolute" and "ordinary" powers of the king, and we will give this remark the close scrutiny it deserves.

From this case, it emerges that the king's power is double, both ordinary and absolute, and that these two powers have several and different laws and ends. Ordinary powers are possessed for the *particular* profit of the *subjects*, the execution of civil justice in ordinary courts, and are nominated by the civilians under the rubric of the *jus privatum*. In England, these powers belong to the realm of the common law.[12] These laws cannot be changed without a parliamentary vote, yet they can never really be changed in substance, as they seem to express rather universal and immutable principles of justice.

On the contrary, the *absolute* power of the King is that which is applied for the general benefit of the *people*, for the *salus populi*: as the people are the body, and the king is the head.[13] It follows that this power is most properly named "Policy and Government". As the constitution of the body of the people varies with time, so too does this "absolute law" vary according to the wisdom of the king and for the common good.

There is then an absolute and a common law, as there are ordinary and absolute powers, a distinction that already appeared in the Year Book for 1469 under the Latin names of *potentia ordinata* and *absoluta*.[14]

Of course, here we face a distinction destined to have great impact.

---

10. Geoffrey Elton, *England under the Tudors* (London: Routledge, 1960) 403; Francis Oakley "Jacobean Political Theology: The Absolute and Ordinary Powers of the King" *Journal of the History of Ideas* 29 (1968) 323, 346.

11. *Bate's Case or Case of Impositions* [1606] 2 State Trial 371; see also James W. Allen, *English Political Thought*, 1603–1660 (London, Methuen & Co, 1938) 8.

12. Francis Oakley "Jacobean Political Theology: the Absolute and Ordinary Powers of the King" 327.

13. *Money Case* [1637] in Thomas Howell (ed), *A Complete Collection of State Trials and Proceedings for High Treason and Other Crimes and Misdemeanors from the Earliest Period to the Year 1783, with Notes and Other Illustrations*, vol 2 (London: Longman, Hurst, Rees, Orme and Brown, 1816) 389.

14. Year Book 9, Edward IV, Trinity 9; F Oakley, "Jacobean Political Theology: the Absolute and Ordinary Powers of the King" 324.

It was Dr. James Cowell, Professor of Civil Law at Cambridge, who in 1607 described the king as supra legem because of his absolute powers, reigning beyond the ordinary course of the common law.[15]

In the words of Davies, Attorney General for Ireland, the king exercises a double power, namely, an absolute power, or *merum Imperium*, when he 'doth use Prerogatives only, which is not bound by positive law',[16] and an ordinary power of jurisdiction. Moreover, as we know, following James, Blackstone paralleled these prerogatives with the *mysteries* of the *bona dea*, ranking them among the *arcana imperii*. In particular, Blackstone reaches the point of speaking of a necessary "initiation" into the mysteries of the royal prerogatives.[17]

Through this distinction between *potestas ordinata* and *potestas absoluta*, we can conceive of the king as *having a large and indefinite reserve of power*, which he could on *occasion* use for the benefit of the state.[18] Significantly, the existence of that reserve of power goes beyond definition, constitution and words, as awe and charisma, as a *sublime* political power to deal with matters of state. As hidden powers, they are *mysteries*. This hidden and unspeakable *residue* constitutes the essence of the political sublime. This is the most important point.

The shift toward an *occultism* of royal prerogatives was widespread. It goes far beyond the neutralizing concept of *absolutism* by which we normally try to capture this form of monarchy. Absolutism is, rather, a royal occultism. As we know, Baldus[19] spoke of the prince as being capable of derogating from the ordinary right by his absolute power, *though* not from the laws of "God and of nature", in this sense using the same words as Spinoza and his devastating formula of *Deus sive Natura*, whose implications are still to be fully apprehended. It is not just a matter of emphasis on Roman law, or the revival of forms used by Cynus of Pistoia or Bartolus.[20] As Oakley reports, Baldus also had introduced the terms absolute and ordinary in his gloss on the *Lex*

---

15. Francis Oakley, *Kingship: the Politics of Enchantment* (Malden: Blackwell Publishing, 2006) 129.

16. John Davies, The Question Concerning Impositions, Tonnage, Poundage ... Fully Stated and Argued from Reason, Law and Policy (London: H Twyford, 1656) 30–31; see Oakley, "Jacobean Political Theology" 325.

17. William Blackstone, *Commentaries on the Laws of England, Volume 1: A Facsimile of the First Edition of 1765–1769* (Chicago: The University of Chicago Press, 1979) book 1, ch 7, 231.

18. Charles McIlwain, *Constitutionalism Ancient and Modern* (London: The Lawbook Exchange, 2005) 94.

19. Baldus [Cod 1.14.4].

20. Bartolus, *Commentaria in primam Codicis partem* (Venetiis: Baptista de Tortis, 1493) fol 36; Cynus of Pistoia, *Lectura super aurea volumine Codicis* (Venetiis: Andrea de Thoresanis de Asula, 1493) fol b 8 v; see Oakley, "Jacobean Political Theology" 330.

Digna (Cod 1.14.4) in an attempt to clarify that the prince was bound to live according to the laws out of his benevolence, not out of necessity. The point – for us – is rather the sovereign possessing an occult dimension that supersedes orthodox political theologies.

All of this is lost in the standard accounts of Romanists for the good reason that, to a large extent, it was the *canon* law that deeply influenced conceptions of modern sovereignty. The insertion of canonist principles into the body of Roman law led to a kind of *double modality* in the exercise of sovereign powers: a modality – to use the words of Oakley – running in accordance with the common law, or the common course of nature; and an exercise of the *plenitudo potestatis*, or of the *special* providence of the Lord. We could say that, according to these speculations, in God and in the pope resides a plenitude of power, a residue of an undefinable power to act.

This residue is the one that Schmitt tried to capture in his analogies between the state of exception and miracles. God can act outside the laws of nature and perform a miracle, just as when He did when He enabled Shadrach, Meshach, and Abednego to emerge unscathed from the flames of Nebuchadnezzar's fiery furnace.[21] In the same way, the pope can perform a papal miracle[22] by an exercise of his absolute power. But can a king perform miracles? It is hard not to see here a strong heterodox normative inversion where that which is unorthodox becomes political.

Of course, we may find several references[23] to the omnipotence of God in St. Jerome (347–420), through Gratian (359–383) and St. Peter Damian (1007–1073), in Hugo of Saint Victor (1096–1141), Peter Abelard (1079–1142), Peter Lombard (1096–1160) and in William of Ockham (1280–1349). Albert the Great (1200–1280) was, perhaps, the first scholastic to have used the precise distinction between *potentia absoluta* and *potentia ordinata*.[24] Given this theoretical background and the revival of theological concepts in the twentieth century, what distinguishes Schmitt's conception of political theology from the medieval discourse is his neutralization of the pure political dimension of modern sovereignty. For us, his theory is a conscious *cover up* of the change in values that occurred after the Reformation. Its real purpose is to reactivate Roman Catholicism and its philosophical-his-

---

21. Daniel 3:20 ff.
22. See Oakley, "Jacobean Political Theology" 333 with reference to Aegidius Romanus, *De ecclesiastica potestate* (Richard Scholz ed, Weimar, Hermann Bohlaus Nachfolger, 1929) 158 and 192.
23. For all references see Oakley, "Jacobean Political Theology" 334.
24. Francis Oakley, *Politics and Eternity: Studies in the History of Medieval and Early Modern Political Thought* (Leiden: Brill, 1999) 261.

torical tradition against the heterodox political forces that prevailed in modernity.

If we place the sovereign as the *locus* of exception, his position lies on the threshold where the *Dominus*, the guardian of order, merges with Belial, the angel of anomy (2 Cortinthians 6:15). We could say that the angel of anomy operates in a state of exception, in an extraordinary state of affairs. In his *Speech of the Star Chamber* in 1616 on his prerogatives, James placed a particular emphasis on the "extraordinary".[25]

There are multiple examples from this age. In 1528, Henry VIII asked for a dispensation to proceed with a second marriage, something that the pope could not do using his ordinary power, but that, the king claimed, he could dispense out of his *mere* and *absolute* power above the law.[26] But, we insist, it is one thing to ask the pope to act in a miraculous way; it is another to take possession of the extraordinary and locate it at the center of political sovereignty as the power to act *praeter legem vel contra eam* (beyond and against law).[27]

As we have already seen, Bartolus elaborated on this dichotomy in his representation of the figure of the *Dominus Mundi*. Nevertheless, as long as we speak of the exceptional powers of the pope, we remain in the realm of orthodoxy. When we start to speak of the circumstances by which the king can do things *de facto* which he cannot do *de jure*, and especially when we clearly speak of a reserve of power possessed by the king for extraordinary cases[28] (or as Charleton put it in 1652, a royal "reserved power"[29]), we get out of the pure economy of salvation. We face an explicit normative inversion, either in relation to the pope, or in relation to the emperor. It is in this perspective that we can really appreciate the work of Bloch as an antithesis to Schmitt's efforts to bridge the disjuncture between prior theological concepts and those of the modern theory of law and the state.

Certainly, royal prerogatives derive from the consideration that God Himself has created a general law of nature, but he has made no law for miracles. There is no logically necessary connection between

---

25. James I, "Speech of the Star Chamber" (1616) in Charles McIlwain (ed), *The Political Works of James I* 333; and see Blackstone, *Commentaries on the Law of England*, book 1, ch 7, 231.

26. Henry VIII, "Instructions to Sir Francis Bryan and Peter Vannes, Rome" in John Brewer (ed), *Letters and Papers, Foreign and Domestic of the Reign of Henry VIII*, vol 4 (London: Royal Commission for State Papers, 1870) part 2, n 4977, 2158.

27. Oakley, "Jacobean Political Theology" 334.

28. James I, "A Speech to the Lords and Commons of the Parliament at White-Hall" (1609), in Charles McIlwain (ed), *The Political Works of James I* 309–310.

29. Walter Charleton, *The Darkness of Atheism Dispelled by the Light of Nature: a Physico-Theological Treatise* [1652] (Bristol: Thoemmes, 2002) 329.

this premise and the conclusion that the prerogatives of the king, like those of God, clearly transcend the ordinary. Indeed, there is a gap, a *Kluft*, between the two propositions, which is bridged over by an usurpation, legitimated by the fact that the sovereign must act *pro bono publico*. This is something that could be justified long before Christianity ever entered the stage of history. A political *refoulé* reemerges in the heterodoxy of modernity, not in orthodoxy. This heterodoxy was denied by political theology and the parallel created between earthly institutions and divine power. It was Schmitt who established a link between miracles and exception so stringent as to appear logical. The kings never had a government of exorcism or the miraculous. They had *magic* powers in Bloch's reconstruction, and this magic of the royals was transmuted into a theory of their power backed by theological prerogatives. The path from magic to theology is not a logical necessity, as magic is independent from theology. The disconnection between magic and theology could be bridged by the large and indefinite reserve of power that could be triggered by the exception, *ratione status*. This term, here, is not meant in the derived sense of *State reason*, but in the original sense of the necessary measures to be taken in *reason of the state of things*.

In this way, the exception is then located within the mysterious residue of indefinite power residing in the prerogatives of the Sovereign. That sublime and terrific reserve of power that can end up reversing the legal order.

2 James and Royal Occultism

From our standpoint, there is a still more occult side in James's thought that must be apprehended here. It has to do with the general framework of James's idea of order and the argument by correspondence between kings and God on which James leaned so heavily in his political writings,[30] and that can ultimately be deemed if not "blasphemy" certainly "heterodox".

This theory of the parallel, or theory of correspondence, between God as Dominus in heaven and the monarch as *Dominus* on Earth reached its ideological peak in the works of Dante where it was mingled with the imagery of the Roman people as the 'flesh' of the composite corporate body of the empire. According to us, this parallel took a rather heterodox turn starting with James, especially concerning the abyss of tacit powers.

The matter of royal prerogatives is echoed in both James's Star

---

30. William H. Greenleaf, "James the I and the Divine right of King" *Political Studies* 5 (1957) 36.

Chamber Speech in 1616 and earlier in 1609 in his important address to Parliament, which is central to understanding his particular political theory.[31] In the Star Chamber Speech, James clearly developed a mystical view of his powers:

> *The mysteries of the Kings power is not lawfully to be disputed…*
>
> *It would amount to take away to mystical reverence that belongs unto them that sit in the Throne of God.*[32]

This is a peculiarly heterodox position. Not even Frederick I could admit to sitting on the Throne of God, even if he proclaimed himself to be the Lord of the World and conceived his mission in messianic terms. Only the Son of Man (Mark 14:62; Daniel 7:13; Psalm 110:1) could have been elevated to the point of sitting in heaven with God on his *left*.

Once he established this heterodox correspondence, James considerably elaborated his ideas by the introduction of a further analogy between on the one hand, the absolute and ordinary powers of God, and, on the other, the absolute and ordinary, or regulated, powers of the king.

> *I desire you to give much more right in my private Prerogative, that you give to any Subject; and therein will I be acquiescent: As to the absolute Prerogative of the Crowne, that is no Subject for the tongue of a lawyer, nor is lawful to be disputed.*
>
> *As it is Atheisme and blasphemy to dispute what God can doe: good Christians content themselves with his will revealed in his word. So, it is presumption and high contempt in a Subject to dispute what a King can doe; but rest in that which is the Kings revealed will in his Law.*[33]

Here the distinction between the private prerogatives of the person of the monarch and the absolute prerogatives of the Crown is strikingly clear. James's argument relies on a metonymy where the king is represented by the *objective* nature of kingship, which is the crown, and not the person of the king. In this sense, kingship is elevated beyond the holder. We can also stress the value of the term *"absolute"* from its meaning of a power being beyond laws and regulations, to the very idea that this prerogative is *beyond words and language*.

---

31. Oakley, "Jacobean Political Theology2 337; Greenleaf, *Order, Empiricism and Politics: Two Traditions of English Political Thought: 1500–1700* (Oxford: Oxford University Press, 1964) 58 ff.

32. James I, "Speech of the Star Chamber" (1616) in Charles McIlwain (ed), *The Political Works of James I* 333.

33. James I, "Speech of the Star Chamber" (1616) 333–34.

In substance, for James it would have been blasphemy to try to ontologize royal mysteries through the use of language, even if done by a lawyer, because not even a lawyer, an oracle of the law, or a *sacerdos* (in this view a priest of royal cult) can articulate those mysteries. Such absolute powers are ineffable. We are certainly shifting toward the aesthetic of the political sublime of modern royal authority in a way that we think would have been completely alien to previous medieval conceptions of the prince.

We would also highlight the distinction between the terms absolute and ordinary, something that offers a different perspective to the term absolute monarchy: if absolute is contrary to ordinary, it is because it is exceptional. Just as in the case of Innocent IV against Frederick II, the mystic of absolute power lies in the fact that it is simultaneously beyond law, beyond language and beyond the ordinary. It is the terrific unspeakable power that can manifest itself in a state of exception, or, if you prefer, in the midst of the storm as in the Book of Job. This power is so unfathomable that indeed, it does not belong, and cannot belong to an ordinary man and consequently, it is rhetorically transferred to the crown.

It is in this light that James's address to Parliament in 1609 must be understood, with all its surrounding hints of paganism:

> *Kings are justly called Gods, for that they exercise a manner or resemblance of Divine power upon earth.*[34]

If kings are justly called gods, can they command the spirits? Can they perform an exorcism? Do they also have jurisdiction over the fairy world? Given James's attitude toward witchcraft revealed in his *Demonologie*, these questions are not unfounded.

Oakley argued that the distinction between the absolute and ordinary powers of the king was in effect a piece of political theology, generated by the cognate distinction between absolute and ordinary powers of God that emerged in the scholastic theology of the twelfth century and subsequently survived as a commonplace.[35] Later he suggested considering that 16th and 17th century lawyers were thinking not in terms of two coordinate or parallel powers each confined by law to its proper sphere, but rather of two powers. One power (the absolute) was in essence superior to the other (the ordinary) and "in times of necessity" or for "reason of state" the former could transcend the latter, and, by reaching "above the ordinary course of the law",

---

34. James I, "A Speech to the Lords and Commons" 307.
35. Oakley, "The «Hidden» and «Revealed» Wills of James I: More Political Theology" 15 *Studia Gratiana* (1972) 367–368.

encroach upon its domain. This implied that there could have been the perception of a strong difference between the nature of one power and that of the other.

If we emphasize the distinction made by James, as we did, one power is mysterious, unlimited and "not lawful to be disputed", whereas the other is clearly fit for discussion, for it is "the Kings' revealed will in his law". In sum, we confront a revealed power and an occult power of the kings – the same distinction meaning, on one side, the "hidden" will of God, and on the other side, God's "revealed" will.

Here, we face a concealed, secret or hidden will of God and/or of the Sovereign, and a revealed will of God/Sovereign, that is revealed in the word of God contained in the Holy Scriptures, just as the will of the sovereign is revealed in his laws. This is along the same lines as an unorthodox Gnostic revelation of the existence of a hidden, or occult divine beyond the revealed truth of the scriptures. Even the laws have a visible revealed side but also a hidden occult side pertaining to the sublime of the legal. There is always occult excess, an unfathomable and unexhausted reserve of sense in political action and in the law. There is also something in the juridical-political domain which exceeds it, bypassing and superseding our capacities of verbalization, and which redirects us toward the excessive nature of the title of the Dominus Mundi. The occultism of the political and of hegemony goes far beyond its tentative capture in irenic notions of soft-power.[36]

The distinction between the absolute and ordinary powers had enjoyed a long history, as well as the parallel distinction between the *potentia Dei absoluta* and ordinata with which it was linked. The intent of this distinction was to stress the retention in the hands of God or of the king of an absolute, unlimited power whereby the ordinary dispositions of the law could be transcended.[37]

What we want to stress here is the connection with occultism, emphasized by the insistence on the dark side of law and politics, which was reserved for those who were initiated in its mysteries. After all, this was also at the root of the counterargument used by Coke (1552–1634) to deny the king in court: he was not initiated into the mysteries of the temple.[38] The mysteries cannot be deduced by reason, even we cannot know if the occult God has any resemblance to the

---

36. Joseph Nye, *Soft Power: The Means to Success in Foreign Politics* (New York: Public Affairs, 2009).

37. See W(illiam of) Ockham, *Quodlibeta Septem*, VI.1.1, nn 13–40, in Guglielmus de Ockham, *Opera Theologica*, vol 9 (New York: The Franciscan Institute of St. Bonaventure University, 1980) 585 f.

38. William Holdsworth, "Sir Edward Coke" *The Cambridge Law Journal* 5 (1935) 332.

revealed one. We call this device of a political occultism the too-much-ness device, as it is rooted both in Gramscian theory of hegemony as well as in other philosophical theories of the last century.

From certain passages of James's works we could derive Oakley's conclusion that:

> ...*the vital thing for man is to eschew futile speculation about the dispositions of God's hidden will, and to acquaint himself, instead, with that revealed will thereby God makes known to man the divine modus operandi in the moral sphere and in the economy of salvation*[39] [...]

...*but also* in the political sphere. James's conception that his subjects could not even discuss the royal prerogatives seems like the political equivalent of the philosophical statement that 'What we cannot speak about we must pass over in silence'.[40] This was particularly true here because for James to indulge in futile speculations about royal prerogatives was also a crime of treason: "As it is blasphemy... it is treason...".

We must literally pass over in silence what is unlawful to speak about, and that is the essence of *legitimate* power. Legitimacy is surrounded by its unfathomable occult nature.

3 The Devil and the King

At this point, however, more than James's conceptions of God in relation to the Crown Prerogative, it may be of great interest for us to analyze his theory of the devil. According to Orr, James's articulation of divine right kingship also served as a bulwark against the perceived *threat of the supernatural* to his rule, starting from the demonic threat to the peace and stability of his rule in Scotland, and the panics provoked by the spread of witchcraft in 1590–91 and 1596–97.[41]

Stuart Clark[42] was the first one to point out the political dimensions of early modern demonological writings. As we know, James was actively interested in witchcraft at a time when witches were seen as the devil's sworn servants, tacitly or formally covenanted to

---

39. Oakley, "The «Hidden» and «Revealed» Wills of James I" 373.

40. Ludwig Wittgenstein, *Tractatus Logicus-Philosophicus* (London: Kegan Paul, 1922) proposition n 7.

41. David Orr, "'God's Hangman': James VI, the Divine Right of Kings, and the Devil" *Reformation & Renaissance Review* 18 (2016) 137.

42. Stuart Clark, "King James's *Daemonologie*: Witchcraft and Kingship" in Sydney Anglo (ed), *The Damned Art: Essays in the Literature of Witchcraft* (London: Routledge & K Paul, 1977) 159; James Wormald, "The Witches, the Devil and the King" in Tom Brotherstone and David Ditchburn (eds), *Freedom and Authority: Scotland, c. 1050 – c. 1650: Historical and Historiographical Essays Presented to Grant G. Simpson* (East Linton: Tuckwell Press, 2001) 174–75.

a power other than that of God and his lawful lieutenant on Earth. Moreover, James was involved in the witch hunt, and in particular in the prosecution of North Berwick in 1590–99, taking a personal role in the interrogation of the accused witches.[43] We cannot overlook this element as it is well represented by his contemporaries and by Shakespeare, in particular in *Macbeth*. The regicide perpetrated in the drama represents the worst kind of treason because it originated in the prophecy of witches, and in the tacit pact that Macbeth formed with demonic instances in seeking to fulfill that prophecy.

In a way, we can say that James's reflections articulated a fully developed political theory serving to legitimize the king's role as God's chosen instrument for combating the devil, in a context where the theory of witchcraft evolved in strict connection with the events closely examined by Maxwell Stuart. We refer in particular to the connection between the circumstances of the North Berwick witch hunt and the troublesome Earl of Bothwell, a detail which also strongly interested Schmitt in his study on Hamlet.[44] In these trials, witnesses were collected to prove that the Devil appeared personally to his adepts, declaring that he hated the king, because James was the greatest enemy he had on Earth. It was not then by chance that in his theory of prerogatives, James asserted that the rights of kingship were strictly linked to the king being the child and servant of God.[45]

Indeed, James's *Demonologie* was written during the panics, a time that can easily be described in modern terms as a prolonged state of exception due to supernatural attacks against the peace of the realm. In his vision, in parallel with the theories of Bodin,[46] the kings enjoy a special immunity from the power of witchcraft by virtue of their divinely ordained offices, such that the witches are disarmed of their occult powers if brought face-to-face with the godly magistrate.

Here, we encounter the issue of control over evil spirits once again at work in political matters, as occurred during the discussions between Pope Gregory VII (1010–1085) and Emperor Henry IV (1050–1106), when the former denied the latter the authority to

---

43. Peter Maxwell-Stuart, *Satan's Conspiracy: Magic and Witchcraft in Sixteenth-century Scotland* (East Linton: Tuckwell Press, 2001); Peter Maxwell-Stuart, "King James's Experience of Witches, and the 1604 English Witchcraft Act" in James Newton and John Bath (eds), *Witchcraft and the Act of 1604* (Leiden: Brill, 2008) 31–46.

44. Carl Schmitt, *Hamlet or Hecuba. The Irruption of Time into Play* (Corvallis: Plutarch Press, 2006) 16.

45. Orr, "'God's hangman': James VI, the Divine Right of Kings, and the Devil" 142.

46. Orr, "'God's hangman': James VI, the Divine Right of Kings, and the Devil" 143.

practice exorcisms. On this point, James had strong opinions, as he believed that papally licensed exorcists were frauds, the holy water to be at best a cold shower and at worst blasphemous vanity.[47] For him, only inward sincere faith had any efficacy in holding the Devil at bay. But one of James's most intriguing speculations is on the theological justification for the existence of witches and their powers. The *Malleus Maleficarum* (1487)[48] – the most used book of instructions for judges during the witch hunt trials – had emphasized the notion of a divine permission for witchcraft in which God permitted the Devil and his followers to act in the world, but did not actively will them to do evil. Based on this view, it was possible to sustain that the demons that tormented Job were acting with God's permission. James operated consistently with the *Malleus Maleficarum*, asserting that witchcraft depended on the Devil but that his followers were acting as God's "hangmen" in the world.[49]

This notion, rightly emphasized by Orr in his study on James, became particularly relevant for a theory of world lordship through the thoughts expressed by the king in his treatise on *The True Law of Free Monarchies*.[50] The treatise can be seen as an attempt to re-legitimize James's kingship in the face of Buchanan's explosive legacy as interpreted by radical Presbyterians as a claim to a right of resistance,[51] some holding that kings could be deposed, exiled, and even executed should they fall into tyranny or *heresy*.[52] Indeed, a real Presbyterian *coup d'état* was attempted in Edinburgh in December 1596 during the witchcraft panic.[53]

The two rival claims, that of the divine right of kings, and that of an equally divine right of resistance against a tyrannical or heretic

---

47. James I, *Daemonologie, in Forme of a Dialogue, Divided into Three Bookes* (Edinburgh: Robert Waldegrave, 1597) 78.

48. Henricus Institoris (alias Jacob Sprenger), *Malleus Maleficarum* [1487] *The Hammer of Witches. A Complete Translation of the Malleus Malleficarum* (Cambridge: Cambridge University Press, 2009).

49. Lawrence Normand and Gareth Roberts (eds), *Witchcraft in Early Modern Scotland: James VI's Demonology and the North Berwick Witches* (Exeter: University of Exeter Press, 2000) 331; Orr, "'God's hangman': James VI, the Divine Right of Kings, and the Devil" 146.

50. James I, "The True Law of Free Monarchies", in Charles McIlwain (ed), *The Political Works of James I* 53 ff.

51. James Burns, *The True Law of Kingship: Concepts of Monarchy in Early-modern Scotland* (Oxford: The Clarendon Press, 1996) 234.

52. Orr, "'God's Hangman': James VI, the Divine Right of Kings, and the Devil" 146.

53. Julian Goodare, "The Attempted Scottish Coup of 1596" in Julian Goodare and Andrew MacDonald (eds), *Sixteenth Century Scotland. Essays in honour of M Lynch* (Leiden: Brill, 2008) 311–336.

monarch, came to clash on a supernatural level. In this context, James reaffirmed that the kings were *divinely appointed guardians* charged with combatting the Devil and his servants in the world, and that rebellion was very much like witchcraft, the work of the Devil acting in the world as God's hangman.[54]

This parallel is of extraordinary importance, bypassing the usual analogy traced between the government of heaven and that of the Earth, because it emphasises that it is the presence of the devil that legitimises the prerogatives of the kings. Rebellion and witchcraft are equated, and both are a crime against the king (not the Church) because the king is appointed in his political office as the guardian of demons. The political and the supernatural were perhaps never before so intertwined theoretically as they were in this passage of James's.

What then about the tyrant? James's answer is given in his *Basilikon doron*[55] where he affirms that only God could judge *wicked* kings and hold them accountable. The king, then, and not the pope or the emperor, becomes the ultimate court on Earth who can judge magic and witchcraft. People cannot rebel against a wicked king for the formal reason that they cannot judge magic. Only the king can, and only God can hold him accountable for witchcraft.[56] This is the sovereign's *monopoly*, not of earthly powers but of *supernatural* powers. Magic became the essence of sovereignty as a guardianship of the devils.

---

54. Orr, "'God's Hangman': James VI, the Divine Right of Kings, and the Devil" 147.

55. James I, "Basilikon Doron" in Charles McIlwain (ed), *The Political Works of James I* 20.

56. Orr, "'God's hangman': James VI, the Divine Right of Kings, and the Devil" 148.

Chapter II: Analysis

It should not surprise you, that like the Hillsong, Prosperity, Word-of-Faith (WoF), and New Apostolic Reformation (NAR) advocates that have used Psalm 82:6 to argue that we are little gods, and thus gods, King James I used the same verse:

> I said, "You are gods, sons of the Most High, all of you." (Psalm 82:6 ESV)

Commenting on this Derek Kidner states that:

> A second view is that these 'gods' are 'principalities and powers', 'the world rulers of this present darkness' (cf. Eph. 6:12). There are a few Old Testament references to such potentates, good and bad (Isa. 24:21; Dan. 10:13, 20f.; 12:1), for whom the New Testament uses the term 'angels' (Rev. 12:7). Admittedly they are shown as princes rather than judges, but the distinction is not a sharp one in Scripture (cf. Ps. 72). On the whole this view seems truer than the former to the language of the psalm (e.g. verse 7) and to the occasional Old Testament use of the term 'gods' or 'sons of God' for angels (see on Ps. 8:5; cf. Job 1:6; 38:7).
>
> A third interpretation sees here a relic of polytheism, that these are the gods of the heathen, not yet denied but domesticated and brought to account. It is true that 1 Corinthians 10:20 speaks of pagan worship as the worship of demons, but this is to make the point that idolatry is never neutral but a surrender to Belial and his hosts; it is not an acceptance by Paul of heathen mythologies. Likewise the Old Testament never wavers in its abhorrence of heathen gods. For Yahweh to authenticate their claim with the words, 'I say, "You are gods"' (6), would be totally out of character.[1]

In the context of this verse, it is talking about a spiritual reality apart from the here and now. Within wherever heaven is, Yahweh held council among angels and fallen angels to say that he is the one that holds judgment over the earth and all false gods (fallen angels) will do nothing but meet the same end as human beings. These fallen gods

---

1. Derek Kidner, *Psalms 73–150: An Introduction and Commentary*, vol. 16, *Tyndale Old Testament* Commentaries (Downers Grove, Illinois: InterVarsity Press, 1975), p. 328.

are shown that

> with verse 7 it underlines the principle that not even the highest credentials can be brandished against God their giver: cf. his word to the presumptuous Eli: ' "I promised …"; but now the Lord declares: "Far be it from me …" ' (1 Sam. 2:30). If this can be said to the most exalted, it is also a warning to the least.[2]

This is a condemnation, not a praising and affirming that like God, these demonic forces are also gods, but pitiful creatures that can be condemned like human beings. For the movers and shakers in Hillsong, Prosperity, WoF, and NAR teachers to be pushing the idea that they are literally gods (or, little gods)[3] means there is a theological problem here. Benny Hinn, likewise, on TBN in 1990 said that he was a "little messiah", and also that "we are all divine". Again, this is pointing to thinking that, Hinn and we as Christian believers are gods.[4] This Psalm is condemning these teachers and not praising them. Kidner believes that Yahweh in Psalm 82 is talking to mortal kings and princes, but I am not so sure. Even if Yahweh was talking to mortal men there is no indication here, in the least, that human beings are being called literal gods. Jesus used this verse to rebuke the Pharisees, but it was never indicated, even by Jesus, that any of us were "gods" in any kind of way.

To enforce this point:

> The psalm itself is straightforward and describes the LORD's judgment on the other gods. In that, it makes the theological claim that Israel's god is the king and chief god of all of the other gods. Its structure is clear, and the only issue of interpretation centers on the identity of the *they* in v. 5.[5]

Tanner continues:

> Most scholars see the *they* here as the other gods. But the *they* could al-

---

2. Kidner, *Psalms*, p. 329.

3. See, BattleDungeon, "Joyce Meyer – Little Gods," *YouTube*, July 12, 2023, https://www.youtube.com/watch?v=9-hsd7MTq24. And, Polite Leader, "Kenneth Copeland 'Adam Was God,'" *YouTube*, July 12, 2023, https://www.youtube.com/watch?v=J0PokWF4ees. Also, Salt and Light, "Bill Johnson teaches 'little god' heresy – 'You are the one'," *YouTube*, July 12, 2023, https://www.youtube.com/watch?v=o1nkAq00aBo.

4. Lori Eldridge, "Benny Hinn's False Teachings About God Exposed," *Endtime Prophets*, July 22, 2023, https://www.endtime-prophets.com/hinn.html.

5. Beth Tanner, "Book Three of the Psalter: Psalms 73–89," in *The Book of Psalms*, ed. E. J. Young, R. K. Harrison, and Robert L. Hubbard Jr., The New International Commentary on the Old Testament (Grand Rapids, MI; Cambridge, U.K.: William B. Eerdmans Publishing Company, 2014), p. 641.

so be the result of the gods' failure and reflect the impact of their acts on the people. It is certainly possible that the *they* is not one or the other but is both the gods and the people whom the acts of the gods impact. Either way, the result of the acts is quite serious because *the foundations of the earth* are in jeopardy. The situation must be addressed.

6–7 Verses 6–7 place the *gods* on equal footing with the humans. They have lost their immortality, hence their god status. This ability for the God of Israel to demote the others speaks of the power of the king of the council. The king alone can control all of the other gods. This divine trial also demonstrates the fairness of Israel's god. This god is not capricious, but sentences the other gods for their refusal to act in ways that reflect the values of God's kingdom. (italics in original)[6]

Again, there is a strict condemnation here and not any affirmation that anyone, let alone human beings, are in way true "gods".

Kris Vallotton, the "prophet" of Bethel church in Redding, California says that

[t]he power of the cross not only dealt with the forgiveness of our sins but it also changed our very nature. Some people have isolated the effects of the born-again experience to the spirit. That's not accurate. Salvation changed our entire being! Peter says that we are "partakers of the divine nature" (2 Pet. 1:4). Think of it, your very nature is now divine! Paul said that we our "new creatures" in Christ (2 Cor. 5:17). He didn't say we are new spirits, He said "new creatures!" If we believe that we are still sinners, we dilute the power of the blood and then, like Jacob, spend our days trying to be good.[7]

Another notorious WoF teacher, Andrew Wommack, says that

[y]ou are one with Jesus Christ right now. "But he that is joined unto the Lord is one spirit" (1 Cor. 6:17). The Greek word translated "one" here means "a singular one to the exclusion of another." It's much deeper than mere similarity (i.e., being joined together as "one" in purpose); this speaks of complete union. If there are molecules and atoms in the spirit realm, then you are molecule-for-molecule and atom-for-atom identical to Jesus. As He is, so are you in this world. In your spirit, you are completely one with Him![8]

Wommack heretically continues to say that you will not

experience the power and ability of God within if you can't perceive things beyond your body and soul. If you think that God's power is with

---

6. Tanner, *Psalms*, p. 643.

7. Kris Vallotton and Bill Johnson, *The Supernatural Ways of Royalty: Discovering Your Rights and Privileges of Being a Son or Daughter of God* (Shippensburg, PA: Destiny Image, 2006), Logos Edition.

8. Andrew Wommack, *Spirit, Soul and Body* (Colorado Springs, Colorado: Andrew Wommack Ministries, 2005), pp. 31–32, Kindle Edition.

Him somewhere out there, eventually you'll become discouraged. It's not that you won't believe God has power, but you'll doubt you can ever attain it. You must believe you are one with Him in spirit and that it's your responsibility to release His power from within in order to see it manifest.[9]

Again

> I realized I'm not just a man anymore. One-third of me is complete. One-third of me is identical to and one with Jesus. One-third of me is wall-to-wall Holy Ghost![10]

The trend here is not hard to see. You are "molecule-for-molecule ... like Jesus", "you'll doubt you can ever attain it" (referencing God's power in every form), "I'm not just a man anymore ... One-third of me is identical to and one with Jesus". Despite what Wommack would say, none of this is possible, unless you are God himself. But since, Wommack would say we are not "God", the fact remains that Wommack's theology makes us a "god" instead. And a god that Wommack believes can do greater things than God because of pulling John 14:12 out of context. "Truly, truly, I say to you, whoever believes in me will also do the works that I do; and greater works than these will he do, because I am going to the Father" (John 14:12 ESV). Looking at the rest of the chapter, there is a very distinct emphasis on Jesus making the Father known.

> If you had known me, you would have known my Father also. From now on you do know him and have seen him. (John 14:7 ESV)

> Jesus said to him, "Have I been with you so long, and you still do not know me, Philip? Whoever has seen me has seen the Father. How can you say, 'Show us the Father'? Do you not believe that I am in the Father and the Father is in me? The words that I say to you I do not speak on my own authority, but the Father who dwells in me does his works. Believe me that I am in the Father and the Father is in me, or else believe on account of the works themselves. (John 14:9-11 ESV)

So, the greater context of John 14 shows that Jesus came to make the Father known, but to who? Matthew tells us: "He answered, 'I was sent only to the lost sheep of the house of Israel.'" (Matthew 15:24 ESV) Jesus was not intending to focus his work outside of Israel. By telling the disciples they would do greater works of making the Father known, Jesus was telling the disciples this greater work would happen by going outside of Israel and preaching to the Roman world

---

9. Wommack, *Spirit*, pp. 32–33.
10. Wommack, *Spirit*, pp. 33–34.

(See Acts 1).
Answering that point

> [i]f the works of Jesus included his miracles, his teaching, even his entire ministry, how can it be said that the works of his disciples would be greater than his? One suggestion is that, after Jesus' return to the Father and the coming of the Spirit, the works the disciples would perform in the expanding mission of the church would be quantitatively greater than his—more works performed by many disciples in many different places. But the word translated greater (*meizona*) does not mean greater in number, but greater in quality—more important or more impressive—and it is used in this way throughout the Gospel of John (cf. 1:50; 4:12; 5:20, 36; 8:53; 10:29; 13:16; 14:12, 28; 15:13, 20; 19:11). Did Jesus mean, then, that the disciples' works would be qualitatively greater than those he performed? This is highly unlikely. The disciples did later heal and exorcise in Jesus' name, Peter did pray and Dorcas was restored to life (Acts 9:36–42), and through Paul's ministry Eutychus may have been restored to life (Acts 20:7–12). But they did not miraculously feed multitudes, calm storms, restore sight to those who had been born blind or call people out of their graves when they had been already dead for four days. The disciples' works did not reveal the Father in the same way as Jesus did in his ministry and teaching. From apostolic times until now, as far as we know, Jesus' followers have never performed works that were qualitatively the same, let alone qualitatively greater, than those of Jesus. [...] If we apply this to the difference between Jesus' works and those of his disciples, we might say that the disciples' works were greater than his because they had the privilege of testifying by word and deed to the finished work of Christ, and to the fuller coming of the kingdom that it ushered in, whereas Jesus' ministry prior to his death and resurrection only foreshadowed these things. As they testified to these things, they witnessed God's promises to Abraham being fulfilled, as Gentiles were converted and included in the people of God.[11]

However, because according to Hillsong, Prosperity, WoF, and NAR teachers, we are divine "little" gods, and we have the ability to do greater things than God.[12] This is a claim not just to divinity, but a form of Satanism.

---

11. Colin G. Kruse, *John: An Introduction and Commentary*, ed. Eckhard J. Schnabel, Second edition., vol. 4, Tyndale New Testament Commentaries (London: InterVarsity Press, 2017), pp. 348–349.

12. LongforTruth1, "8 Reasons You Should Stop Listening to Andrew Wommack," *YouTube*, July 12, 2023, https://www.youtube.com/watch?v=B8wQasfaYto.

Chapter III: Defining Esotericism

Before going any further, I need to take a couple chapters to define exactly what the Right-Hand Path (RHP), or esotericism, and the Left-Hand Path (LHP), or Satanism is. These terms are often confused with implied meanings from individuals that have not done the work to discover what is meant by these terms. I will take this chapter and chapter four to help you to understand what these terms mean.

***

It is interesting to read through Irenæus's *Against Heresies*. With the discovery of the Nag Hammadi codices in Egypt several decades ago, it made this ancient work not as important in general Gnostic studies as before. *Against Heresies* up until this point was pretty much the textbook of what ancient Gnosticism was for nearly two-thousand years. While other texts such as Augustine's *Against the Manichaeans* did exist, there was no other text that had as much knowledge or information about ancient Gnostic beliefs as this book by Irenæus.

When the Nag Hammadi codices were found, all this information had to be reconsidered. Even within ancient early church fathers' books, there were references to many different Gnostic sects that scholars knew very little if anything about. Some of these sects' our academia knew the name of only. Even today, with some of those Gnostic sects, that can still be the case. However, with the discovery of the Nag Hammadi codices many different forms and sects of ancient Gnosticism have been discovered that have allowed modern scholarship to either confirm the texts of ancient church fathers or else find information that seemed vague or unknown about the church fathers' claims.

Anyone reading through *Against Heresies* will start to notice references to the right- and left-hand path of Bythos, the true "God" of some Gnostic sects. The God of the Old Testament that Christians know very well as the same God the Father of the New Testament, was not considered to be the same God by Gnostics. This trend has started to re-emerge within western society as many Christians are once again disregarding the God of the Old Testament as not being the same as the Father in the New Testament. This may seem strange, but many will argue that expectations and rules of the law are completely different in the two covenants (testaments). While the law works differently in the new covenant, the law does not change. Also, the way of redemption and the work of faith for salvation is the same in both covenants. Following the law itself was not what saved someone, it was faith in the coming seed of Genesis 3:15. This shift in "God" is what is known as Marcionism. Marcion was a first century heretic that fed into a lot of Gnostic errors about the biblical God.

What could these errors be? One was that the God of the Old Testament was an evil "god", or Demiurge, known as Yaldabaoth, or Ialdabaoth, that created the evil material world in rebellion to Bythos, the true Father of the New Testament. In this same ideology, Lucifer, not Satan, came down as the nahash (נחש, nā·ḥāš, serpent) in Eden to free humanity from the material oppression of the Demiurge. So, Lucifer, becoming known as the "Light Bearer" or "Light Bringer" freed humanity from the oppression of evil.[1] Satan continued to be an evil aeon (angel/god) of the Gnostic system some of whom believed that the Demiurge was Satan instead of some other being.

The ideology of the right- and left-hand path does not seem to be

---

1. Despite what traditional Christianity has argued, the text in Isaiah 14:12 is not speaking about Satan or a "Lucifer". The name that the KJV and other translations of the Bible interpreted as "Lucifer" is the Hebrew word, הילל (hêlēl). There is no direct textual evidence of a being known as "Lucifer" here. That name comes from the Latin Vulgate in the late 4th century. Since the KJV, which many claim is using only the Hebrew and Greek which is false, used the Latin Vulgate to fill in missing "gaps" of text, the name Lucifer got imported into traditional Christian thinking. With the arrival of the argument of "textus receptus" which states that "this is the text that has been received over time as scripture, thus it is scripture" is in fact an appeal to tradition. The appeal to tradition is a logical fallacy that states that since tradition says it is true, it is true. The Roman Catholic Church uses this fallacy to say that their man-made traditions guide them in how to interpret the Bible. Even the KJV's textus receptus has failed however, since even as late as the 1900 KJV, still included the apocrypha, and even apocryphal books that the Roman Catholic Church at this point had rejected. However, many in Protestant churches will still hold to the argument that "Lucifer" is Satan's true name when in the Hebrew and Greek there is no textual evidence that such a name ever existed until the 4th century. The faulty acceptance of "Lucifer" has led to many different social, religious and cult problems since many have associated the two different names as being two separate beings. It is possible that the problem's created by the name "Lucifer" would have never existed if the team that translated the original KJV had kept the name "Lucifer" out of the text.

something new. Even though what is known as Satanism today became well known through the teaching of Anton LaVey in the 1960's, where the idea of these paths came from is mostly either unknown or goes back before this information started being recorded. This is important because many things that these two "paths" teach is very similar to different "forces" or "powers" that come from the right and left hand of Bythos. These ideologies of the "power" from the right and left hand of Bythos also is merged with the ideas of the Light Bringer from Gnostic thought. What this shows is that so much of what Gnostics taught is proving to be part of modern New Age, or esoteric and RHP, thought. That is important to remember. Some New Age books try to deny or limit the amount of "Gnostic" teaching in their system, but the ideology is there, and it is impossible to just write it off so candidly.

Is there similarity between the Gnostic teaching and current ideologies of the right- and left-hand paths? We need to take this under consideration. The ideology of the left-hand path will be looked at more closely in chapter four.

Ideology of Merkavah Mysticism

When talking about the occult, many have no idea, especially within the church, about the ancient Judaic form of occultism known as Merkavah or Merkabah Mysticism, depending on how the Hebrew letter Bet ב (v) or בּ (b) is written. Since both spellings are relevant, it is fair to assume that certain Hekhalot texts contained the dagesh (the dot in the middle of the Bet) and others did not.

Merkavah Mysticism writings first emerged around the 6th century AD. Since Hebrew tales were mostly passed on by oral tradition before being written down it can be fair to say that Merkavah Mysticism teachings probably emerged from much earlier in Jewish history. At this time, the oral tradition of passing on stories was much more reliable than even written documents. Today the idea of oral tradition is completely foreign to us. We believe what is written is more reliable than what is said.

The reason that some have believed that Merkavah Mysticism traditions were earlier is that some scholars have tried to claim that the story of the person being brought up to heaven in 2 Corinthians 12 may have come from Merkavah Mysticism thought.[2] This thinking that Paul was a Merkavah Mystic to us as Christians is ridiculous and Merkavah Mysticism traditions adopted this story after the fact rather than the New Testament adopting it after these occult traditions.

---

2. James R. Davila, *Hekhalot Literature in Translation: Major Texts of Merkavah Mysticism* (Leiden, Netherlands: Brill, 2013), pp. 14–15.

Regardless of this point, the Merkavah Mysticism belief structures were centred on what are known as the "Hekhalot Texts". These texts were used to describe how someone would be "raptured" down to the Merkavah (מרכבה, chariot) often seen similarly to the theophany of God in Ezekiel by the river (Ezekiel 1-10). The descent to this chariot would then take the mystic up to the highest heaven where the mystic would approach the first of seven Hekhalot (היכל) or palaces. An angel would stand guard at the gate to each palace. Different texts describe different tests, questions or seals required for entry. Once a mystic was admitted past the first angel, they would enter the palace and come to the gate of the second palace within the first palace. Apparently, each palace inside the next was larger than the one before, within occultic traditions such "physics" are possible. The mystic would proceed much like before with the risk to the mystic being much greater with each successive palace. If the mystic at the sixth palace failed in their tests, angels would come down to kill the mystic on the spot.

If the mystic succeeded in entering the seventh palace, that mystic would be in the throne room of Yahweh. The mystic would then see the four living creatures, and there are texts that describe very vividly what this apparently looked like, one ironically also mentioning lilitr or Lilith's. The mystic would then be brought on to the knee of Yahweh and granted any desire that mystic had. Even the desire to ascend to become an angel, or even like a god, would be granted to the mystic. The idea of becoming an angel is similar to the belief of what the RHP today are trying to achieve in becoming "God". It is not the same, but it is eerily similar.[3]

The most popular and widely known Hekhalot text is that of *3 Enoch* or the *Sefer Hekhalot*. What is highly controversial about this text is the presence of the angel Metatron. *3 (Hebrew) Enoch* identifies this angel as the ascended or assumed (in this case: taken up) Enoch of Genesis 5:21-24. The belief here was that Enoch found favour with God and was given the position of highest angel. When reading through the text, this Metatron is almost identical to Yahweh himself in authority and power. The comparison is easy to make that Metatron (Enoch) was being presupposed as a possible future Messiah. See chapter nine where this is detailed much more thoroughly.

Metatron makes appearances in different Hekhalot texts as well, so we cannot just discard this identification so easily. Enoch is a highly controversial figure even today. Many people calling themselves Christians are convinced that 1 Enoch is scripture despite some of the troubling passages within it. These include prayer to angels 1 Enoch

---

3. Davila, *Hekhalot*, pp. 1–3.

9:1–3, Azazel as the source of evil 1 Enoch 10:8–9 and pagan practices of offering gifts to the natural world 1 Enoch 100:10–13.[4] There are many other problematic passages in 1 Enoch that flat out contradict the testimony of the Bible.[5]

Why bring this up? Many have tried to use the legitimacy of 1 Enoch to prove that the Bible gets things wrong or to add demon-

---

4. Ryan Pitterson, *Judgment of the Nephilim* (New York, New York: Day of Noe Publishing, 2017), pp. 211–218. Please note, this book gets a lot, and I mean a lot, of stuff wrong. Be very careful and show literate biblical discernment when reading it.

5. The most recent of this error is Michael S. Heiser who in his book *Reversing Hermon* argues that Jesus' primary mission was to overturn the sin of the watchers (demons) in 1 Enoch, "[t]he birth of Jesus would have alerted literate first-century Jews that the Messiah's arrival would reverse the sin of the Watchers" (p. 55) and also that Jesus was part watcher and not completely human. The first indication is that "New Testament scholar Amy Richter believes that what she calls the 'Enochic Watchers Template' is essential for understanding the women in the genealogy of Jesus" (p. 72). The second, in Heiser quoting Richter claims that the

> women of the Hebrew Bible named by Matthew in his genealogy of Jesus foreshadow the reversal of the watchers' transgression. All four of them are connected with the Enochic watchers' template. They use the illicit arts, but the use of these skills leads to righteousness rather than evil. The women are also connected with other aspects of the Enochic watchers' template, including sexual interaction which connects the earthly and heavenly realms, interaction with angels, unusual aspects of their offspring, and connections with giants. In the birth narrative, Matthew shows the birth of Jesus occurring in a way that reverses the watchers' transgression and evil in the world as it occurs in the Enochic template. Specifically, the birth of Jesus occurs through the union of a woman and a celestial being, but in contrast to the watchers' story, no sexual relations are involved. Further, in Matthew's narrative, the first humans outside of Jesus' immediate family to interact with the child Jesus are the magi who are practitioners of the illicit arts taught by the watchers and use astrological knowledge to find Jesus. In the Enochic template, the watchers bring idolatry into the world; in Matthew, the magi worship the appropriate object of worship—Jesus. (p. 73)

Heiser confirms this belief by saying that the

> links between these four women and the aforementioned elements of the Enochic template are not always obvious or clear to English readers. This is due in part to dependence on English translations. In other instances, the connections are part of Second Temple Jewish readings of the biblical material that may seem foreign to modern readers. Our modern traditional perspective impedes understanding. (pp. 74-75)

The first about Jesus' true mission falls under a heretical gospel and the second belief brings in the idea of a not fully human Jesus which presupposes a different Christ into the biblical text. If Christ was not fully human, Christ could not have been the last Adam. For more information see: Michael S. Heiser, *Reversing Hermon: Enoch, The Watchers & The Forgotten Mission of Jesus Christ* (Bellingham, Washington: Lexham Press, 2017), Logos Edition.

ology nonsense to the biblical story. When we allow for problematic, and even heretical texts like 1 Enoch, to be counted as scripture, this opens the door to occult texts like 3 Enoch as well. Some would argue against this, but the problem is that the occult, in a general sense, is very aware of the existence and the stories in 1 Enoch. Some groups of the occult need these stories to be true in order to help validate their beliefs. Once we give way to this, other texts like 3 Enoch and other Hekhalot texts will be next in line to be requestioned and accepted as legitimate.

Another interesting point with the Herkhalot texts is that the mystics went up to heaven to get better mystical understanding of the Torah. Torah in the New Testament can mean anything from what we call the Pentateuch to the entire Hebrew Bible, or Old Testament itself. The mystic would go up in this case to learn about the Pentateuch and have the mysterious and magical meanings behind it revealed to them. This is important when you start to read Kabbalistic books such as the Zohar which give magical and hidden understandings of the Old Testament.

These texts also show the mystic how to gain control over angels and get these angels to do the mystics bidding. This is important since many people in today's world are obsessed with angels and the false images that they believe angels are involved in. Many of these "angel worshipers" use occultic rituals like this to gain control over angels. Even within the secular world, and sometimes the Christian one, there are people that believe we become angels when we die. This is wrong and not taught in any way in the Bible. In fact, after reading all the above, it is easy to see where this belief comes from. There are other sources in the Greek culture that affirm we can become δαιμόνιον (daimonion) or demons when we die.[6] I go into more detail about necromancy (praying for angels) in chapter seven.

The problem of this belief being in the Christian church should make us realize that it is from the occult and is not biblical at all. If the Greek origins of the daimonion do not worry you, then Merkavah Mysticism beliefs of people becoming angels should worry you. Christians need to be questioning where these beliefs come from. Often these ideas are assumed into the Bible rather than discerning where these ideas truly come from. The text where Jesus says that "For in the resurrection they neither marry nor are given in marriage, but are like angels in heaven" (Matthew 22:30 ESV) has nothing to do with what our physical bodies will be like. Within the context it means that when

---

6. Walter Burkert, *Greek Religion* (Malden, Massachusetts: Blackwell Publishing, 1985), pp. 179–181.

it comes to romantic relationships, we will be like the angels who have no need of them. Do not let people in your church convince you that the Bible affirms the ideas of Merkavah Mysticism, 3 (*Hebrew*) *Enoch* or the Greek pagan beliefs. These ideas are all occultic in origin.

Another important factor to keep in mind is the hymns and poetry used in Hekhalot texts, and ritual spells. When reading these texts with proper biblical literacy and biblical discernment, someone will come up with one or more of three conclusions about the hymns: 1) they are outright heretical and blasphemous, 2) this is weird but not altogether wrong, or 3) that this actually has better theology in it than many "worship" songs we sing in Sunday morning liturgy (services). All three of these conclusions can be applied to different Hekhalot hymns. Having read through them, there is indication to class each different hymn in one, or more, of these three conclusions. I show an example in chapter ten.

We need to be careful of the origins of these hymns. Just because it sounds good does not immediately make it applicable and useable in church liturgy. We must always consider the source of the music we are singing on Sunday mornings. The issue of music on Sunday's is an issue of conscience for some, and I do disagree with that, and the rest of this book will show why this is no longer a conscience issue. The source of the music always matters. People caught in sin can write godly music and even be used by God to accomplish things for his kingdom, I cannot deny that. The issue here is that these hymns were directly intended for an occult purpose. When taking that into consideration we have to realize that just because it sounds good it cannot be normalized for our corporate or personal worship. This music must be avoided.

Ideology of the Right-Hand Path

Before I get into the hard teachings of the Right-Hand Path there needs to be a few definitions of what exactly these New Agers (Esotericists/RHP) believe. This needs to be done because many of the things that New Agers believe, sound biblical. This may seem strange, but the New Age movement does arise out of the Judeo-Christian traditions, being the descendants of Merkavah Mysticism. Keeping this in mind, it should not be a surprise that many of the terms we use in every day Christendom are also being used by New Age followers in their practices and beliefs.

One thing that is important to realize about them is the idea of As Above, So Below. Since I describe the concept of As Above, So Below extensively in chapter six in the section *Andrew Denton and the Occult*, I will not redescribe those details here. However, this idea is key in making what these individuals believe understandable. Remember that as biblical as this phrase sounds, from the "Lord's Prayer" in Matthew 6, "let it be on earth as it is in heaven", it is far from biblical in its totality and in the way it is used in the New Age movement.

Next, what is important to remember is that there are many uses of Judeo-Christian imagery that are being used by New Age followers that many will believe are biblical. For instance, I will show what a possible charm pendant crafted by a New Age person could look like. See if any of this seems strange to you:

This would show up on a medallion that is self-carved, maybe one to two inches in diameter. This charm does not seem problematic at all does it? The only thing that may seem strange is the number "9" on the bottom.

Note: this is not an actual magical pendant. It is simply an example of what such a pendant could look like.[7]

Anyone familiar with Hebrew will recognize the top name as that of "Yahweh" and of course the Star of David. The Star of David is really in controversy right now since the symbol is not confirmed in biblical Judaism. Always keep in mind that today's Rabbinical Judaism is not the same as biblical Judaism. Today's Judaism is a child of the first-century Pharisees that was encoded into the Babylonian and Jerusalem Talmud's. Rabbinical Jews today are not all that familiar with the teachings of the Torah. Some are, but if you were to go to their synagogues, you would hear "sermons" (for lack of a better term) that are based on the Talmud, not the Torah.

Why say all this? Because the Star of David is not in fact a Jewish symbol. It is a Middle Eastern symbol that is embedded in pagan esotericism of the Ancient Near East. Many do not know that and just accept the symbol as biblical because "the Jews are using it." Let me

---

7. David Conway, *Magic: An Occult Primer* (Newport, Rhode Island: The Witches' Almanac, 2019), pp. 209–229.

once again be clear, the Jews today are in every way, Torah violators. And as such, because they are using this symbol does not immediately give it legitimacy. Since the symbol originates in Ancient Near Eastern pagan esotericism, this symbol needs to be taken as a warning.

Even if you did not realize the truth of the Star of David, the number "9" should have seemed strange. This is a kabbalistic gematria number that is calculated to indicate an entire ritual or "spell" that is intended for a specific purpose.[8] The number is an indication of what kind of power, astrological importance, numerological significance and more that the charm has.[9]

Since many in the RHP are aware of how these symbols are being accepted by the Christian church, it is not difficult for them to bring these symbols into the Christian church and people think it is biblical when it really is not.

Another term that is often heard and misunderstood by many in the church is that of the "Tree of Life."[10] Whenever someone in the New Age is referring to the Tree of Life, they are not indicating the tree in the Garden of Eden. While they may refer to that actual tree as a metaphorical symbol of the tree, they say is real, there is a distinctive difference.

See Figure 1 (Fig. 1) for an example of the Kabbalistic Tree of Life.

This seems strange right? What is it? What this represents is all the areas of the physical and spiritual universe that "God" is in. The very bottom "Malkuth" is the physical world we are living on now.[11]

Depending on whether you come from a Judaic background or Christian background, in teaching, the goal would be to descend the

---

8. Richard Cavendish, *The Black Arts*: *An Absorbing Account of Witchcraft, Demonology*, *Astrology*, *and other Mystical Practices Throughout the Ages* (New York, New York: TarcherPerigee, 2017), pp. 110–114.

9. There have been recent scholars that have denied that gematria is ever used in the New Testament. This is more of an attempt to hide the way that Matthew and John (in Revelation) were trying to link Jesus to David (Matthew 1) and the Beast to Nero (Revelation). Ancient gematria and kabbalistic gematria are two completely different things. There are a number of ancient documents coming out of the early first-century BC that show that gematria was known and being used by the old covenant community. This does not mean that gematria was used in the Old Testament. I have had lengthy arguments with people online about this. They kept making claims that I said it was used in the Old Testament when it was not. Remember that the old covenant era lasted until Christ was resurrected. Since Matthew and John both knew about it, and used it to show who Christ was/is and to hide who Nero really was, is again a show that gematria (the none kabbalistic kind) was known and being used in the later years of the old covenant era.

10. Conway, *Magic*, pp. 58–69.

11. Conway, *Magic*, pp. 60–62.

Tree of Life from the throne of God (the top) as Judaism teaches, or as the Christian tradition teaches start from the bottom (Malkuth) and work your way up the Tree of Life to the throne of God.[12] Once you get access to the throne of "God" you become absorbed into the greater "god" and become part of "god".

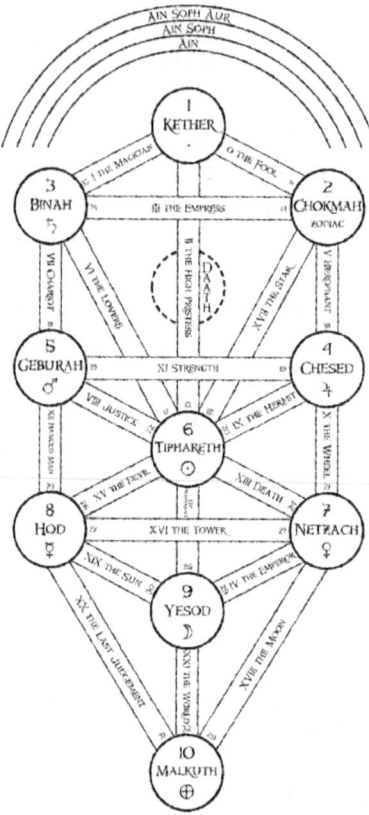

TREE OF LIFE

Fig. 1. This Image is in the Public Domain.

The ultimate goal of the RHP that it claims is that it "stands for '*order, light and restriction*' ... the Right Hand Path is used for occultists striving for a union with the divine with a resulting resolution of the magician's individuality." (italics in orignal)[13] What this is saying is that the occultist of the RHP is seeking to "become God". In other words, all occultists become part of the same "god" that they will be

---

12. Aaron Leitch, *The Angelical Language Volume I* (Woodbury, Minnesota: Llewellyn Publications, 2010), pp. 12–19.

13. Kennet Granholm, *Embracing the Dark: The Magic Order of the Dragon Rouge – Its Practice in Dark Magic and Meaning Making* (Sarrijärvi, Suomi: Åbo Akademi University Press, 2005), p. 28.

absorbed into, lose any trace of their own "selves", and become part of the greater "god".

The question now is, what are the gnostic connections to all of this?

> Now Pistis Sophia set him apart from the darkness and summoned him to her right, | and the prime parent she put at her left. Since that day, right has been called justice, and left called wickedness. Now because of this they all received | a realm (kosmos) in the congregation of justice and wickedness, ... stand ... upon a creature ... all.[14]

Also,

> He cleansed his soul from the transgressions | which he had committed with an alien hand. He stood up, being upright within himself, because he exists in everyone, and because he has | death and life within himself, and he exists | in the midst of both of them. And when he had received the power he turned towards the parts of the right, | and he entered into the truth, having forsaken all things pertaining to the left, | having been filled with wisdom, with counsel, with understanding and with insight, and an | eternal power. [And] he broke open his bonds. [Those who had] formed the whole place [he] condemned. [But they did not] find [...] hidden within him.[15]

That is interesting too. When we take into consideration everything I have shown about the beliefs about the RHP, it is not hard to see where this "ideology" comes from.

The idea of ascending the Tree of Life so that you become more like "god" and eventually able to merge with "god" is evident in the quote by Pearson. Look at how the Gnostic writer says that, "He cleansed his soul from the transgressions | which he had committed with an alien hand. He stood up, being upright within himself, because he exists in everyone, and because he has | death and life within himself, and he exists | in the midst of both of them." This is a very evident belief in the RHP. God is in all, and it is our ultimate goal to re-merge with "god". To do so, we need to purge of the evils of this material world and control the powers of life and death. This belief about purging evils from the material world is something that is held as an important belief in the New Age.

Let us also look at the quote by Robinson and Smith, "Since that

---

14. James McConkey Robinson and Richard Smith, *Coptic Gnostic Library Project, "On," in The Nag Hammadi Library in English*, 4th rev. ed. (Leiden, Netherlands: Brill, 1996), p. 176, Logos Edition.

15. Birger A. Pearson, "The Testimony of Truth (IX, 3)," in *The Nag Hammadi Library in English*, ed. James M. Robinson, trans. Søren Giversen, 4th rev. ed. (Leiden; New York: E. J. Brill, 1996), p. 453, Logos Edition.

day, right has been called justice, and left called wickedness. Now because of this they all received | a realm (kosmos) in the congregation of justice and wickedness." Again, this is evident in RHP belief. They stand for what they call justice. The question is however, is it Godly justice? The evidence of that "justice" says that no, it is not Godly justice. All these things they refer to as goodness and light, as the Granholm quote shows, is not that at all in the light of biblical truth.

How so? Remember that the New Age believes in a highly syncretistic form of belief. Ever since Helena Blavatsky with her Theosophical Society merging Western Hermeticism (a combination of Kabbalistic beliefs, gnostic beliefs, and European and Ancient Near Eastern pagan beliefs) with Far East beliefs like Hinduism, thus creating the New Age movement, the idea of the New Age is a "whatever works for you" kind of spiritual soup. All these beliefs and ideologies are mixed into one pot of "soup". Whatever helps you "merge" with "god" they will encourage and say you need to use to get there.

The problem is that many of the New Age movements support open sexuality, transgender movements and also the progressive movements in heretical churches. All these ideologies push the idea that "who you are inside is the real you." Again, that is Gnostic ideology that the New Age is wanting you to believe. The material world that made your physical self, got it wrong, and your own inner "god" is able to tell you what the "truth" is. This is "justice" to them. This is "right and good" to them, but it is not. I detail with the issue of the current divergent sexual movements more in chapter eight.

Dealing with the issue of what the RHP is trying to accomplish, we will never be "united" or "merged" with God. That is not the goal of our salvation.

> So is it with the resurrection of the dead. What is sown is perishable; what is raised is imperishable. It is sown in dishonor; it is raised in glory. It is sown in weakness; it is raised in power. It is sown a natural body; it is raised a spiritual body. If there is a natural body, there is also a spiritual body. Thus it is written, 'The first man Adam became a living being'; the last Adam became a life-giving spirit. But it is not the spiritual that is first but the natural, and then the spiritual. The first man was from the earth, a man of dust; the second man is from heaven. As was the man of dust, so also are those who are of the dust, and as is the man of heaven, so also are those who are of heaven. Just as we have borne the image of the man of dust, we shall also bear the image of the man of heaven. (1 Corinthians 15:42–49 ESV)

I have heard a number of people misquote this verse to say that we will have "spiritual" bodies, but that is both a yes and no. We will have bodies the same as Jesus' resurrected body. It will be a physical body and also capable of some spiritual things. What these spiritual things all will be we do not know. Christ could walk through locked doors with his resurrected body, it would be reasonable to think we could do the same when the final judgment comes, and we are resurrected with our physical bodies. This is the hope we live for. The return of Christ and to be raised with our new resurrected bodies to praise God forever.

> Then I saw a great white throne and him who was seated on it. From his presence earth and sky fled away, and no place was found for them. And I saw the dead, great and small, standing before the throne, and books were opened. Then another book was opened, which is the book of life. And the dead were judged by what was written in the books, according to what they had done. And the sea gave up the dead who were in it, Death and Hades gave up the dead who were in them, and they were judged, each one of them, according to what they had done. Then Death and Hades were thrown into the lake of fire. This is the second death, the lake of fire. And if anyone's name was not found written in the book of life, he was thrown into the lake of fire. (Revelation 20:11–15 ESV)

> And I heard a loud voice from the throne saying, "Behold, the dwelling place of God is with man. He will dwell with them, and they will be his people, and God himself will be with them as their God. He will wipe away every tear from their eyes, and death shall be no more, neither shall there be mourning, nor crying, nor pain anymore, for the former things have passed away." (Revelation 21:3–4 ESV)

> Then the angel showed me the river of the water of life, bright as crystal, flowing from the throne of God and of the Lamb through the middle of the street of the city; also, on either side of the river, the tree of life with its twelve kinds of fruit, yielding its fruit each month. The leaves of the tree were for the healing of the nations. No longer will there be anything accursed, but the throne of God and of the Lamb will be in it, and his servants will worship him. They will see his face, and his name will be on their foreheads. And night will be no more. They will need no light of lamp or sun, for the Lord God will be their light, and they will reign forever and ever. (Revelation 22:1–5 ESV)

There is a lot of scripture there to go through but hopefully you can see what it is saying. When Jesus returns, all will be resurrected, the righteous and the unrighteous. The unrighteous will be sent to the lake of fire for eternity and the righteous will live and be with God forever. Note what it does not say. We will not rule "as part of God" forever. We will have our own bodies, our own personhood, our perfect glorified selves will be with our God, worshiping him as the only true God "forever and ever." This is the hope that the truth has. Not that we will be "merged" with "god" by whatever magical direction you want to take.

"Jesus said to him, 'I am the way, and the truth, and the life. No one comes to the Father except through me. If you had known me, you would have known my Father also.'" (John 14:6–7 ESV) Going back to the syncretism of the New Age beliefs, the Bible shows it is all garbage. This quote by Jesus in John 14 shows that Jesus is the only way to the Father. There is no other. It does not matter what is in that New Age "soup", the only way to be saved, is to have the hope of a glorified resurrection body that will worship God for eternity is through Christ alone. No one else can save you. No other "magic" or "god" can save you. And none of these will "merge" you with "god". All these "soup" teachings will do is send you into the eternal fire.

Chapter IV: Defining Satanism

For many years now, the most popular books on the Christian market that either have to do with spiritual warfare (biblical demonology) or the occult have mostly been written by Pentecostals or those coming from the Pentecostal tradition. The majority of these texts, from Pentecostal tradition, are being written by those in the very movements I am writing against. These books are almost all written by Prosperity, WoF, and NAR teachers or self-proclaimed "prophets" and "apostles". Therefore, as they are the ones that are writing a majority of the biblical demonology books, the terminology has been theirs to define.

As a result: most Christian's believe that when talking about Satanism, you are speaking about a traditional form of Satan worship. Much like Christian's worship God, Satanists apparently worship Satan.

Before going too deeply, first I want to connect the gnostic origins of the Right-Hand Path (RHP) also to the Left-Hand Path (LHP) so that a coherent argument can be made.

The Gnostic Roots

In order to connect the LHP to the RHP we need to go over what the Gnostic roots of the LHP are. Many people will look at Gnosticism as some occultic "university level teaching" form of ancient Christianity. While that "university level" concept is complete nonsense, the fact is that Gnosticism is still highly connected to the Christian faith. To say that the Left-Hand Path likewise has Gnostic connections may seem strange since so many of these occultists are determined to defy the commands of the Bible.

> But one receives the unction of the [...] of the power of the cross. This power the apostles called "the right and the left." For this person is no longer a Christian but a Christ. [...] he said, "I came to make [the things below] like the things [above, and the things] outside like those [inside.

> I came to unite] them in the place." [...] For it is the first of these two heavenly [men], the one who is revealed, that they call "the one who is below"; and he to whom the hidden belongs is (supposed to be) that one who is above him. For it would be better for them to say, "The inner and the outer, and what is outside the outer." Because of this the lord called destruction "the outer darkness": there is not another outside of it. [...] But that which is within them all is the fullness. Beyond it there is nothing else within it. This is that of which they say, "That which is above them."[1]

If you have been reading closely, you will pick up on some clear things. First, in dropping the name "Christian" and becoming a "Christ", the Gnostics affirmed that the point of the false Christ they believed in was to make you a Christ like him. In other words, the purpose of "God" was to make you your own "god" that acted independently from him. Possibly, even becoming greater. The quote further shows the importance in the LHP ideology from Gnostic thought, of the idea of "As Above, So Below."

Note what also happens in Gnostic thought:

> And Sophia took her daughter Zoe and had her sit upon his right to teach him about the things that exist in [...] (heaven); and the angel [of] wrath she placed upon his left. [...] [his right] has been called life; and the left has come to represent the unrighteousness of the realm of absolute power above. [...] Now when Yaldabaoth saw him in this great splendor and at this height, he envied him; [...] And envy engendered death; and death engendered his offspring and gave each of them charge of its heaven; and all the heavens of chaos became full of their multitudes.[2]

To explain this, Sophia is often thought to be a truer "god" than Yahweh in the Old Testament. This Sophia is thought to be a first manifestation of a female "saviour" that would reach down and save humanity by sending the "Light Bringer," or Lucifer. Also, Yaldabaoth (the Demiurge, or Yahweh) is, in Gnostic thought, a deviant child of Sophia. Keeping that in mind, notice the elevation of evil and depravity or "unrighteousness", also engendering "death", and having its own heavens of chaos filled with multitudes. Taking all the quotes and references above, it is pretty clear where the ideology of the LHP has

---

1. Wesley W. Isenberg, "The Gospel of Philip (II, 3)," in *The Nag Hammadi Library in English*, ed. James M. Robinson, 4th rev. ed. (Leiden, Netherlands: Brill, 1996), p. 150, Logos Edition.

2. Note that is this quote is a reference to someone known as "Yaldabaoth", this is the "official" name of the Demiurge, or Yahweh to the Gnostics who is also often called Satan by those same heretics. Roger A. Bullard, "The Hypostasis of the Archons (II, 4)," in *The Nag Hammadi Library in English*, ed. James M. Robinson, trans. Bentley Layton, 4th rev. ed. (Leiden, Netherlands: Brill, 1996), p. 168, Logos Edition.

come from. The LHP is Gnostic in its origins. These self-proclaimed "truths" and "knowledge" given to the LHP by an "enemy" that they in a round-about way worship, gives them "gnosis" or "knowledge" that allows them to be guided to be their own "god" or "Christ."

The Biblical Truth

There are many things that can be said against the Left-Hand Path.

First, Jesus states that "I am the way, the truth, and the life. No one comes to the Father but by me." (John 14:6 ESV) Jesus is the only way to the Father. We do not become the Father, we do not become a Christ or a "god". Rather we are brought into communion with God so that we can know the Father the way that was intended in Eden.

Second, read through all of Psalm 2. It is clear from that Psalm that Yahweh is in control of all things. The kingdoms of the world, the plots to overthrow God will not work. "He who sits in the heavens laughs; the Lord holds them in derision. Then he will speak to them in his wrath, and terrify them in his fury." (Psalm 2:4–5 ESV) This section of Psalm 2 is highly comforting. Keeping in mind everything that has been happening to this world in the last two years in particular at the time of writing, Yahweh, God, is laughing at it. The problems of the last few years (at time of writing) are nothing to him or his plans for this world. Jesus came and did the work that many of these cults and groups are trying to accomplish. These groups are a mockery to God, and he laughs about it, but will also respond in wrath and fury.

Third, this points to one original statement made by the nahash (נחש, serpent/dragon/Satan) in Eden: "But the serpent said to the woman, 'You will not surely die. For God knows that when you eat of it your eyes will be opened, and you will be like God, knowing good and evil.'" (Genesis 3:4–5 ESV) It is pretty clear what all these occultic movements revolve around. The LHP and the RHP all revolve around the idea of the adherent becoming either a god, or god himself (small g intentional). The entire system of everything in this book so far is pointing to the original lie that "You will be like God." Sorry to tell these Hell bound occultists, you will never be like God. You will only die in the attempt. God mocks you and will respond in fury towards you for trying. The only way to avoid this, is to repent and believe in the true saviour, Jesus Christ.

Back to Defining Satanism

In an academic observation of Satanic movements, Massimo Introvigne defines Satanism in this way

Satanism is (1) the worship of the character identified with the name of Satan or Lucifer in the Bible, (2) by organized groups with at least a minimal organization and hierarchy, (3) through ritual or liturgical practices.[3]

Introvigne spends some time explaining why he has defined Satanism the way he has, but other scholars, like Kennet Granholm have disagreed with him.[4] Granholm defines Satanism such that

> morality issue ramblers on the Left Hand Path usually discard a once-for all outlined and valid-on-all-occasions ethical code for an individual situational morality. [...] Satanism is said to be the Left Hand Path of the west. [...] In the west the Left Hand Path is usually used for the occultists whose goal is self-deification with a maintained individuality.[5]

This is important to remember. Satanism, or the LHP (from here on in Satanism/Satanists/Satanic will refer to Hillsong, Prosperity, WoF and NAR movements), is the pursuit of self-deification which is remarkably similar to Hillsong, Prosperity, WoF and NAR movements. To these Satanists, you are divine and are a god.

In printing Anton LaVey's book *The Satanic Bible*, Abel Lawrence shows the following basic teaching in the LHP.

> It is a common misunderstanding that Satanists do not believe in God. Because man's interpretation of "God" has been so varied throughout history, the Satanist just embraces the definition that best fits him. Rather than his gods creating him, man has always created his gods. To some, God is benevolent; to others, he is terrifying. To the Satanist, "God"—by whatever name he is given, or by no name at all—is seen as nature's balancing component, not as a source of pain.[6]

LaVey himself says that

> THE GOD YOU SAVE MAY BE YOURSELF ALL religions of a spiritual nature are inventions of man. He has created an entire system of gods with nothing more than his carnal brain. Just because he has an ego, and cannot accept it, he has to externalize it into some great spiritual device which he calls "God".[7]

> The Satanist feels: "Why not really be honest and if you are going to create a god in your image, why not create that god as yourself." Every

---

3. Massimo Introvigne, *Satanism: A Social History* (Leiden, Netherlands: Brill, 2016), p. 3.

4. Introvigne, *Satanism*, pp. 4–5.

5. Granholm, *Embracing*, p. 28.

6. Abel Lawrence, *The Books of Forbidden Knowledge: Witchcraft, The Satanic Bible and Necronomicon: Black Arts, Practical Magick, Demonology and Other Mystical Practices* (Independently Published, 2021), p. 471. Kindle Edition.

7. Anton Szandor LaVey, *The Satanic Bible: Central Religious Text of LaVeyan Satanism* (New York, New York: William Morrow, 2022), p. 20, Kindle Edition.

man is a god if he chooses to recognize himself as one.[8]

Again, looking at what LaVey is saying, Hillsong, Prosperity, WoF, and NAR movements beliefs about themselves being divine and little gods is right in line with what LaVey taught in *The Satanic Bible*.

Granholm and LaVey are not the only ones to hold this view.

> Luciferians do not worship nor believe in the devil, god or any outer consciousness.
>
> Instead Luciferians are free to accept responsibility for their life and in turn maintain a self-determined life of indulgence with disciplined control, fostering self-excellence and building a strong spiritual foundation which supports self-deification by the process of Apotheosis; literally transformation into divine consciousness.[9]

After saying this, a couple pages later, Hope Marie makes the comment that, "YOU ARE THE ONLY GOD WHICH IS!"[10]

Looking at the first quote by Marie, the Hillsong, Prosperity, WoF, and NAR adherents definitely live a life of "indulgence", "self-excellence", "building a strong spiritual foundation" and definitely "self-deification." Going back to Wommack's comment that "I realized I'm not just a man anymore. One-third of me is complete. One-third of me is identical to and one with Jesus. One-third of me is wall-to-wall Holy Ghost!", and further back to Vallotton's "[s]alvation changed our entire being! Peter says that we are 'partakers of the divine nature' (2 Pet. 1:4). Think of it, your very nature is now divine!" both of these statements speak of an experience in which you are made divine and have a divine spirit, or consciousness, inside you.

Notice what Bill Johnson says that in

> reality, my sinful past no longer exists. The Lamb of God purchased it with a payment in blood, forever removing my sins from the records of Heaven. The atoning blood of Jesus covers my sin, never to be uncovered again. Sin's power to destroy us is itself destroyed by a superior reality: forgiveness.
>
> [...]
>
> To maintain consciousness of our sinful past to help us become more humble is the cruelty of a religious spirit; it requires us to keep something in our minds that isn't in God's. In reality, it is much more humbling to live in the liberty of unearned forgiveness. When we are forgiven, the King gives us permission to live as though we had never sinned.
>
> [...]

---

8. LaVey, *Satanic*, p. 75.
9. Hope Marie, "Luciferianism & Our Origins" in *Wisdom of Eosphoros*, ed. Michael Ford (Houston, Texas: Succubus Productions, 2015), p. 27.
10. Marie, *Wisdom*, p. 30.

> "For as he thinks within himself, so he is" (Prov. 23:7). When we are charged to think of ourselves dead to sin, it is more than a suggestion to think positively about our conversion. It is an invitation to step into the momentum of a reality made available only through the cross. The supernatural power released in this way of thinking is what creates a lifestyle of freedom. It is able to do this because it is TRUTH. To say that I have sinned is true. To say I am free of sin is truer still. The renewed mind is necessary to more consistently taste the supernatural life, which God intended to be the normal Christian life.[11]

Notice the number of references to your mind and consciousness that gives you the ability to live a lifestyle of freedom because of "supernatural power". If these statements by Johnson now sound like LaVey, Ford and Marie's Satanism, it is because they are.

The accusation, however, could be made that LaVey, Ford and Marie all do not believe in either a "God" or a "devil/Satan/Lucifer". Stephen Flowers argues that

> The left-hand path considers the position of humanity as it is; it takes into account the manifest and deep-seated desire of each human being to be a free, empowered, independent actor within his or her world. The pleasure and pain made possible by independent existence are seen as something to be embraced and as the most reasonable signs of the highest, most noble destiny possible for humans to attain—a kind of independent existence on a level usually thought of as divine. [...] Essentially, the left-hand path is the path of nonunion with the objective universe. It is the way of isolating consciousness within the subjective universe and, in a state of self-imposed psychic solitude, refining the soul or psyche to ever more perfect levels. The objective universe is then made to harmonize itself with the will of the individual psyche instead of the other way around.[12]

Flowers continues that

> There was—and still is—the practice of the left-hand philosophy in a purely pagan or heathen (i.e., pre-Christian) religious context, which does not need to refer to Satan or Lucifer to be intelligible. The left-hand path would have existed in Europe without the advent of Christianity (as was, and still is, the case in India).[13]

Putting both of these quotes together, an independent "divine" existence is possible, the goal is to be just like it, even to "harmonize" with it. Also, the big thing to notice is that the LHP does not need Satan, or

---

11. Vallotton, *Supernatural*, Logos Edition.
12. Stephen E. Flowers Ph.D., *Lords of the Left-Hand Path: Forbidden Practices and Spiritual Heresies* (Toronto, Ontario, Canada: Inner Traditions/Bear & Company, 2012), p. 19, Kindle Edition.
13. Flowers, *Left-Hand*, p. 54.

Lucifer to be "intelligible". Which means, in order to be an adherent of the LHP, you do not have to believe, in a literal, or literary (fictional) non-existent, Satan. This means that this external supernatural intelligence could be defined as what the Bible calls "God".

Flowers on whether there is a theism in Satanism and the person of the "Prince of Darkness" is

> first form or general principle of isolate intelligence from which all the particular manifestations of individual consciousness (or subjective universes) are derived: the ultimate deity of the left-hand path. An element of the nonnatural universe objectively within the universe itself, and therefore an independent sentient being in the objective sense because it is the very principle of that quality within the cosmos. Because of its categorical separateness, it is seen as rebellious and "evil" from the right-hand-path perspective. It is a more culturally neutral term for the same entity known in various left-hand-path schools as Satan, Lucifer, Set, and so on.[14]

Again, there is nothing here that says the LHP cannot have God has its focus. Ford continues in *The Bible of the Adversary: 10th Anniversary Edition* they

> do not worship Satan, nor do we bow before anything else. There are many types of Luciferians; some are Theistic: believing deeply in the spirit of the Adversary yet view this Spirit as a guide.[15]

Ford continues later that every

> Deific Mask has specific types of energy which can be shaped and directed towards a visualized goal. When you enter the ritual chamber, you are free to invest belief in any manner of Theistic, Polytheistic, Atheistic or Agnostic mind-frames which ignites your imagination.[16]

Looking at this definition, it is easy for the Hillsong, Prosperity, WoF, and NAR teachers to assume the "deific mask" as being what they claim is the biblical "God" in the effort to promote their false ideology and deify themselves.

Now we need to go back to King James and how, like the Prosperity, WoF, NAR and Hillsong Satanists, have used Psalm 82:6 to falsely declare themselves their own Satanic divinity. James, like the rest, is permitted to do whatever he likes to whom and with what he likes and no matter what laws he may also make, he can do whatever he likes with no legal or moral objection from others.

---

14. Flowers, *Left-Hand*, p. 317.
15. Michael W. Ford, *The Bible of the Adversary: 10th Anniversary Edition* (Houston, Texas: Succubus Productions, 2017), p. 22, Kindle Edition.
16. Ford, *Adversary*, p. 56.

Look what R. Douglas Geivett and Holly Pivec says about the NAR movement:

> NAR apostles establish the foundational government of the church, first, by 'hearing what the Holy Spirit is saying to the churches.' In other words, they receive new revelation from God. This new revelation is often referred to by NAR leaders as 'present truth' or 'new truths.' Wagner says the new revelation can only be received by apostles and prophets.
> Apostles either receive the revelation directly from God, or they receive it from prophets. Some apostles receive revelation that applies only to churches in their own apostolic networks. But other apostles—whom Wagner calls 'broadband apostles'—receive revelation for the entire body of Christ. Examples of revelation intended for the entire church include key NAR teachings, such as the revelation that God would restore apostles and prophets to the church. They also include the revelation that social transformation is 'one of the highest items on God's current agenda for His people.' After the apostles receive new revelation, they must go about 'setting things in order accordingly.' This means that apostles must implement the revelation they receive in the churches and ministries that come under their authority.[17]

The reality is, that these churches have declared themselves gods, and as gods they have a divine authority given to them, making them gods and apostles who are able to reshape the church anyway they desire.

While some have criticized that Hillsong is not a NAR church, the fact is that Houston, and the other leadership of that church since Houston has been removed temporarily at this point, do believe in the apostolic office and the redefinition that Wagner and others have given:

> Christians who share the load are the ones who will do whatever it takes to fulfil the vision. Religion has developed a concept that clergy is separate from laity, but there is nothing biblical about that belief. A flourishing church involves more people than the senior leadership alone. Paul described the purpose of the five-fold ministry: '...for the equipping of the saints for the work of the ministry, for the edifying of the body of Christ...' (Ephesians 4:12) Apostles, prophets, evangelists, pastors and teachers are given to inspire and teach everyone involved. The 'work of the ministry' is actually the responsibility of every believer. Church life is comprised of all four types of believers and at the core of a healthy church are those who own the vision and help carry the load of responsibility.[18]

---

17. R. Douglas Geivett and Holly Pivec, *A New Apostolic Reformation?: A Biblical Response to a Worldwide Movement* (Bellingham, Washington: Lexham Press, 2014), pp. 38–39. Logos Edition.

18. Brian Houston, *How To Maximise Your Life* (Sydney, Australia: Hillsong Music Australia), Kindle Edition.

Note another section of a different book:

> I hear people talking about a 'prosperity gospel.' There is no such thing. There is only one gospel—the gospel of Jesus Christ. The gospel contains promises born out of sacrifice, which apply to every aspect of life and living. I believe unashamedly that God wants people's lives to move forward and enlarge in every area, but for a greater purpose than ourselves.[19]

A Catholic writer looking into the absurdity of the Prosperity Gospel has this to say in defining what exactly it is:

> In fact, the morality inculcated by this generalized American religiosity had little or no interest in questions of money, or with the desire to become rich. As a result, the preachers of the Prosperity Gospel are not seen as violating any core principle of Christian morality, as would be the case if they promoted, instead of riches, unrestricted and unlimited sexual enjoyment. They cater to our desire for riches, something which is not usually seen as a serious matter of religious conduct. For in the last analysis, but rarely admitted, the tenets of religious faith are seen to rest upon an illusion, useful for ensuring social order and helpful for psychological comfort, but hardly to be compared with the actual world of work. This comparative lack of interest in doctrine and corresponding preoccupation with personal morality has colored American thinking about religion, even by those altogether opposed to religious belief. For example, beginning in 2008, certain atheists sponsored an ad campaign featuring a (black) man dressed in a Santa Claus suit with the caption, "Why believe in a god? Just be good for goodness's sake." What is so interesting about these ads is that they did not offer arguments against the existence of God or on behalf of the self-subsistence of matter or anything of that sort whatsoever. They did not address the question of whether God exists at all. They simply exhorted one to be good without the help of God. They assumed, what Americans generally have assumed, that religion is first of all about morality, not about proclaiming or asserting truths, such as the Trinity or the incarnation or the resurrection of Our Lord. In taking the line they did, it would seem that the sponsors of the ads either shared in the general American understanding of religion or supposed that the vast majority of those who read the ads would do so.[20]

Storck here is unfortunately correct. The Prosperity gospel that Houston says is the true gospel really has no interest in doctrinal truth or holding to biblical moral and ethical standards. Reading through Houston's and other Hillsong, Prosperity, WoF, and NAR churches lit-

---

19. Brain Houston, *For This I Was Born* (Nashville, Tennessee, Thomas Nelson), pp. 129–130 Kindle Edition.
20. Thomas Storck, *The Prosperity Gospel: How Greed and Bad Philosophy Distorted Christ's Teachings* (Ashland, Ohio: TAN Books, 2023), Logos Edition.

erature, the basic message is, if you do good things, by whatever standard that may mean, and you do good things with what "God" has given you, usually meaning giving it all to that church, then you will gain more and have all that you want in this life.

So, Houston, like the other Prosperity, WoF and NAR churches believe that their prosperity and Satanist fuelled doctrine, as defined by Storck, is in fact the true gospel. Not penal substitutionary atonement which is the true gospel of the Bible. Realize this, Houston is telling us, that the prosperity gospel, is the gospel of Jesus Christ, and not penal substitutionary atonement that is shown in the entirety of the biblical testimony. To define what penal substitutionary atonement is Charles Hodge comments that

> A third and more satisfactory answer to the objection in question is that the words penal and penalty do not designate any particular kind or degree of suffering, but any kind or any degree which is judicially inflicted in satisfaction of justice. The word death, as used in Scripture to designate the wages or reward of sin, includes all kinds and degrees of suffering inflicted as its punishment. By the words penal and penalty, therefore, we express nothing concerning the nature of the sufferings endured, but only the design of their infliction. Suffering without any reference to the reason of its occurrence is calamity; if inflicted for the benefit of the sufferer, it is chastisement; if for the satisfaction of justice, it is punishment. The very same kind and amount of suffering may in one case be a calamity; in another a chastisement; in another a punishment. If a man is killed by accident, it is a calamity. If he is put to death on account of crime and in execution of a judicial sentence, it is punishment. A man may be imprisoned to protect him from unjust violence. His incarceration is then an act of kindness. But if he be imprisoned in execution of a judicial sentence, then it is punishment. In both cases the evil suffered may be precisely the same. Luther was imprisoned for years to save him from the fury of the Pope. When, therefore, we say that Christ's sufferings were penal, or that He suffered the penalty of the law, we say nothing as to the nature or the degree of the pains which He endured. We only say, on the one hand, that his sufferings were neither mere calamities, nor chastisements designed for his own benefit, nor merely dogmatic, or symbolical, or exemplary, or the necessary attendants of the conflict between good and evil; and, on the other hand, we affirm that they were designed for the satisfaction of justice. He died in order that God might be just in justifying the ungodly.
>
> It is not to be inferred from this, however, that either the kind or degree of our Lord's sufferings was a matter of indifference. We are not authorized to say, as has so often been said, that one drop of his blood would have been sufficient to redeem the world. This may express a pious sentiment, but not a Scriptural truth. He would not have suffered as He did, nor to the degree He did, unless there had been an adequate reason for it. There must be some proportion between the evil endured,

and the benefit to be secured. If a man were saved from death or bondage by a prince's paying a shilling, it would be absurd to call that either a satisfaction or a ransom. There must be enough of self-sacrifice and suffering to give dignity and inherent value to the proffered atonement. While, therefore, the value of Christ's sufferings is due mainly to the dignity of his person, their character and intensity are essential elements in their worth. Nevertheless, their character as penal depends not on their nature, but on their design.[21]

The gospel here is described in a way that cannot be denied. Christ took the place of us, who deserved to be condemned and died as the perfect substitute for all that would come to faith. Houston, and all the others associated with him, deny this as the true gospel in the favour of prosperity, and Satanism.

L. Michael Morales brilliantly comments that

> Leviticus 1:4 reads, 'Then he shall lean [sāmak] his hand on the head of the ascension offering, and it will be accepted on his behalf to make atonement for him.' The result of this gesture, therefore, is that the animal now stands as a vicarious substitute for the worshipper, with the specific end of making atonement on his behalf—that is, of presenting the Israelite before God, reconciled and accepted.[22]

In being called a lamb, Christ is therefore the atoning sacrifice for all of us and therefore the Old Testament Levitical system is finished. Penal substitutionary atonement is the gospel. The gospel is not that we are gods that are responsible for amounting prosperity to spread this Satanic version of the gospel all over the world.

To enforce their authority to do this, these Prosperity, WoF, and NAR preachers have called themselves apostles. Earlier in the same book by Geivett and Pivec, it is noted that

> NAR apostles establish the foundational government of the church, first, by "hearing what the Holy Spirit is saying to the churches." In other words, they receive new revelation from God. This new revelation is often referred to by NAR leaders as "present truth" or "new truths."[23]

New revelation, which means the former revelation is not enough or insufficient. Is there evidence that Hillsong has in fact, countered the "revelation" or "commands" of scripture? In fact, there is evidence

---

21. Charles Hodge, *Hodge's Systematic Theology Volume II – Anthropology* (Ingersoll, Ontario, Canada: Devoted Publishing, 2019), pp. 346–347.

22. L. Michael Morales, *Who Shall Ascend the Mountain of the Lord?: A Biblical Theology of the Book of Leviticus*, ed. D. A. Carson, vol. 37, New Studies in Biblical Theology (England; Downers Grove, Illinois: Apollos; InterVarsity Press, 2015), pp. 127–128. Logos Edition.

23. Pivec, *Apostolic*, p. 38.

that Hillsong has believed in some new for of revelation. Look at this comment from another former member of Hillsong:

> Communion is no longer taken at Hillsong.[24]

Note how this contradicts the following command from Christ:

> [a]nd he took bread, and when he had given thanks, he broke it and gave it to them, saying, "This is my body, which is given for you. Do this in remembrance of me." And likewise the cup after they had eaten, saying, "This cup that is poured out for you is the new covenant in my blood." (Luke 22:19–20 ESV)

Christ here is pretty direct that communion must be observed. There was no "if you want to" here. The word in the above "do" is Greek ποιεῖτε which is a second person (you) imperative verb. Look how William Mounce, an expert in Koine Greek, describes the imperative:

> There is no more forceful way in the Greek language to tell someone to do something than a simple imperative—particularly the second person imperative. Especially when such a command is given regarding a specific situation, the one giving that command sees himself as an authority figure. He expects those addressed to do exactly as he has ordered.[25]

In other words, communion is not an option. Communion must be observed. If a church refuses to observe communion, it cannot be called a Christian church in any way at all. Because, Hillsong has received some kind of new revelation, that communion is no longer required, then all you have is what that false teacher from the front is telling you. Because the commands of the Bible, the simplest imperative by Christ himself, is no longer law at Hillsong.

> Jesus follows up the bread word with instruction to "Do this in remembrance of me." The notion of "remembrance" is pivotal to the celebration of Passover and cannot be limited, as it often is in English usage, to the idea of cognitive recall of a prior occurrence. In the biblical tradition, cognitive (or affective) recall is often triggered by verbal communication for that purpose, and this provides the impetus for some response or action. In a related sense, "remembrance" is often employed with the sense of "the effect of the recollection of the past for present or future benefit." With the repeated celebration of Passover as precursor, and with this linguistic background for the understanding of remembrance, we may understand Jesus as instructing his followers not

---

24. Tanya Levin, *People in Glass Houses* (Collingwood, Victoria, Australia: Schwartz Publishing Pty. Inc., 2015), p. 33. Ltd. Kindle Edition.

25. William D. Mounce, *Basics of Biblical Greek Grammar*, ed. Verlyn D. Verbrugge and Christopher A. Beetham, Fourth Edition (Grand Rapids, Michigan: Zondervan, 2019), p. 379. Logos Edition.

only to continue sharing meals together, but to do so in a way that their fellowship meals recalled the significance of his own life and death in obedience to God on behalf of others. This recollection should have the effect of drawing forth responses reminiscent of Jesus' own table manners—his openness to outsiders, his comportment as a servant, his indifference toward issues of status honor, and the like—so that these features of his life would come to be embodied in the community of those who call him Lord.[26]

Joel B. Green also agrees that communion is not an option and needs to be celebrated as a remembrance of Christ and what he came to do, but also of who Christ was here on earth both as a person and as God.

Similarly, Leon Morris says that "[d]o this in remembrance of me, does not mean, as some claim, that the communion is essentially a pleading of Christ before the Father."[27]

And since as C. Peter Wagner explains:

> For one thing, I believe that God was waiting for the biblical government of the Church to come into place under apostles and prophets. But this happened in 2001 when, at least according to my estimates, the Second Apostolic Age began. What more? I now think that in order for us to be able to handle the wealth responsibly, we need to recognize, identify, affirm, and encourage the ministry of apostles in the six non-religion mountains. They may or may not want to use the term "apostle," but they will function in Kingdom-based leadership roles characterized by supernaturally empowered wisdom and authority. [...] it serves the apostles who already have Kingdom-advancing projects in place all over the world and who will responsibly monitor their progress.[28]

Realize that Wagner is not saying that the original twelve apostles were the ones imbued with God's authority to spread "the kingdom". This authority was given to these new apostles in the twenty-first century, and these new apostles alone, who according to the requirements of Acts 1 could never fill the biblical role of an apostle to begin with. However, the entirety of Wagner's arguments about the new apostolic office is that these new apostles have more authority, to even rewrite the Bible, than the original apostles had. This claim by Wagner is entirely blasphemy and heresy.

---

26. Leon Morris, *Luke: An Introduction and Commentary*, vol. 3, Tyndale New Testament Commentaries (Downers Grove, Illinois: InterVarsity Press, 1988), p. 325, Logos Edition.

27. Joel B. Green, *The Gospel of Luke*, The New International Commentary on the New Testament (Grand Rapids, Michigan: Wm. B. Eerdmans Publishing Co., 1997), p. 762. Logos Edition.

28. Lance Wallnau, Bill Johnson, and Bill Johnson Lance Wallnau Alan Vincent C. Peter Wagner Ché Ahn Patricia King, *Invading Babylon: The 7 Mountain Mandate* (Shippensburg, Pennsylvania: Destiny Image, 2013), Logos Edition.

These men are frauds, and like King James, have claimed a spiritual authority that is to never be questioned in any way at all. The Hillsong, Prosperity, WoF, and NAR men and women are not to be questioned as apostles or as Satanic gods.

Note how these men treat those that they think are pitiful in some way:

> Donna was single and, refreshingly, never mentioned not having a boyfriend. Mainly this was because Brian did it all for her. Week after week, Brian would make comments from the pulpit. He was trying to find a husband for Donna. At any opportunity, Brian would make a joke at Donna's expense about her mid-twenties spinsterhood. He would laughingly allude to a romantic opportunity for her if a visiting pastor was a bachelor. This got uncomfortable after a while. It was repetitive and I didn't appreciate feeling forced to laugh at someone, not with them. By 1992, Donna found a husband. I attended the wedding with the rest of the youth group and hoped Brian was happy now. Our single female role model was officially gone. Donna had never planned on getting married. It was a lovely wedding, but I was just sorry things had to be that way. Donna doesn't remember it that way at all. She tells her story very differently from the pulpit. She says that it was her own private unmarried angst that drove her to Brian's office. 'I asked him, "What's wrong with me?"' she recalls. '"Why aren't I married? I'm nearly 30."' 'Nothing wrong with you,' Brian looked up to say. 'You're great, mate.' No wonder she finds he and Bobbie so supportive. She told me they were awesome.[29]

So, one of these leaders, stands up publicly then emotionally and spiritually abuses someone from his own church. Houston even gets the entire congregation of the young Hillsong church to laugh in mockery at Donna as well. When she is broken and asks Houston what is wrong with her, he again emotionally manipulates her by telling her that there is nothing wrong with her. So, in public, he is treating her like human garbage for not being married. Yet, when questioned by her about what must be wrong with her, Houston turns around and gaslights Donna.[30] This gaslighting is typical. Whenever questioning these leaders about why they are mistreating people, or what is wrong with the person that the elevated leader is mistreating them, the person is now gaslighted into believing that these leaders actually "love" them when these leaders, like Houston, are really treating them like human garbage. When questioned, you are gaslighted. Churches that are influenced by Hillsong and these Prosperity, WoF, and NAR churches and their music,

---

29. Levin, *Houses*, p. 40.

30. For a definition of what gaslighting is see: Psychology Today Staff, "Gaslighting," *Psychology Today*, July 20, 2023, https://www.psychologytoday.com/us/basics/gaslighting.

treat members the same way for questioning their wisdom in involving themselves with these Satanic churches.

There is no questioning the leaders of these apparently "biblical" churches at all. These leaders are right, and you are always wrong. If you think there is something wrong with you, even when the leaders are publicly mocking you, you are wrong again. There is a blind submission to their authority because these individuals firmly believe that these leaders have some special spiritual authority, just like Wagner claims they do.

The question needs to be asked: does this abuse and authority remain within Hillsong and these Prosperity, WoF and NAR churches, or has it spread around the world to Satanically dominate and even physically kill innocent people? That is where we must go now.

Chapter V: This is Spiritual Warfare. They Are Not People. They Are Demons.

Elle Hardy's book *Beyond Belief: How Pentecostal Christianity is Taking Over the World* is an eye-opener about what is happening with the Satanist church in the world. Hardy's testimony about her research in the documentary *Hillsong: A Megachurch Exposed* was alarming enough. Hardy's book goes to show how far churches like Hillsong, and other Satanist churches are willing to go like with when the following is mentioned:

> the modern third wave of Pentecostalism with C. Peter Wagner in the '80s. That wave, of course, led to Wagner coining the phrase 'spiritual warfare', giving a new name to the old idea of slaying demons in our midst. Spiritual warfare rests on the assumption that everything bad in the world is the result of demonic forces—whether due to 'satanic' beliefs, such as those held by Indigenous Mayans; or to what spiritual warriors see as the bastardisation of Christianity, [...] A student of faith in the Global South, Wagner's time as a missionary in South America gave him the idea that the world is in an apocalyptic struggle between good and evil.[1]

> Another way of looking at it is that dehumanising your opponent is the oldest trick in the book of conflict. For almost 40 years, Guatemala has been a testing ground for spiritual warfare, and it appears to be succeeding. A series of political leaders have put on their biblical armour, and shown how to take strategic-level spiritual warfare from the page into practice. Fully realised, spiritual warfare is a dictatorship of the faithful, going into battle against anyone who doesn't believe their claims.[2]

---

1. Elle Hardy, *Beyond Belief: How Pentecostal Christianity Is Taking Over the World* (London, England: C. Hurst & Company, 2021), p. 233, Kindle Edition.
2. Hardy, *Beyond Belief*, p. 234.

Nine months into Ríos Montt's reign, a pastor at El Verbo told a group of Americans that "we hold brother Efraín Ríos Montt like King David", the biblical figure who defeated Goliath and went on to become the first king of Israel. "The army doesn't massacre the Indians," the pastor continued. "It massacres demons, and the Indians are demon-possessed; they are communists." In the context of the Cold War, this Pentecostal justification was the soft-power sheen over decades of monetary and military might. It offered a moral impetus, beyond protecting America's interests, that people in the region could actually believe in. It was, quite possibly, the first time that spiritual warfare had been put into practice.[3]

Under Ríos Montt, the military launched what can only be described as a final solution, attacking 4,000 villages, wiping 626 of them off the map, [...] Foetuses were ripped from mothers' bodies, children had their heads caved in and were thrown into wells, women were gang-raped, men castrated. It's estimated that 80 per cent of the victims were Mayan.[4]

These quotes are pretty startling. How does the Hillsong, Prosperity, WoF, and NAR movements relate to all this? Hardy again comments that:

Peter Wagner saw fertile ground for strategic spiritual warfare in Latin American countries, which had seen decades of instability. He advocated a "fiercely pragmatic" approach, arguing that leaders "ought to see clearly that the end *does* justify the means."[5] Wagner believed that Christians of the Global South were leading the way when it came to the spiritual battlefield, and the idea is now finding purchase beyond his traditional mission grounds. (italics in original)[6]

In confirming what exactly Wagner said, hoping that it was not quite this bad, I looked into the book *Your Church Can Grow* by C. Peter Wagner to find him say that

[w]henever we imply that evangelistic methods are up for grabs, we are unashamedly recommending a fiercely pragmatic approach to evangelism. Likewise, it is a common mistake to associate pragmatism with a lack of spirituality. Some are rightly afraid that pragmatism can degenerate to the point that ungodly methods are used, and this is not at all what church growth people advocate. The Bible does not allow us to sin that grace may abound or to use whatever means that God has prohibited in order to accomplish those ends He has recommended.

But, with this proviso, we out to see clearly that the end *does* justi-

---

3. Hardy, *Beyond Belief*, p. 238.
4. Hardy, *Beyond Belief*, pp. 238–239.
5. C. Peter Wagner, *Your Church Can Grow: Seven Vital Signs of a Healthy Church* (Eugene, Oregon; Wipf & Stock Publishers, 1998), pp. 160–161. As quoted by Hardy in Beyond Belief.
6. Hardy, *Beyond Belief*, p. 244.

fy the means. What else could possibly justify the means? *If the method I am using accomplishes the goal I am aiming at, it is for that reason a good method.* If, on the other hand, my method is not accomplishing the goal, how can I be justified in continuing to use it? (italics on "does" in original, other italics mine)[7]

So, according to Wagner, and the other Satanist churches that hold Wagner up to the level of a new messiah with his New Apostolic Reformation and seven-mountain mandate eschatology, whatever it takes to spread *their* church, if it works, it is not wrong. If mass murder, assassinations, torture, etc., are effective in spreading *their* Satanic gospel, then it is justified and *not* sinful. Remember that Houston in chapter four directly said that the prosperity gospel is the true gospel. Hardy was being kind to Wagner in the way that she quoted him. The reality of what Wagner is really saying, is many times worse, pragmatically, than we could possibly imagine.

Before someone turns around and says that this is a strawman argument, read what Hardy showed about the civil war in Guatemala, and Wagner's influence on it. Wagner did not renounce or condemn the actions the Guatemala soldiers took when using his strategic-level spiritual warfare to murder innocent people and even rip babies out of their mother's wombs. There is no strawman argument here. Wagner fully believes that if it takes wiping a village and that villages people off the face of the earth to spread *his* gospel, then it is not sinful and is justified.

In his commentary on Acts, Wagner says that:

> Strategic-level spiritual warfare is one expression of the power given by the Holy Spirit that has been spreading rapidly on all continents over the past few years. As I mentioned in the first chapter, it deals with confronting the principalities and powers described by Paul in Ephesians 6:12. Strategic-level spiritual warfare is significantly different from ground-level spiritual warfare (casting out demons from individuals) and occult-level spiritual warfare (dealing with witches, curses, Eastern religions, New Age channelers and the like). A substantial body of literature has been forthcoming in this relatively new field.[8]

So, now we need to draw the line of thinking here: 1) Wagner goes as a missionary to South America. One of the countries he influences is Guatemala in Central America. Wagner at this time is teaching about strategic-level spiritual warfare. 2) While Wagner is in the country, a

---

7. C. Peter Wagner, *Your Church Can Grow: Seven Vital Signs of a Healthy Church* (Eugene, Oregon; Wipf & Stock Publishers, 1998), pp. 160–161.

8. C. Peter Wagner, *The Book of Acts: A Commentary* (Ventura, California: Regal, 2008), pp. 53–54.

civil war is being fought and this is where Mayan natives are called demons to justify their slaughter because of "strategic-level spiritual warfare." 3) 1981, the original publishing date of *Your Church Can Grow*, Wagner publishes this book that shows that a "vital sign" of growth is that the "church" takes whatever steps are necessary to grow the church. To try and say that Wagner was not aware of what was happening in a country where he had been a missionary, and the reasons for that mass-murder is to be wilfully ignorant. Wagner knew what was going on and why it was happening. Instead of rebuking the killing, he praised it for being "the ends always justify the means." This is scary bit of information to rake into consideration with the Satanist church.

Hardy further warns that what happened in Guatemala is a grim warning of what might be happening in other parts of the world.[9] Could it happen here in North America or other "western" nations? Might as well take a look and see.

The New Inquisition

A question needs to be asked in looking at all of the above: have these Satanists, by saying they have the true gospel, that other "churches" do not, tried to take over government, especially here in North America? While there have been no direct influences here in Canada to elected politicians from Satanist churches to this point, when Trump was facing his first impeachment trial, he invited a number of prominent "preachers" to pray for him in the oval office.

When the first impeachment against President Trump was under way, Trump invited a bunch of people to come into the oval office and pray for him that he would remain in office. A picture was taken of all the participants in this group prayer. In the picture you can see, unsurprisingly, Trump's spiritual advisor Paula White, right behind her is Brian Houston, you can also see Sean Feucht there as well with his hand on Trump's arm.[10] Paula White is a well-known NAR preacher, and Feucht has been grossly involved in Satanic Christianity and outright New Age practices for years calling it "Christian". All three of these individuals are seven-mountain mandate individuals and are all pushing the idea that we must take over the world with their form of Satanism. These three people are in direct contact, and in direct influence, of one of the most influential men in the United States at the time of writing. In the article posted by Fox News in footnote 10

---

9. Hardy, *Beyond Belief*, p. 246.

10. Caleb Parke, "Pastors, worship leaders pray for Trump in Oval Office amid impeachment fight," *Fox News*, July 21, 2023, https://www.foxnews.com/politics/pastors-worship-leaders-pray-for-trump-in-oval-office-amid-impeachment-fight.

(this chapter) there is also a video by Brian Houston praising the "faith based event."

Also note, that Trump invited Kenneth Copeland to pray for his rally for re-election in November 2022 and called Copeland a great man. Copeland, as is no secret, is a well-known NAR activist.[11] Another video of Paula White initiating a prayer for the launch of *Evangelicals for Trump Coalition* shows a moment that White directly calls Guillermo Maldonado an "apostle" when introducing the "Christian" leaders.[12] The number of NAR Satanists that are actively influencing one of the most powerful men in United States politics cannot be understated. In her book, Hardy, shows how some these same Prosperity, WoF, and NAR preachers have many politicians paid off in African countries.

> Redeemed's Adeboye and Winners Chapel's Oyedepo, are content to be kingmakers—or, as they're more politely described, 'spiritual advisors'—seeing to a long line of Christian and Muslim politicians willing to bend the knee in return for a public endorsement, an electoral blessing. What the megachurch leaders get in return is a different kind of power.[13]

If these internationally politically powerful men and women who are pushing a global take over of their heretical Satanist apostles, and to push a takeover by any means necessary, are we as true, biblical Christians safe? There is a very long history in the entire world of politicians looking for "divine" or "Godly" blessing from prominent religious figures in order to support their political, or sometimes outright tyrannical, push for power.

Here is a quote from a Christian friend of mine on social media that I am quoting with permission:

> You know I've often wondered if it'll be the NAR who will be persecuting Christians in the west since we refuse to bow to their progressive ideologies.[14]

Tara Storm here raised an interesting question. All the evidence that I have shown and come across points directly that Storm may very well be on to something here.

Prosperity, WoF, and NAR churches, along with Hillsong, have

---

11. RevAlexMeadows, "Kenneth Copeland Prays For Trump (Latrobe, PA)," *YouTube*, July 21, 2023, https://www.youtube.com/watch?v=uw40kns811c.

12. NBC News, "Christian Leaders Pray Over Trump During Launch Of Evangelicals For Trump Coalition | NBC News," *YouTube*, July 21, 2023, https://www.youtube.com/watch?v=HrBvMFJ_drs.

13. Hardy, *Beyond Belief*, p. 201.

14. Tara Storm, "Facebook Reply Post," *Facebook*, July 12, 2023, https://www.facebook.com/anthony.uyl/.

clearly shown that they will stop at nothing to fulfill their world conquering mandate, including the brutal slaughter of entire villages. No office is off limits for these Satanists, no moral guides are in place since these new "apostles" are the final authority on all things. Since the most direct command from Christ about taking communion is not even being followed, what model are these men and women following? As I have shown that they are in fact teaching Satanism in what they believe, it is not unfair to say that their world domination will result in the persecution and murder of biblical Christians. Remember that these churches believe that their prosperity gospel, is the true gospel. Not the true gospel of penal substitutionary atonement that has shown its power and freedom for so long. If our gospel is false, and thus, we are not Christian's, to them we are nothing but "demons" that must be removed. These churches have already laid down this mandate and accepted it by saying "the ends justify the means."

While the inquisition of the Roman Catholic Church in the 1500's was mostly targeted at women that they accused of being "pagans" without precedent, a new inquisition is trying to take hold that will have Satanists, claiming to be Christians, coming after God's true church.

The model and the framework of a Satanist war machine has been shown in this chapter. To call the seven-mountain mandate anything but a Satanist war machine would be a plea to wilful ignorance which is something God will not tolerate as an excuse. When will the gate of fire be poured out on the world? Hopefully this gate will never open. To prevent that gate from opening is why we need to take a stand now.

Chapter VI: An Example of Hillsong's Music Coming from the Occult

Over the last few years, some but not all, people within the Christian church have started to raise questions about the legitimacy of Hillsong Church based out of Sydney, Australia.

The first "warning" signs were when the empty words of the songs of Hillsong's music team, *Hillsong* UNITED, became more and more obvious. While the songs would always mention God, Christ, or the Holy Spirit in some way, the songs were very self-centred, focused on the person more than the songs that are shown in the scriptures themselves. There is a large element of personal references to personal issues in many Psalms, but in every case, those Psalms turn the focus to God in order to call on him to intervene or to soothe the soul of the writer during a time of outright murder and mayhem in some cases.

However, last year (2022), another issue with Hillsong came to the front. That issue came to light with the release of the three-part docuseries called *Hillsong: A Megachurch Exposed.* Many people took the sexual misconduct of Carl Lentz and also of the paedophilia of Brian Houston's father seriously. The coverup by Houston especially rocked many people to their very souls. This was not the whole issue brought up with Hillsong. The other issue with Hillsong Church in the entire world was the money driving aspect of it. While many people will say that it is just greedy men pushing a business model instead of the gospel like Hillsong should, we need to ask is there more going on here? While the docuseries mentioned above was written by a secular film company, some critics have taken that as an ad hominem way to accuse the film makers of saying that the church needs to be paying its staff and "volunteers" and because it is a secular company that they do not understand that churches are run off of volunteer help.

In most cases it is true that some churches cannot survive without volunteers. Most churches simply cannot survive with the meagre budgets they have and so volunteers are needed in order to keep the church running. In Canada at least, the very people running the church, the board of directors (or "elders") are required to be volunteers and not to have family members that are paid in any way by the church for services of any kind. This requirement for volunteer leadership is made clear in Canadian Charity Law. If a church wants to maintain a tax-free charity status, the board of directors cannot be paid or related to paid members of a church. That being said however, note the commands of scripture:

> You shall give him his wages on the same day, before the sun sets (for he is poor and counts on it), lest he cry against you to the LORD, and you be guilty of sin (Deuteronomy 24:15 ESV).

> Then I will draw near to you for judgment. I will be a swift witness against the sorcerers, against the adulterers, against those who swear falsely, against those who oppress the hired worker in his wages, the widow and the fatherless, against those who thrust aside the sojourner, and do not fear me, says the LORD of hosts (Malachi 3:5 ESV).

Christ said

> Soldiers also asked him, "And we, what shall we do?" And he said to them, "Do not extort money from anyone by threats or by false accusation, and be content with your wages" (Luke 3:14 ESV).

Paul

> Now to the one who works, his wages are not counted as a gift but as his due (Romans 4:4 ESV).

> He who plants and he who waters are one, and each will receive his wages according to his labor (1 Corinthians 3:8 ESV).

> For the Scripture says, "You shall not muzzle an ox when it treads out the grain," and, "The laborer deserves his wages" (1 Timothy 5:18 ESV).

Notice that in these verses, there are absolutely no exceptions made for those that are "working" for a church in any way. What I am saying here is: if a church can afford to pay its volunteers, as Hillsong can without doubt, then by scripture it is required to do so. However, since the docuseries *Hillsong: A Megachurch Exposed* showed that Hillsong volunteers are often emotionally abused and physically mistreated, Hillsong is treating its workforce more as willing slaves than workers worth their wages as the Bible from the Pentateuch to the Epistles commands. To be quite honest, it would not hurt Hillsong's bottom line financially in any way to pay its volunteers for one day of work per week.

Are these the only issues with Hillsong Church? As the main title of this chapter shows that it is indeed not the only problem. There are in fact many other problems going on with Hillsong, and Chris Tomlin in this chapter, that need to be dealt with. Since I have shown without a doubt that all the Hillsong, Prosperity, WoF, and NAR movements are Satanism, and also note that Elevations' Steven Furtick has claimed that "I am God Almighty" (again, Satanism), it needs to be shown how this music that is nothing but occultic hymns, needs to be kept out of our churches because of the intentions behind it which is covered extensively in chapter nine. While some have tried to use the defense of "but the words are okay..." or "the Doctrinal Smell Test" excuse, later in chapter ten I will prove that this defense does not in any way work.

So, in a proper critique, let us go and see what Brian Houston and one of his more notable elders, Andrew Denton, then Darlene Zschech and finally Chris Tomlin are saying and teaching.

Brian Houston and the Occult

First, the below quote is not the first Brian Houston book I read. The first one *Live Love Lead* had within it certain words and certain phrasing that made the "red flags" go up. Really though, the book *Live Love Lead* was not enough to base an accusation of being based in the occult on. That Houston book led to what is more known as circumstantial evidence. Circumstantial evidence is evidence that if you know what is being said, you know what is being said. However, with this type of evidence, it is not enough to prove without a question the accusation brought against the person. Once the accusation is proven, then circumstantial evidence can be used to backup the main evidence.

So, when I read the second Houston book *There is More* I was not surprised when I found the following:

> There is a reason our church begins every church service with praise and thanksgiving. I once heard someone write off the faster praise songs at the beginning of a service as the cocktails served before the meal. But there is a whole lot more to the songs of praise that we commence every service with than simply giving the latecomers a chance to arrive. Praise is always an entry point and often precedes the miracle: Enter his gates with thanksgiving and his courts with praise. (Psalm 100:4, NIV11) Besides the tradition of worship being the right thing to do, singing and speaking the Word of God can actually bring a felt shift to the atmosphere of a church service. Worship brings a tangible sense of joy and peace, power and awe, into the room as we confess with our lips the

greatness of who God is. Worship is also filling the human spirit with the content of God's Word, which is why we take such great care when approving the lyrics of our songs. We know that songs can shape theology and that theology builds faith.[1]

The above quote shows that music is being used for magical means. In stating that "[p]raise is always an entry point and often precedes the miracle," this is a direct point of evidence of occultism within Hillsong's music. What makes this quote even worse, is what kind of "miracle" and "spiritual" forces that Houston and his church are trying to call down. What Houston is trying to do with the music will be shown in chapter nine.

In showing that music can be used to manipulate the church attendees. As the following quote shows, Bach

> was beholden to provide a constant flow of church music for the city's main churches, especially St Thomas and St Nikolai. The express purpose of this church music was the utilization of musical means to render the congregants more receptive to the Lutheran orthodoxy of the day and thus intensify its articulation in ways that the spoken word alone, it was assumed, could not. In implementing this agenda, Bach presumably thought of himself not so much as a great artist but primarily as a consummate artisan. Against this backdrop it is ultimately more or less irrelevant what he may have thought or felt in his heart of hearts about certain tenets of the Lutheran orthodoxy of his day. He had a task to perform and we have reason to assume that he was determined to perform that task to the best of his abilities.[2]

It has been a common practice for churches, and now even Satanic ones, to use music to influence and change their congregations' perspectives. Even if the songs pass the "Doctrinal Smell Test", the change will be inevitable. Observing what music can do, note that in a participant study:

> Spiritual or mystical experiences. Finally, all but one of our participants described having had some sort of spiritual or mystical experience involving visions, direct communication with deities, feeling the presence of the divine, or a gut feeling that something remarkable was occurring. Some described everyday experiences as being spiritual or mystical. John said that he has "encountered entities from another time and place", Samantha described playing drums at a bonfire as a mystical experience when she "felt exhilarated, like a skydive", and Jonathan

---

1. Brian Houston, *There is More* (New York, New York: Waterbrook, 2018), pp. 69–70. Kindle Edition.
2. Lars Fischer, "The Legacy of Anti-Judaism in Bach's Sacred Cantatas," in *Jews and Protestants*, ed. Irene Aue-Ben-David, Aya Elyada, Moshe Sluhovsky and Christian Wiese (Ingersoll, Ontario, Canada: Devoted Publishing, 2023), pp. 79–80.

said that he has "visions... while meditating". Jack described "appreciation of great art... forests... music... being on top of a mountain" as spiritual experiences.³

The above quote shows a direct link between magical experiences through the use of music. Music is always apart of occult experiences as is shown near the end of the quote. An occult goeticist, what the Bible would refer to as a "necromancer" (I will deal with this in chapter seven), by the name of Jake-Stratton Kent makes a direct connection between ancient gods, music and summoning demonic spirits.

> The Phoenicians considered [Kothar or Hephaestus] to be patron of magic; they also considered him to be the inventor of incantations, and cognate with this also the first poet. [...] poetry and incantation were seen as actual devices. It also points to the pre-Greek antiquity of the connection of poetry and magic, and their relation to the goetic fire cults.⁴

In speaking about goetic, demon summoning rituals, Stratton-Kent comments that

> Afterwards they went in procession in the streets, dancing in measured motions. At some points they would dance singularly, at others all together, while musical instruments were played before them.⁵

Music, the occult, and even summoning of spirits can be in and the same thing. Since, Hillsong teaches a Satanic gospel, and the above quote from Houston shows that the music draws in power to do miracles, there really is no questions as to what the music is really doing in our churches.

To make the point even further about what Houston is saying, speaking about spoken praise, or just spoken words as "always an entry point and often precedes the miracle" as the problematic part.

To bring the point home, on the next page of this book that will once again show what Houston is speaking of, look below

> [w]ords are not just for communication; words are for creation. Before Adam and Eve ever fell into sin, they knew God only as Elohim: the God who creates. Before they ever needed Jehovah-Jireh (Provider) or Jehovah-Rapha (Healer), they were in communion with the Creator God. You see, the Lord created the world with His words. He said,

---

3. Kevin A. Harris, Kate M. Panzica, and Ruth A. Crocker, "Paganism and Counseling: The Development of a Clinical Resource," *Open Theology*, vol. 2, no. 1, (2016): p. 867.

4. Jake Stratton-Kent, *Geosophia: I* (London, United Kingdom: Scarlet Imprint, 2010), p. 195.

5. Stratton-Kent, *Geosophia: I*, p. 201.

> "Let there be light" (Genesis 1:3). And there was light. Our words still hold creative power. They can breathe life into dead situations, create hope where there was none. You can speak life into your marriage, your spouse, your partner. You can speak destiny and purpose into your children's little bodies, helping them create belief around the words you choose. You can speak life into your well-being and your finances. It's as easy as thanking God for what you do have and trusting Him with your words for what you don't. Recall scriptures that relate to your circumstances and speak them out over your life. For example, you might echo Philippians 4:19: "Thank You, God, that You supply all my needs in accordance to Your riches in glory!"[6]

To claim that we have the same miraculous, "creative" power in the words that we speak is to be saying that our words have the same power as magic, or spells. We, as people do not have that power, God alone does. To claim that we have the ability to access that power at a moment's whim is to say that we ourselves are gods and that the true God, must do as we command because he "loves" us too much. Realize the addition that Houston is making in the first quoted piece. "But there is a whole lot more to the songs of praise that we commence every service with than simply giving the latecomers a chance to arrive. Praise is always an entry point and often precedes the miracle." I hope you are reading that right. The songs Hillsong is putting out, are designed to invite in miraculous power. Miraculous power that allows you to claim the power of only God himself, to do "creative" works. In short: Hillsong's music are magical mantras/spells designed to give you the power of God himself.

Note some interesting occultic use of words in the Hugo Odeberg translation of *3 (Hebrew) Enoch*

> And there is a court before the Throne of Glory, which no seraph nor angel can enter, and it is 36,000 myriads of parasangs, as it is written (Is.6:2): "and the Seraphim are standing above him" (the last word of the scriptural passage being 'Lamech-Vav' [numerical value: 36]). As the numerical value Lamech-Vav (36) the number of the bridges there. And there are 24 myriads of wheels of fire. And the ministering angels are 12,000 myriads. And there are 12,000 rivers of hail, and 12,000 treasuries of snow. And in the seven Halls are chariots of fire and flames, without reckoning, or end or searching. (3 Enoch 22b:1–4a)

> And why is he called Raderiel? Because out of every word that goes forth from his mouth an angel is created: and he stands in the songs (in the singing company) of the ministering angels and utters a song before the Holy One, blessed be He when the time draws nigh for the recitation of the (Thrice) Holy. (3 Enoch 27:3)

---

6. Houston, *More*, p. 71.

to smite kings by his speech, to turn kings away from their paths, to set up(the) rulers over their dominion as it is written (Dan. 2:21): "and he changeth the times and the seasons, and to give wisdom unto all the set wise of the world and understanding (and) knowledge to all who understand knowledge, as it is given (Dan. 2:21): "and knowledge to them that know understanding", to reveal to them the secrets of my words and to teach the decree of my righteous judgement, 10as it is written (Is. 55:11): "so shall my word be that goeth forth out of my mouth; it shall not return unto me void but shall accomplish (that which I please)." 'E'eseh' (I shall accomplish) is not written here, but "asdh' (he shall accomplish), meaning, that whatever word and whatever utterance goes forth from before the Holy One, blessed be He, Metatron stands and carries it out. And he establishes the decrees of the Holy One, blessed be He. (3 Enoch 47:9–10)

Before pulling all of this apart look at a statement made in the Sefer Yetzirah:

They consist of a decade out of nothing and of twenty-two fundamental letters. He divided the twenty-two consonants into three divisions.[7]

The idea here of words, and letters that have the power to create are evident in both Hekhalot and Kabbalistic literature. The Lamech-Vav being a gematria word that can be used to create is in the first quote from 3 Enoch. The second quote indicates an angelic being that is given the ability to create new angels with words alone, and lastly, Metatron is given the power to verbally bring down entire kingdoms because of the decree of Yahweh himself. Since Houston, like the rest of his Satanist allies, believe they are gods, they can pervert the biblical ideology to try to claim that their words are just as effective as "God's" and will accomplish the same thing. Unsurprisingly, if these "creative words" do work, it will be at the hands of something demonic, a Metatron-like demon (there is no such demon or angel named in the Bible), that will accomplish the task. The last quote is from the Sefer Yetzirah, an early Kabbalah text that also shows in the greater context that there a "magical" letters and words that were used to create the cosmos. Words that Kabbalists, and Houston, seem to be able to use to their will.

Do you realize the deception there? Houston, and others of his ilk, like Bill Johnson, Kris Vallotton, Kenneth Copeland, and as will be shown later, Chris Tomlin promoting necromancy, are claiming that you, since you have the power of God, are a god yourself and have the same creative "words" as God. This is usually defended with the termi-

---

7. Rev. Dr. Isidor Kalisch, יצירה *Sepher Yezirah*: *A Book on Creation; or, The Jewish Metaphysics of Remote Antiquity* (Ingersoll, Ontario, Canada: Devoted Publishing, 2020), p. 8.

nology that we are "little gods". This is not only heresy but Satanism. We are not gods. We are not divine, and neither do our words have the same creative power as God's to cause the miraculous to happen. The verse of John 14:12 that we will do greater things than God is a reference to the spread of the gospel. Again, context is important, as I have explained earlier, the context of John 14 talks about Jesus coming to make the Father known. In other parts of John and other gospels, Jesus says he came to make the Father known to Israel first. In Acts 1, Jesus commissions the apostles to carry the gospel to the ends of the earth. Jesus did not do that while on earth. Hence, the greater work of making the Father known was given to the apostles.

Houston continues with his occult ideology that

> the list goes on. What are you believing for? What is the "more" when it comes to your calling that stirs you to make a confession of faith? Speak, proclaim, command, and call down the blessing that is promised to you. Lift your eyes and lift your confession; then watch our High Priest lift your spirits and cause to rise within you hope and faith that He will do abundantly above all you could ever ask or imagine.[8]

See here what else Houston has to say, "In the eyes of God and with his leading, wisdom, favor, and provision—if you hold fast to that which he has placed in your heart and do it with a pioneering spirit, I believe you will see it come to pass."[9] and also,

> Consider that the first three individuals outside of Jerusalem whose lives were transformed by the gospel were not only outsiders but way outsiders. The first was a sorcerer, a wizard named Simon who confounded people with his magic tricks.[10]

The first quote is problematic in that Houston is making you the reason why a dream or "gifting of God" will or will not come true. The idea of fostering or "growing" something in your heart, despite what some charismatics say, is not biblical. God is the one that makes these things happen. It is not up to us whether God's plans will happen. God alone decides what will happen and how God will use us in his grand plans. By us "hold[ing] fast" to what we feel we want and doing so "with a pioneering spirit", Houston is again feeding into occultic, I am a Satanic god, type of thinking. Again, on the surface it may not seem so. But once the "key" of the first quote I showed from Houston about the "music" making miracles happen, the idea of self-deification is lit-

---

8. Houston, *More*, p. 72.
9. Brian Houston, *Live Love Lead* (New York, New York: Faithwords, 2015), p. 60. Kindle Edition.
10. Houston, *Lead*, p. 61.

tered throughout Houston's writings.

The second quote is problematic because in fact, Simon did not convert. I am not sure how Houston is making this claim. The scripture is clear that Simon converted because he wanted the power of the Holy Spirit for deceptive, and most likely, magical purposes. In response to Simon's request to get this "God power" from the apostles, Peter rebuked Simon and sent the occultist on his way.

See how Peter rebukes Simon:

> Even Simon himself believed, and after being baptized he continued with Philip. And seeing signs and great miracles performed, he was amazed (Acts 8:13 ESV).

> Now when Simon saw that the Spirit was given through the laying on of the apostles' hands, he offered them money, saying, "Give me this power also, so that anyone on whom I lay my hands may receive the Holy Spirit." But Peter said to him, "May your silver perish with you, because you thought you could obtain the gift of God with money! You have neither part nor lot in this matter, for your heart is not right before God. Repent, therefore, of this wickedness of yours, and pray to the Lord that, if possible, the intent of your heart may be forgiven you. For I see that you are in the gall of bitterness and in the bond of iniquity." And Simon answered, "Pray for me to the Lord, that nothing of what you have said may come upon me" (Acts 8:18–24 ESV).

Verse 13 shows that the miracles performed amazed Simon, he then approaches Peter when Simon sees that the apostles placing their hands upon people allowed for the Holy Spirit (at that time) to come to people. Simon wanted to do the signs and miracles. Even though he confessed and was baptized, Peter recognized it as a false conversion. A false conversion that was based on the desire to gain more occultic power.

Houston here is misquoting scripture to claim something as untrue. Since Hillsong through the docuseries *Hillsong: A Megachurch Exposed* was proven to be a business and not a true church, it should not be surprising that Houston would use a verse, out of context, to say that someone that offered to buy God's power was a true believer. Even though the words of Peter make it clear that Simon was a false convert and a deceiver doomed to destruction.

The evidence of this is given in many different early church fathers books claiming that "[n]ow this Simon of Samaria, from whom all sorts of heresies derive their origin, formed his sect out of the following materials"[11] or that Simon continued to use magical power

---

11. Irenæus, *Against Heresies* (Ingersoll, Ontario, Canada: Devoted Publishing, 2020), p. 79.

in Rome. In that account, Peter himself called on God to rebuke Simon and Simon, while floating in the air, was brought crashing down to the ground (*The Acts of Peter*). Church history shows the true heart of Simon Magus. Simon Magus's heart was one of the demonic, and not of God.

A defense will likely come up at this point that Houston quotes scripture and the words of Hillsong music are directed to God. Later I will show the flawed argument of the Doctrinal Smell Test to use as a defence in chapter ten. Just because it talks about God, Jesus, and/or the Holy Spirit does not mean those songs, or hymns, are meant that way. Likewise, many of us have seen people in the past, or presently, who claim to be Christians, but it is plain they are not. Again, the name of Jesus is on their lips, but the content of their heart is far from being regenerate.

To the first point of Houston quoting scripture, the occult regularly uses the Bible itself for goetic/necromantic purposes. In the text from a Latin Medieval text called *Secrets of Solomon: A Witch's Handbook from the trial records of the Venetian Inquisition* Joseph H. Peterson translates a spell that is meant to purify a ritual fire by exorcising the "evil spirits" out of it. The way this is done, is by the "witch" speaking Psalm 119:113–117.

> You should have fire exorcised as we have said in the chapter on the pentacle. For a good incense, take equal parts of aloe, myrrh, musk, and natural balsam; mix them in a consecrated mixing vessel, the lid of which should be perforated, and when needed for the work, throw it into the exorcised fire, while saying this prayer:
>
> O Lord I have hated the unjust, and I esteemed your law. You are my helper and my supporter, and I have always [*greatly] trusted in your word. Turn away from me, O spiteful ones, and I will study the commands of my God. Support me according to your pronouncement, and I will live, and don't dash my hopes. Help me and I will be safe, and I will always reflect on your judgments.[12]

Some of you may think that is absurd as the occult does not use the Bible in any way. The truth is that many New Agers and those involved in the darker occultic arts know the Bible better than a majority of Christians attending church every Sunday. It is hard to believe but it is true. This does not mean that they understand the true message of the Bible and the salvation of Christ, but they can quote the Bible verbatim much better than a majority of Christians warming seats every

---

12. The Bible reference in the footnotes says Psalm 118 (according to the Latin Vulgate) with Psalm 119 in brackets for the KJV. Joseph H. Peterson, *Secrets of Solomon: A Witch's Handbook from the trial records of the Venetian Inquisition* (Kasson, Minnesota: Twilit Grotto Press, 2018), p. 78.

Sunday.

Whether Houston intends for this to be the way he is using the Bible, we cannot know for sure. However, in the docuseries *Hillsong: A Megachurch Exposed*, Elle Hardy mentions that Houston, when his new church was not doing well, which is something you do not hear from Houston mainly because he does not want you to know that, that Houston went to the United States and learned from some of the best Word-of-Faith and Prosperity teachers that the United States had at the time. In the end, Houston learned how to use magic, from active Satanists, to grow his church. Houston may not have realized it is magic, or that it is demonic and even properly labelled, Satanism, but I believe he does. Only time will tell exactly where Houston knows this occultism comes from.

Andrew Denton and the Occult

First, I must comment on who Andrew Denton is. Denton is one of the elders of Hillsong Church in Sydney, Australia. Denton admits in the opening chapters of his book *Kingdom Builders* that he is not Bible College or Seminary trained. Denton even mentions that he did not finish high school either. Despite the hiring requirements of many churches, a lack of college, and even high school, training are not disqualifiers for ministry or even preaching the gospel.

But what these facts do show is that Denton has been part of Hillsong Church since its earliest days, and therefore the hermeneutical training Denton has received has been from Brian Houston himself. Since the above section shows that what Houston is teaching, preaching, and publishing through his church's music is all steeped in the occult and to be used to promote and spread Satanism, it should not surprise any of us what Denton is going to say in this book about how to make money and give it all to your church. Not a bad idea in principle, but the ways Denton argues for you to make this money happen is coming from the occult.

I am not going to spend a lot of time on it, as I do not think I need to, but I will deal with the idea of *The Source* extensively in chapter nine when talking about the *Age of Aquarius*. There are three places in Denton's book that he refers to God either as *Source* or *The Source*.[13] It should not be hard to believe after reading this book up to this point that you will easily see that (*The*) *Source* is a common name given by the occult to the universe, nature, God, or Satan. God being named *Source* is not in the Bible. When *Source* is used as a proper noun, a

---

13. Andrew Denton, *Kingdom Builders* (Castle Hill, New South Wales, Australia: Shout! Publishing, 2020), p. 54, 59, 72. Kindle Edition.

name, identifier such as "he is a Canadian", Canadian being a proper noun, this is a reference to a New Age and occult version of a god. People again will argue against this pseudonym for God as "Source". God is named as a source of blessing and promise. But God is not named as "Source, the source of blessing and promise." This is a very important distinction to make. I will explain more about the origins of "Source" in chapter nine.

Why is this distinction important? Denton says that

> I'm telling you, over the years, I've seen God provide, and provide, and provide. Susan and I have continually seen Ephesians 3:20 in our lives. You see, the world is looking for the one thing it can do to unlock blessing and fortune. Libraries and bookstores are full of these books. And, I believe as Christians, we've got it. When you put God first, everything flows as a consequence. Opportunity flows. Resources flow. The heavens literally are poured out.[14]

This is a reference to the occult concept of As Above, So Below.

To explain the concept of As Above, So Below, I must shift the conversation back to Johnson, Vallotton and Wommack again. This needs to be done because before I go any further, I need to explain the origin of "As Above, So Below" to show that it is from the occult. This occultic belief is the most basic of occult philosophies in the New Age, and more specifically, the LHP.[15] The quote comes from below:

> This is true, and far distant from a Lie; whatever is below, is like that which is above; and that which is above, is like that which is below: By this are acquired and perfected the Miracles of the One Thing.[16]

---

14. Denton, *Kingdom*, p. 45.

15. When I was having the fight with my church, the goetic necromancer (see chapter seven to understand that praying for angels, even for God to send them, is goetic necromancy) I told you about in the introduction had for decades been telling the church that he had extensive knowledge and experience with the occult. In a meeting where the head pastor and this elder confronted me about my studies, I asked the elder about As Above, So Below and he believed it was biblical. If someone claims to have lots of experience and knowledge about the occult, they will know what As Above, So Below is and that it is *not* biblical, but anti-biblical. This confession by the elder showed that he knew nothing about what he claimed. What it came down to is, he dabbled with a ouija board a few times, got his astrology charts done a few times as well, and bought a spell book to try it out, but was never actively involved in occultism. When people come into your church and make these claims, you need to verify them. The reason being that this elder was actively engaged in occultism on behalf of the church for decades but because of his deceptive belief in his "extensive knowledge", everyone believed what he was doing was biblical. This elder may have believed that he had all this knowledge, the truth is he did not and was easily swayed by "deceptive philosophies" like the Bible warns us about.

16. Hermes Trismegistus, *The Emerald Tablet of Hermes*, (Unknown Location: iap, 2009), Locations 97–100, Kindle Edition.

So, you can see very easily where the paraphrase of "As Above, So Below" comes from. What we must also recognize is what the further lines of the Emerald Tablets say. These lines are within the next few lines of the Emerald Tables. Honestly, the entire document can be read very quickly.

> It Ascends from the Earth up to Heaven, and descends again from the Heaven to the Earth, and receives the Powers and Efficacy of the Superiors and Inferiors. [...] In this Work, you acquire to your self the Wealth and Glory of the whole World: Drive therefore from you all Cloudiness or Obscurity, Darkness and Blindness.[17]

The basis of these phrases is that what you "pray" for or what you are performing a spell ritual for can only be affected by what is in "Heaven" already. Your petition goes up to heaven, and then from that reality in heaven it goes back down to the petitioner. These realities must be co-existent. If what you are petitioning for is not already a reality in heaven, not just a metaphorical or hyperbolic reality, but a literal spiritual reality, it cannot be made a reality in the material world. What is ironic, is that this document that is centuries old at the least, and maybe a single millennium at most, is that this ritual practice can be used to gain "Wealth and Glory of the whole World." Ironic? You should all know that I do not believe in that kind of irony. The beliefs that these Satanist preachers are teaching you and the way they are perverting the Bible, comes right from magical teachings from hundreds of years ago.

We will have to go look at the Ephesians verse from chapter one that is argued by these Satanists that heavenly blessings are awaiting to be brought down to earth. This time however, I will quote the entirety of the immediate context.

> Blessed be the God and Father of our Lord Jesus Christ, who has blessed us in Christ with every spiritual blessing in the heavenly places, even as he chose us in him before the foundation of the world, that we should be holy and blameless before him. In love he predestined us for adoption to himself as sons through Jesus Christ, according to the purpose of his will, to the praise of his glorious grace, with which he has blessed us in the Beloved. In him we have redemption through his blood, the forgiveness of our trespasses, according to the riches of his grace, which he lavished upon us, in all wisdom and insight making known to us the mystery of his will, according to his purpose, which he set forth in Christ as a plan for the fullness of time, to unite all things in him, things in heaven and things on earth. (Ephesians 1:3–10 ESV)

Reading from the point of "heavenly places" forward, Paul here spills

---

17. Hermes, *Emerald*, Locations 107–111.

out what exactly these spiritual blessings are. Paul does indicate that these are benefits of an "already and not yet" state. When looking at that idea we can realize that "[t]he benefits of this 'already and not yet,' Paul has already stated: grace and peace (Eph. 1:2). We face difficulty, danger, and the deceit of our own hearts, but heaven and all its benefits are already ours."[18]

These benefits and spiritual blessings ultimately find fulfillment in the idea of our receiving "grace and peace" from God.

The blessings do not end there, however. From verse four onwards those blessings are spilled out. Paul directly tells us what spiritual blessings in the heavenly places we have. The reality of what blessings we have is important to remember because

> Paul uses the term καθώς (kathōs, inasmuch as) to link his opening blessing of God with an account of the specific ways God has blessed those who bless him. [...] Paul begins his description of God's blessings by saying that God "chose us" (ἐξελέξατο ἡμᾶς, exelexato hēmas).[19]

The reason we have these blessings is because God chose us from since before the world was created. Since we have been chosen, all the results of Christs' crucifixion and resurrection are the blessings that have been given to us in the heavenly places. Are we going to live forever in our current flesh? No. We are going to wait in heaven after we die until the final resurrection. When that happens, we have then those blessings of eternal life in the heavenly places. This is a reality that there is now in heaven eternal life, but it is not here on earth, yet. It will be one day, but the As Above, So Below "doctrine" that Satanist heretics use to eisegete (read theology into) this verse would mean that we have that eternal life in the here and now. That interpretation is nonsense.

Context is the most important thing to keep in mind when exegeting any portion of scripture. So

> the context indicates that the apostle is thinking particularly of—or subsuming all these benefits under—those that are mentioned in the present paragraph, namely, election (and its accompaniment, foreordination to adoption), redemption (implying forgiveness and grace overflowing in the form of all wisdom and insight), and certification ("sealing") as sons and heirs.[20]

---

18. Bryan Chapell, Ephesians, ed. Richard D. Phillips, Philip Graham Ryken, and Daniel M. Doriani, *Reformed Expository Commentary* (Phillipsburg, New Jersey: P&R Publishing, 2009), p. 21.

19. Frank Thielman, Ephesians, *Baker Exegetical Commentary on the New Testament* (Grand Rapids, Michigan: Baker Academic, 2010), pp. 47–48.

20. William Hendriksen and Simon J. Kistemaker, *Exposition of Ephesians*, vol.

There is absolutely no promise of health and wealth in these verses. The redemption that Christ came to accomplish on the cross and resurrection are the blessings in the heavenly places we have inherited as sons and daughters. It is very easy to see that Paul, who was a Pharisee and as such would have had access to vast amounts of wealth that we could not imagine, worked in some of the poorest jobs to pay for his ministry and also suffered great "thorns" and "sufferings" for the sake of the gospel. The way the Satanists are eisegeting this verse, out of context, Paul would not have had to suffer in that way. In the way that these Satanic heretics use this verse, they would have to say that Paul either did not have enough faith or was not blessed by God. Since his letters are included within our canon of scripture, these teachers cannot say that Paul had little faith and/or was not blessed.

To emphasize how Bill Johnson has used this verse and the Matthew 6 "Lord's Prayer" I will quote the following:

> This is called stewardship. When we use correctly that which belongs to another, we become qualified for that which is our own. This amazes me. Even though I belong to Jesus and everything I have belongs to Him, He still wants to reward me with that which is my own. The bottom line is that good stewardship is the way to increase in the things of God. Favor is one of those heavenly commodities that we seldom pursue, study or understand. While it can be said that God loves everyone the same, not everyone has the same measure of favor. It is the reason behind one person receiving five talents, another two and another one. Remember that a talent was a sum of money, so the story about the talents in Matthew 25:14–30 is a business illustration that gives us insight into the nature and function of the Kingdom of God. Proper use brings increase. Neglect or abuse causes deep personal loss.[21]

You see the perversion here, right? Favour is what Johnson in the previous paragraph says is that which is your own. In the next paragraph, ironically, Johnson uses the example of "money" to show that favour. If you use your material stuff properly, it will increase. Where does the Bible say that using our material wealth properly brings increase? The Bible never says that. That parable was not intended to tell us that to get rich we have to use God, or "Satanic gods", resources correctly. This is nothing but Satan driven materialism.

Later in the same book Johnson says that

> These verses in Isaiah 61 add that we will experience prosperity and priestly ministry to God, while benefiting from the resources of those

---

7, *New Testament Commentary* (Grand Rapids, Michigan: Baker Book House, 1953–2001), pp. 73–74.

21. Bill Johnson, *The Mind of God: How His Wisdom Can Transform Our World* (Grand Rapids, Michigan: Chosen, 2020), Logos Edition.

who refuse to follow Christ. All this is for the purpose of advancing the Kingdom. Double portion blessing and extreme joy will accompany the people of God in this season. Is this possible in our lifetime? I think so. It is worth bringing before the Father.[22]

Andrew Wommack says that:

[r]ight now, you are as full of God as you believe to be. He doesn't determine how full of love, joy, and peace you are. You do. God is always willing for every single person to be healed, delivered, and prospered. It's never the Lord who doesn't move in your life—it's you who aren't receiving from Him. That's why I want to encourage you in how to receive.[23]

Also,

[t]he good news that truly releases God's power and draws people to Him in droves is the gospel: God is good and He loves you. Through Christ's atonement, everything you need for abundant life—both in heaven to come and on earth here and now—has already been provided. All you must do is believe and receive. This is what we should be preaching.[24]

Bill Johnson is infamous for pulling the following verse out of context to try and bring heaven, and all its benefits literally down to earth. The verse he tends to use is this:

Pray then like this: 'Our Father in heaven, hallowed be your name. Your kingdom come, your will be done, on earth as it is in heaven. (Matthew 6:9–10 ESV)

Look how Eugene Peterson's *The Message* paraphrases these verses:

Like this: Our Father in heaven, reveal who you are. Set the world right; do what's best—as above, so below. (Matthew 6:9–10 MSG)

The Message is used very often along with *The Passion Translation* for these Satanists' studies. Just seeing this verse, and the explanation I gave in this section, you should immediately realize there is a problem here. With how Wommack, Johnson, Vallotton and now Denton and Houston have used the "As Above, So Below" ideology to promote their theology, hopefully you can see that there is a problem. What these men are teaching you, is being used to subvertly deceive you. As Above, So Below sounds biblical, it sounds correct, but it is

---

22. Johnson, *Mind*, Logos Edition.
23. Andrew Wommack, *Discover the Keys to Staying Full of God* (Shippensburg: Pennsylvania: Harrison House Publishers, 2008), Location 42–44, Kindle Edition.
24. Wommack, *Discover*, Location 88--90.

not. These men are using occultic doctrine and calling it Christianity.

In the end, it is easy to see that the idea that "God has blessings for you in heaven that you need to declare or pray down to earth" is not biblical, in fact, it is anti-biblical. The idea that there are blessings we need to get God to send down to us from heaven, is an As Above, So Below idea. This does not mean that God does not send blessings from heaven. But they are not pre-existent in heaven. In other words, the blessings that God sends to us are sent in the same way the world was created from nothing. God speaks, it happens. God is not sending a pile of money sitting in some corner of heaven already that has Denton's name on it to him if Denton asks for it. The key word that Denton is using that makes that belief obvious is "unlock". We are not unlocking anything. A Bible book, chapter and verse needs be provided for the idea of "unlocking" but there is not one.

Also let us see something else that is problematic in Denton's book that comes from occultic ideology. This one is "[n]ow, a prophecy should only ever confirm what's on someone's heart."[25] Again, a biblical book, chapter and verse are needed on that theology, but none is provided. The reason evidence is needed is because almost all the prophecies in the Bible are not confirming what is on the target audience's hearts, even the ones that are speaking of hope, are speaking of hope in terms of judgment by the coming Day of LORD and not what is "on someone's heart." These prophecies are in fact calling them to repentance for their wicked ways and also to give them hope that God would restore them (again, they were worshipping false gods, hope of Yahweh's restoration was not "on their hearts"). Denton is promoting false teaching that is rooted in occultic practice to tell people what they want to hear instead of the truth.

The next problem item that Denton brings up is interesting too

> then GOD answered: "Write this. Write what you see. Write it out in big block letters so that it can be read on the run." (Habakkuk 2:2) You've got to have goals in all areas of life: ministry, business, family, marriage, health, and finances. You've got to have a clear vision and have dreams to hold on to in crisis. They will stop you from shifting into survival mode. Without written goals, you won't do the things that you need to do to have a healthy and fruitful life.[26]

However, before commenting let us look at that passage in context.

> I will take my stand at my watchpost and station myself on the tower, and look out to see what he will say to me, and what I will answer concerning my complaint. And the LORD answered me: "Write the vi-

---

25. Denton, *Kingdom*, p. 102.
26. Denton, *Kingdom*, p. 128.

sion; make it plain on tablets, so he may run who reads it. For still the vision awaits its appointed time; it hastens to the end—it will not lie. If it seems slow, wait for it; it will surely come; it will not delay. "Behold, his soul is puffed up; it is not upright within him, but the righteous shall live by his faith. "Moreover, wine is a traitor, an arrogant man who is never at rest. His greed is as wide as Sheol; like death he has never enough. He gathers for himself all nations and collects as his own all peoples" (Habakkuk 2:1–5 ESV).

So far, Denton's case for the exegesis of this passage is pretty weak but let us again look earlier on in the text in chapter one.

> O LORD, how long shall I cry for help, and you will not hear? Or cry to you "Violence!" and you will not save (Habakkuk 1:2 ESV)?

> "Look among the nations, and see; wonder and be astounded. For I am doing a work in your days that you would not believe if told. For behold, I am raising up the Chaldeans, that bitter and hasty nation, who march through the breadth of the earth, to seize dwellings not their own. They are dreaded and fearsome; their justice and dignity go forth from themselves. Their horses are swifter than leopards, more fierce than the evening wolves; their horsemen press proudly on. Their horsemen come from afar; they fly like an eagle swift to devour. They all come for violence, all their faces forward. They gather captives like sand. At kings they scoff, and at rulers they laugh. They laugh at every fortress, for they pile up earth and take it. Then they sweep by like the wind and go on, guilty men, whose own might is their god!" Are you not from everlasting, O LORD my God, my Holy One? We shall not die. O LORD, you have ordained them as a judgment, and you, O Rock, have established them for reproof. You who are of purer eyes than to see evil and cannot look at wrong, why do you idly look at traitors and remain silent when the wicked swallows up the man more righteous than he? You make mankind like the fish of the sea, like crawling things that have no ruler. He brings all of them up with a hook; he drags them out with his net; he gathers them in his dragnet; so he rejoices and is glad. Therefore he sacrifices to his net and makes offerings to his dragnet; for by them he lives in luxury, and his food is rich. Is he then to keep on emptying his net and mercilessly killing nations forever (Habakkuk 1:5–17 ESV)?

This can be quite a humorous piece of scripture. Here is a sarcastic paraphrase:

> Habakkuk: Yahweh, help us, c'mon we are dying down here!

> Yahweh: Yeah, sure, I will help you. However, you do not believe how I am going to do it.

> Habakkuk: Oh? How is that?

Yahweh: I am going to send the Babylonians to come kick the living tar out of you.

Habakkuk: WHAT? THEY ARE WORSE THAN WE ARE!

Yahweh: I know. They will get what is coming to them too.

Yahweh: Oh, by the way, you better write this down so that when it happens you and future people will believe that I said what I was going to do is what I did.

However, note how Denton uses this verse: "Write this. Write what you see. Write it out in big block letters so that it can be read on the run. [...] Without written goals, you won't do the things that you need to do to have a healthy and fruitful life." So, if you write it down, it will happen. With the number of "curse tablets" that have been found in archaeological digs in Ancient Near Eastern cities, it should not be surprising that the ancient world in their occultism, believed that something that was written down had more power than something spoken. It should be no wonder that Denton, under the tutelage of the Satanist Houston, believes this as well.

Darlene Zschech and the Occult

Since I have already shown the all-out occult nature of Hillsong's teaching from Brian Houston and the elder Andrew Denton, there is no need to go over the teaching that Zschech is exposed to. As a result, I can go right into the problematic teaching that is present with Zschech.

Here is the first:

> The Word says that God inhabits the praises of His people (Psalm 22:3). It's amazing to think that God, in all His fullness, inhabits and dwells in our praises of Him. When someone asks, "Where is God in this situation?" we know that God is found in our praises. He occupies our praise, and with His presence He brings His love, His healing, His forgiveness, His grace, and His mercy. Whatever is needed to make a situation turn around for the good is present as we praise the Lord.[27]

Before we go on to critique this statement, we need to look at Psalm 22:1–5.

> My God, my God, why have you forsaken me? Why are you so far from saving me, from the words of my groaning? O my God, I cry by day,

---

27. Darlene Zschech and Brian Houston, *Extravagant Worship: Holy, Holy, Holy Is the Lord God Almighty Who Was and Is, and Is to Come...* (Grand Rapids, Michigan: Bethany House, 2004), Logos Edition.

but you do not answer, and by night, but I find no rest. Yet you are holy, enthroned on the praises of Israel. In you our fathers trusted; they trusted, and you delivered them. To you they cried and were rescued; in you they trusted and were not put to shame (Psalm 22:1-5 ESV).

The word the ESV translates "enthroned" is the word Zschech is saying is "inhabits". Other versions of the Bible likely use that word.

Here's the lexical info on that word: ישב [yēšē'b] "vb. sit, remain, dwell."[28]

So, does "inhabit" mean to literally be "inside" of the praises that cause healing and other things as Zschech claims? No, God does not inhabit our songs in that fashion. In fact, it means that God, "dwells" or "inhabits" them in that he is heaven dwelling within the songs of his people as God sits on his throne.

What this means is that Zschech is preaching the music is a magical mantra. This is in line with what Houston taught about music bringing in the power to perform miracles and to speak "words of creation." While I will deal with necromancy more in chapter seven, essentially what is happening here is the summoning of a spirit. If you are not aware of what summoning a spirit is, even an angel or "God", it is again goeticism/necromancy.

This next statement by Zschech is alarming. "Until you know through personal experience who God is, you will never truly know who you are."[29]

Essentially where that statement is coming from is ancient Gnosticism. In gnostic thought, special knowledge of a high god, the true father, often known as Bythos, could only be gained by a magical existential experience that happened outside or inside of yourself. Many have tried to say that Gnosticism is caused by studying the Bible and theology too much. That definition of Gnosticism is in error. Theology is what is identifying these occultic realities for what they are. Gnosticism is knowledge that is gained because some demon showed you something you wanted to be true, and you believed it. Likewise, the Bible never says that we will only know who we truly are until we have a personal experience with God to know who he is. The command from scripture is that we are to know God by knowing the Bible. We can never really know who we are as God's image bearers until we know God, but we do not need a personal experience with God to truly know ourselves. That experience with God is Gnostic heresy.

---

28. Francis Brown, Samuel Rolles Driver, and Charles Augustus Briggs, *Enhanced Brown-Driver-Briggs Hebrew and English Lexicon* (Oxford, England: Clarendon Press, 1977), p. 442. Logos Edition.

29. Zschech, *Worship*, Logos Edition.

Another problematic teaching with Zschech is her belief that we are able to enter into the presence of God. I do not just mean in worship or in "spirit", but literally enter into the presence of God. Remember the first quote from Zschech above. This is not a misconstruing of authorial intent, Zschech is literally saying that God himself, the most holy person that has existed from eternity, is in the very songs we sing. So, the below statement is one where Zschech is saying we can literally enter God's presence.

> We have an invitation to enter into the Most Holy Place, where our heavenly Father sits. Through worship we put Christ as the chief cornerstone of our lives, and the power we have access to in His presence is real. He longs for us to draw closer to Him. He has cleansed our hearts and made them pure so that we can stand in His presence. So we continue to praise our mighty Lord—to sing, clap, dance, celebrate, get soaked in His presence and overwhelmed by His grace.[30]

That is interesting. Remember when Moses asked to see Yahweh's glory?

> Moses said, "Please show me your glory." And he said, "I will make all my goodness pass before you and will proclaim before you my name 'The Lord.' And I will be gracious to whom I will be gracious, and will show mercy on whom I will show mercy. But," he said, "you cannot see my face, for man shall not see me and live" (Exodus 33:18–20 ESV).

We are sanctified and justified before God, however, remember that

> [i]f we say we have no sin, we deceive ourselves, and the truth is not in us. If we confess our sins, he is faithful and just to forgive us our sins and to cleanse us from all unrighteousness. If we say we have not sinned, we make him a liar, and his word is not in us (1 John 1:8–10 ESV).

We still have sin in us. To say we do not is to once again claim a Satanic form of divinity.

The only way for us to be able to stand in the presence of God Almighty in all of his holiness, is if we are without sin. If we stand before God as we are now, in the flesh, his holiness will lash out against us and put us to death. We need to realize the reality of the holiness of God. What is also important to remember is that there is no place in the Bible that talks about God's spirit returning to the temple after it was rebuilt. Therefore, when the curtain was torn at Jesus' death, it was not that the Holy Spirit was being released upon the world. The Holy Spirit is in every place in this world now, but that was not the

---

30. Zschech, *Worship*, Logos Edition.

point of this text. It was a representation that Jesus was the new high priest and there was no need for mediation by a priest or by sacrificial offerings in the Most Holy Place.

People may disagree with this based on the text of Haggai 2

> And I will shake all nations, so that the treasures of all nations shall come in, and I will fill this house with glory, says the LORD of hosts. The silver is mine, and the gold is mine, declares the LORD of hosts. The latter glory of this house shall be greater than the former, says the LORD of hosts. And in this place I will give peace, declares the LORD of hosts'" (Haggai 2:7–9 ESV).

The problem is the historical record of the returned Israelites. First, the second temple was not nearly as glorious as the first. The second temple was not even comparable to Solomon's temple. Also, there was no peace in Israel after the return of the exiles. Soon after the Persians fell, the number of wars, rebellions and tyrants that oppressed the Israelites was a clear indicator that there was no peace in the land like Haggai 2 says will exist. There was no peace in Israel until after the second temple was destroyed. Looking at all this history, it is evident that the second temple, or Herod's Temple, was not the true second temple at all. If this temple was not the true second temple, then whose was?

> Jesus answered them, "Destroy this temple, and in three days I will raise it up." The Jews then said, "It has taken forty-six years to build this temple, and will you raise it up in three days?" But he was speaking about the temple of his body. When therefore he was raised from the dead, his disciples remembered that he had said this, and they believed the Scripture and the word that Jesus had spoken (John 2:19–22 ESV).

The true second temple was Christ himself. Therefore, the basis of the evidence that Zschech would need to prove her point is out of context eisegesis. The historical and textual context say otherwise about Zschech's required point of evidence. Also, the words of Christ himself show that he was and is the second temple. Not the stone building that was constructed after the exiles returned. The Spirit of Yahweh never returned to that temple. Yahweh returned to Israel, and also the false second temple, in the person of Jesus. Zschech's argument does not work. We cannot enter into God's presence, even now in the new covenant.

Here is another text, when you understand the occult stance that Zschech is coming from, this next quote is easily explainable as heretical: "When we do mess up, Jesus stands as our high priest before the Father to defend us. He tells the Father, 'They are the ones you have given me. I am in them, and you are in me. Look at how beautiful they are.'"[31] For all of you: Jesus is not the one living in us. Jesus has a physical body in heaven, seated at the right hand of the Father. "And he said, 'Behold, I see the heavens opened, and the Son of Man standing at the right hand of God'" (Acts 7:56 ESV). "And to which of the angels has he ever said, 'Sit at my right hand until I make your enemies a footstool for your feet'" (Hebrews 1:13 ESV)? Again, Zschech is wrong because Jesus is at the right hand of the Father. It is the Holy Spirit that dwells in all of us. Hence, the claim that God the Father is in us, is a false claim. While it could be argued that the Father is in us because the Holy Spirit is, but that again is theologically incorrect. This teaching by Zschech is from the RHP which argues that we become part of God and are not gods ourselves like Satanism and the LHP teach. Zschech's teachings over all are LHP, but some RHP esotericism does tent to come through her words every now and then.

The next quote you the reader will need to keep the entire context of this book and the previous section about Brian Houston in mind to realize the error here. Zschech's quote is as follows:

> I used to joke with my worship team that the reason Jehoshaphat's enemy was defeated was because the singers and musicians were so bad—perhaps it was more like torture! Their enemies conceded quickly, saying, "Okay, you win, we give up; just stop the singing!" But even if the people were tone deaf and couldn't carry a musical note, the Lord would have eagerly received their praises. It wasn't the harmony that defeated their enemy; it was the presence of God's mighty power that warred on their behalf and won their battles.[32]

The main point to comment against this is that Jude said

> But when the archangel Michael, contending with the devil, was disputing about the body of Moses, he did not presume to pronounce a blasphemous judgment, but said, "The Lord rebuke you." But these people blaspheme all that they do not understand, and they are destroyed by all that they, like unreasoning animals, understand instinctively (Jude 9–10 ESV).

To say that we have the authority to wield the power of God to send the demonic off, according to Michael as quoted by Jude, is blasphemous. Read that again, rebuking the demonic ourselves, is blasphemy. Since Zschech, Houston, Denton and the other Hillsong ilk are arguing for an occultic version of God, a god that is in essence you, Zschech is claiming to bear the authority of God and the magic songs

---

31. Zschech, *Worship*, Logos Edition.
32. Zschech, *Worship*, Logos Edition.

that she writes that apparently have God inhabiting them bodily, is occultism and a claim to self-divinity.

The next quote is interesting as well. If you remember from the section about Denton what I said about Habakkuk 2:2

> I have written my dream down, and the only reason it changes is that it keeps growing! It is a great thing for you to do, to "write down the revelation and make it plain on tablets so that a herald may run with it" (Habakkuk 2:2). Not my dream, your dream. Writing down my dream is not going to help you at all, but writing down your dream will.[33]

Again, like with Denton, Zschech argues that writing down your God-given (apparently) dream, will make it come to pass.

Next look at Zschech's claims about Luke 17:11–19

> Jesus invited ten men to a worship service. They didn't have to drive or get a ride. Jesus just showed up where they were. Imagine that. Being in the presence of our Savior. And this wasn't just any worship service. Ten men were invited, all ten were suffering from a debilitating illness, and all ten men were healed. Wow! Wouldn't you want to be there?[34]

Let us go and look exactly at what the text from that part of Luke's gospel says:

> On the way to Jerusalem he was passing along between Samaria and Galilee. And as he entered a village, he was met by ten lepers, who stood at a distance and lifted up their voices, saying, "Jesus, Master, have mercy on us." When he saw them he said to them, "Go and show yourselves to the priests." And as they went they were cleansed. Then one of them, when he saw that he was healed, turned back, praising God with a loud voice; and he fell on his face at Jesus' feet, giving him thanks. Now he was a Samaritan. Then Jesus answered, "Were not ten cleansed? Where are the nine? Was no one found to return and give praise to God except this foreigner?" And he said to him, "Rise and go your way; your faith has made you well" (Luke 17:11–19 ESV).

So, we need to look at what happened when the lepers cried out for Jesus, Master, to have mercy on them.

> Because of the manifest status of these ten lepers as outcasts, their address to Jesus is startling. One might be tempted to regard their request for "mercy" as simply a request for financial assistance in light of their poverty (i.e., as "alms for the poor"). "To have compassion" could have this sense, and this nuance ought not to be ruled out in favor of, say, some spiritual benefit. On the other hand, the language of their request

---

33. Zschech, *Worship*, Logos Edition.
34. Darlene Zschech, *Worship Changes Everything* (Ada, Michigan: Baker Publishing Group, 2015), p. 56, Kindle Edition.

cannot easily be reduced to this interpretation, and the appellation by which they name Jesus "Master" suggests that much more is at stake here. When used elsewhere in the Third Gospel, "Master" denotes one who has authority consistent with miraculous power, and this is its meaning here.[35]

This is an important fact to remember. As lepers, they were not allowed to enter the local village or even to approach those that were not afflicted with whatever skin disease they had at the time. Leprosy in the Bible does not always mean the type of skin disease we call leprosy today. Whatever the skin disease was, it required these men to be outcasts that could not approach others.

However, knowing that Jesus was nearby, and having have heard of his miraculous power to heal and "make clean" they in fact cried out to him. Jesus in no way makes an invitation to them at all. Jesus, according to the text, did not approach them either. Jesus could have and still maintained his clean status, but there is no indication that they approached Jesus or that Jesus went anywhere near them. For all we know, they were in fact yelling at one another from across a dusty road.

In either case, Jesus tells them to go and make themselves clean according to the requirements of the law.

> Acting on Jesus' directive, the lepers are cleansed. Luke uses the normal word to describe the recovery from a leprous condition, "to be made clean." The same term appears in v 17, but other words are found in vv 15 and 19—"to be healed" and "to be saved"—and all follow as a consequence of the request of the ten lepers for divine mercy.[36]

What Green is observing here is that Jesus made them clean and saved them. This cleansing however was at "the request of the ten lepers for divine mercy." We have no indication here in anyway that Jesus in fact "invited" the ten lepers to anything at all.

To put it more plainly:

> [a]pparently Jesus did not see them at first, but when he did he responded. He did not come to them or touch them. He did not even say, "You are cured!" He told them, leprous as they were, to go and show themselves to the priests, the normal procedure when a leper was cured. The priest acted as a kind of health inspector to certify that the cure had in fact taken place (Lev. 14:2ff.). Jesus was putting their faith to the test by asking these men to act as though they had been cured. And as they

---

35. Joel B. Green, *The Gospel of Luke, The New International Commentary on the New Testament* (Grand Rapids, Michigan: Wm. B. Eerdmans Publishing Co., 1997), p. 623.

36. Green, *Luke*, p. 624.

obeyed so it happened.[37]

Again, this is a different and more truthful take on the situation than Zschech would have us believe. The ten lepers in doing what Jesus commanded, showed that they believed they had been cured simply by turning to show the priest, whomever that may have been, that they were cleansed. The ten lepers did not wait, they turned and went as commanded. There was no indication of an invitation to "worship."

The end of the story indicates something significant. Since the gospel throughout the New Testament consistently speaks about healing, mostly being in the spiritual or being made in a "clean" sense, not immediately the physical sense. While Jesus did heal the sick, it was because in being sick they were "unclean" and by healing them, they were made "clean" again. Being clean, they would once again be made holy.

The invitation was not only to Jews, however. The end of the story shows that Jesus was intending this gospel for all people:

> [b]ecause the gospel was made available to "foreigners" as well as to Jews, Luke included this trenchant remark of Jesus. Earlier, Luke had used the cosmopolitan remark of Jesus that "people will come from all over the world—from east and west, north and south—to take their places in the Kingdom of God" (13:29). Luke thus presents the breadth of God's mercy; by divine intention all people will see the salvation sent from God" (3:6).
>
> The whole incident was significant for Luke, who saw the Christian message as one for all people who would receive it—including Jews, Samaritans, Gentiles, the clean and the unclean. Part of full restoration to health and wholeness was acknowledgement of the one who had performed the healing, so the closing words of the paragraph are significant: "Your faith has healed you" (17:19).[38]

This is now an interesting contradiction to Zschech's claims. Look at how Zschech observes the end of the story:

> sadly, only one experienced true worship. Only one fell at the feet of Jesus and then rose to dance with joy. Ten left, thrilled to be healed, but only one returned to experience deeper levels of being in the presence of Jesus Christ. What brought him back? Gratitude. He came back to say thank you to God, the Creator, the Healer, the Giver of all good gifts. Jesus' response is amazement at how few received the totality of

---

37. Leon Morris, *Luke: An Introduction and Commentary*, vol. 3, *Tyndale New Testament Commentaries* (Downers Grove, Illinois: InterVarsity Press, 1988), p. 275.

38. Allison A. Trites, William J. Larkin, *Cornerstone Biblical Commentary, Vol 12: The Gospel of Luke and Acts* (Carol Stream, Illinois: Tyndale House Publishers, 2006), p. 236.

His offer.[39]

This conclusion is completely incorrect. Yes, one did come back to worship Jesus for healing him, the purpose of the story was not to show "deeper levels of being in the presence of Jesus Christ." That interpretation by Zschech is a complete perversion of the story. The point of the story, as made above, was that the gospel had come to all. The gospel had even come to the Samaritan's who the Jews considered as despicable and sub-human.

Now, recall Zschech's original claim: "Jesus invited ten men to a worship service." Looking at the text and the exegesis, there is absolutely no indication of that. There is nothing in the text that shows Jesus invited them to anything at all, even if it was from across the road. These men instead called out to Jesus for mercy, and by turning and obeying, the ten men were healed. There was no "worship" of any kind that the men were invited to. Jesus simply commanded and they obeyed. That is a type of worship, but there was never an invitation there. Zschech's definition of worship within the book does include obedience but notice that Jesus was not inviting them at all, it was an either "do or die from 'leprosy'" situation.

What we have happening here is the use of a medium to dispense the power of God. Zschech claims that it was the worship that these ten men were invited to that healed them. Recall again that Zschech claimed that: "Being in the presence of our Savior. And this wasn't just any worship service. Ten men were invited, all ten were suffering from a debilitating illness, and all ten men were healed." Again, Zschech's argument here points to the fact that it was the worship that healed them. By claiming that it was the worship that healed them, and not the cleansing holiness of Christ granted to them for their obedience, we once again are falling to the realm of the worship being used to impart the miracle. As you will be shown shortly, and as Houston argued above, this is a plea to necromancy. By performing the ritual, or the "worship", the miracle was given.

Look again at how Zschech needs to pervert the purpose of this story to prove the point. Zschech claims that: "He came back to say thank you to God, the Creator, the Healer, the Giver of all good gifts. Jesus' response is amazement at how few received the totality of His offer." This was not an amazement. When keeping the story in context, we see that Jesus is making it clear that this is an "invading kingdom" moment. The kingdom of God is here, now.

Luke 17:1–10 shows stories of not being tempted to sin, cries

---

39. Zschech, *Everything*, p. 56.

for more faith and unworthy servants that are called to service their Master (the triune-God).

Luke 17:20–21 is interesting as well:

> [b]eing asked by the Pharisees when the kingdom of God would come, he answered them, "The kingdom of God is not coming in ways that can be observed, nor will they say, 'Look, here it is!' or 'There!' for behold, the kingdom of God is in the midst of you" (ESV).

Again, this is an interesting twist that shows that Zschech is not using the story for its intended purpose. The intended purpose was to show that with Christ coming to Jerusalem, that the kingdom was not only coming, but was now here. "The kingdom of God is in the midst of you." Jesus here is saying that the kingdom consisted of those that were holy: Jews, unholy: Gentiles, clean: those that followed the Torah, not the Pharisees traditions, and the unclean: those that either broke the laws or that were sick and afflicted.

The whole chapter is speaking about the coming kingdom and who is acceptable, not that Jesus is inviting you to worship him and that the worship will heal you.

The rest of chapter 17 continues to show similarities to the Olivet Discourse of Matthew 24-25. The kingdom is here and coming in a total and final way. You will know when it is here because of these things. Those things that Jesus was saying to look out for, according to Jesus was "in the midst of you." It was happening, and something cataclysmic was soon coming, that being the destruction of the second temple to end the old covenant once and for all.

As I have said earlier, Houston, Denton, and Zschech firmly believe that the act of worship is what makes miracles happen, brings in the Holy Spirit, brings in as well the power to create. All these beliefs are all entrenched in the occult and not the Bible. Worship itself does not heal; God does. Zschech wants you to believe otherwise. Zschech wants you to believe that by worshipping, it will make God do what you want. This is not the case with a sovereign God. Again, that is a ritualized form of occultism. This one is cleverly hidden, but when keeping in context what Hillsong church as a total has taught and pushed, the connection is easy to see.

Zschech in this case, has taken the miracle of the healing of the ten lepers out of Jesus' hands, and put into the power of some "worship service" that is never indicated in the text. Obedience is worship yes, but there was no such active "service" or active submission to a "worship service" that healed the men. Although only one returned to thank Jesus, the other nine men were still healed and to push Zschech's argument further, if anything, their act of worship in obeying was false worship because they refused to acknowledge Jesus for who he was.

Zschech's claims here are completely fallacious and are showing her preference for ritualized "worship" that will force God to do things and bring in miraculous power. Much like her former pastor Brian Houston has said about what worship does. However, this power belongs to Christ alone. Using worship to "appease God" to get the healing is a form of necromancy and the Bible never commands that this is the way to put our requests before God. The way many do give God their requests are in no way worshipful at all. These requests are actually demands and these individuals once again use the false "worship" to force God to do their will.

Zschech is using her fallacious exegesis, really eisegesis (reading things into scripture), to continue to support the occultic nature of Hillsong's teaching that you can self-divinize and get whatever you want from the God they want you to believe is your slave.

God does not need you to do anything to do as he wishes. You can be healed by not being in worship at the time. He says to make requests, but when the requests turn into demands and those demands are turned into rituals because as Zschech says "you are worshipping", it is now anti-biblical. Zschech has turned it into magic.

One last quick point about the occultic nature of Zschech's teaching, Zschech claims that "[t]his is not just David's theme and testimony. All throughout Scripture, we read that God created all, is in all, and owns all."[40] Reading all the evidence that I have shown about what the LHP teaches and believes, seeing Zschech say that "God [...] is in all" is a confirmation that LHP doctrine proper is part of her ideology.

Chris Tomlin and the Occult

In the book they co-authored together, *Holy Roar*, Tomlin and Whitehead say that

> [m]usic is more powerful than we even understand. It can soften our hearts, soothe our troubled souls. It opens a door to the spiritual world. It paves the road for the Spirit's coming. The patriarchs, psalmists, and prophets of the scriptures understood the power of music especially.[41]

Opening a door to the spiritual world to pave a way for "the Spirit's coming" is an act of goetic necromancy and not biblical practice. However, as a proof text, Tomlin and Whitehead mention the follow-

---

40. Zschech, *Everything*, p. 132.
41. Chris Tomlin, and Darren Whitehead, *Holy Roar* (Nashville, Tennessee: Thomas Nelson, 2017), p. 46, Kindle Edition.

ing:[42]

> But now bring me a musician." And when the musician played, the hand of the LORD came upon him. And he said, "Thus says the LORD, 'I will make this dry streambed full of pools.' For thus says the LORD, 'You shall not see wind or rain, but that streambed shall be filled with water, so that you shall drink, you, your livestock, and your animals' (2 Kings 3:15–17 ESV).

Ironically, Zschech mentions the same passage of evidence for her talk about "warfare music" as well. The problem is this is one of a variety of passages that talk about Yahweh intervening to fight for Israel. Unfortunately, most of these references in no way mention music, at all. Every passage talks about obeying the commands of Yahweh, submitting to God's holiness and justice, and Yahweh would intervene to save them. This instance in 2 Kings 3:15–17 is only a fraction of passages. It is a rare one where music specifically is mentioned. I bring this up to say this: the exceptions do not make the rule.

The biggest problem with the Tomlin quote however is that "[m]usic is more powerful than we even understand. It can soften our hearts, soothe our troubled souls. It opens a door to the spiritual world." Again, as I did with Denton, there needs to be a Bible book, chapter, and verse to show that you can open "doorways to the spiritual world." Again, this is not only unbiblical, but anti-biblical. The reason being that since this again points to an occultic use of music, the music is intending to call on spirits. Realize that this is not the Holy Spirit, but a demonic spirit.

To further the argument about the "magic doorway being open": "[t]he music was a conduit of God's grace, and we felt it in that hospital room."[43] Again, this is occultic nonsense. Music alone does not do that. Music is not the conduit of God's grace. It is not that God cannot use the music to calm people down, but to say that music is a conduit of God's grace in a hospital room where healing was needed, that is occultism. Thankfully, the healing did come, and the baby was saved, but to say that the music is what was the "conduit" to bring that healing, that is nothing more than a plea to magic.

Before anyone gets angry at this claim because Tomlin, like Houston, sings about the Bible and God, I once again ask you to refer to page 78 that shows that the Bible itself is used in occult rituals. The example I reference is in a book called *Secrets of Solomon* and we as Christians need to realize that the occult adherents often know the Bible better than most of us. While I said this earlier, it needs to be

---

42. Tomlin, *Roar*, p. 47.
43. Tomlin, *Roar*, p. 45.

said again. Occultists do not understand the Bible better than Christians, but many, if not most, of them know it better than a majority of people sitting in a pew or chair every Sunday.

If people are still unconvinced of Tomlin's Satanism, after Joyce Meyer's 40th Anniversary Women's Conference held from September 22–24, 2022 at the Dome at America's Center in downtown St. Louis,[44] Tomlin put up a post on his social media feeds that read the following:

> Wonderful night at the 40th anniversary of the Joyce Meyer conference...grateful to be a part of the celebration![45]

Unfortunately, the evidence is there. With the Satanism via necromancy that Tomlin uses for his music and the support of a Satanist in Meyer, who believes in the little gods heresy (see footnote 3, Chapter II, page 28), we cannot sit here and honestly believe that Tomlin himself is not a Satanist along with the Prosperity, WoF, and NAR churches and leaders that he so often associates and does "ministry" with.

---

44. Julie Roy, "Leading Evangelicals Embrace Joyce Meyer at 40th Anniversarty Event," *The Roys Report*, July 13, 2023, https://julieroys.com/leading-evangelicals-embrace-joyce-meyer-at-40th-anniversary-event/.

45. Chris Tomlin, "Wonderful night at the 40th anniversary of the Joyce Meyer conference...grateful to be part of the celebration," *Instagram*, July 13, 2023, https://www.instagram.com/p/Ci8pb2CgFuA/.

Chapter VII: Defining Necromancy

So, first let us look at what the definition for necromancy, for this section necromancy and goeticism are synonymous. The Baker Encyclopedia of the Bible defines necromancy as the "[p]ractice of communicating with the dead; a practice strictly forbidden by the Law (Dt 18:11)."[1]

Easton's Bible Dictionary defines necromancy this way: "i.e., 'one who interrogates the dead,' as the word literally means, with the view of discovering the secrets of futurity (comp. 1 Sam. 28:7)."[2]

The lexical definition of the word translated as necromancer in the ESV is defined this way:

> 2. necromancer, in phr. [אוֹב אִידְעֹנִי] necrom. or wizard Lv 20:27 (H; usually tr. 'a man also or woman that hath a familiar spirit or that is a wizard' RV; but better a man or a woman, if there should be among them, a necromancer or wizard; no suff. reason for exceptional use of phrase here); [...] (where repres. as chirping & muttering, in practice of their art of seeking dead for instruction, prob. ventriloquism) 19:3.[3]

In effect: calling on any spirit, even dead ones (including saints), and angels is really communicating with the demonic.

Zschech and Tomlin Teaching As Above, So Below and Necromancy

When talking about, "As Above, So Below," refer to chapter six in the section on Andrew Denton and the Occult. The application I want to draw here is that the writers of the music are wanting to draw the spir-

---

1. Walter A. Elwell and Barry J. Beitzel, "Necromancer, Necromancy," *Baker Encyclopedia of the Bible* (Grand Rapids, Michigan: Baker Book House, 1988), p. 1535, Logos Edition.

2. M. G. Easton, *Illustrated Bible Dictionary and Treasury of Biblical History, Biography, Geography, Doctrine, and Literature* (New York, New York: Harper & Brothers, 1893), p. 496, Logos Edition.

3. Brown, *Lexicon*, p. 15.

its from heaven and draw heavenly power to make miraculous changes here on earth. In other words: As Above, So Below.

In dealing with the As Above, So Below comment as well with the necromancy comment, the following is from Zschech as well:

> I heard this prophetic word spoken over Russell Fragar: "And the angel of the Lord will stand at the foot of your bed at night and sing songs over you, O great scribe." What a divine way to write, to have songs sung to you straight from heaven that bring revelation, not just beautiful music.[4]

The Bible does talk about God singing over us. This quote however seems a little strange. There is a big and problematic teaching of spiritual or "angel" encounters at night, during the "Witching Hour", which is between 0200 and 0359 hours of when the occult believes that the veil between the spiritual world and material world is weakest. To date I have not heard of one of these angel encounters that sounded completely biblical. Some sounded strange definitely, others commanded people to contravene the commands of the Bible.

> With the help of a discerning friend, I began to realize that the different aspects of that first night had meaning for the broader body of Christ. It was as if I had entered into a prophetic intercessory experience that had implications for the church as a whole. For instance, the intense pressure in my head and the incredible pushing on my back represented God's desire to push fear and unbelief out of His bride. That's why I felt as if my heart had stopped. It was as if Jesus came and said, "I want to rearrange your heart. My own heart cries out for an exclusive relationship with you." That's why I couldn't hold on to Jim in the night; the Lord wanted me to cling to Him alone. The Lord was saying, "I am jealous after you with true jealousy, and I will not be satisfied to have a relationship with you through your husband, your pastor, or anyone else."[5]

This was written by Michal Ann Goll, the wife of James W. Goll, this seems extremely odd and very much unlike the Christ of the Bible and the commands he gives us through Paul in 1 Corinthians. This is not Jesus at all, it is some kind of demonic presence. But both the Goll's have fallen into its service.

Notice how anti-biblical this account, written by Michal, is

> I couldn't imagine going back to regular routines, going to bed and sleeping all the way through the night, waking up thinking about what I was going to do that day, doing chores, going shopping for groceries, cooking dinner. I didn't want to go back to regular life. I was hungry for

---

4. Zschech, *Worship*, Logos Edition.
5. James W. Goll, *Angelic Encounters: Engaging Help from Heaven* (Lake Mary, Florida: Charisma House, 2013). Logos Edition.

more of Him. I came away from this time a changed person. No longer was I intimidated by other people. Now I had a new level of authority, even though I was not really aware of it. Jim said, "I don't know who you are or who you are becoming." I didn't know who I was either. He was shocked at the waves of authority he could feel when I even waved my hand toward him. The changes in me meant changes in our marriage. We had to make some adjustments. Jim says he had thought he was married to the perfect wife, because I was totally compliant. And then when I got delivered from my fear of man, fear of rejection, and so forth, I became, in his words, a lioness. At first he thought he had liked me better before, when I was real quiet, but then we decided that God was remaking both of us into His image. As we were becoming more like Jesus, we'd have to continue to make more adjustments to each other.[6]

Whoever this "Jesus" really was, it told Michal that she was to no longer take on her roles as a caretaker of the family as important. This "Jesus" told Michal that her duties as a mother were to take a backseat. This is not what the Bible commands. Whoever this Jesus was, it was not the real Jesus and was really something demonic that both the Goll's believed.

Going back to Zschech's comment about Fragar, with the support of the evidence about the deception of the Goll's, this seems like another instance where something is ... out of sorts. Since the occultic links between Hillsong and what it teaches is again undeniable, what we have here is a false angel, most likely a demon, showing up during the Witching Hour to "sing songs from heaven" over and also to convince both Goll's to forget biblical commands in an attempt of bringing heaven to earth or bringing: As Above, So Below.

There has been a large interest in psychics in churches, and especially in the enneagram, a divination tool brought together by spirit writing, or necromancy. For those that are not aware, psychics are what the biblical text would refer to as a necromancer. While some might argue that psychics do not talk to the dead all the time but to other spirits there needs to be a discussion about the biblical text on necromancers and what the greater context of the rest of scripture has to say about the issue.

First let us take a look at a direct text from a famous anti-occult law found in Deuteronomy 18:10–12

> There shall not be found among you anyone who burns his son or his daughter as an offering, anyone who practices divination or tells fortunes or interprets omens, or a sorcerer or a charmer or a *medium or a necromancer or one who inquires of the dead,* for whoever does these

---

6. Goll, *Angelic*, Logos Edition.

things is an abomination to the LORD. And because of these abominations the LORD your God is driving them out before you (italics mine) (ESV).

I will not spend a lot of time on this verse as the text is pretty explicit. Anyone that calls on or talks to spirits, of any kind, including the dead, are to be avoided. While many Bible dictionaries will define necromancy as those that speak to the dead, the italicized text above seems to indicate that they are all of the same category. Mediums, necromancers, and those that call on the spirits of the dead are one and the same. So, the question then becomes, can the dead return form Sheol?

> For the living know that they will die, but the dead know nothing, and they have no more reward, for the memory of them is forgotten. Their love and their hate and their envy have already perished, and forever *they have no more share in all that is done under the sun.* [...] Whatever your hand finds to do, do it with your might, for *there is no work or thought or knowledge or wisdom in Sheol, to which you are going* (italics mine) (Ecclesiastes 9:5–6, 10 ESV).

Looking at Ecclesiastes it is certain that death is final. Many ghost-hunters, modern day necromancers, will claim that ghosts only come out at night, there is no distinction within these verses that "under the sun" means only during the day. Under the sun means under the sun. The earth is always "under the sun" whether it is day or night. The dead have no part of this earth in any way. They are in Sheol, and there the dead will stay until Christ returns (Revelation 20).

With these verses in Ecclesiastes plainly saying what they are, then what are these dead spirits that some Pentateuch verses speak about? Easy, those supposed dead spirits are really the demonic. These dead spirits are rebellious angels that were thrown out of heaven for daring to think they could ascend to the throne of God.

Again, many will deny this, once again I would ask for the critics to do more research. There is again a book translated by Joseph H. Peterson entitled: *Elucidation of Necromancy*. In this book Peterson translates texts that do not at any time claim to be summoning the dead, or even a demon. You can probably guess that the entire text of this book is about calling on "angels".[7]

Exegeting Leviticus 19:31

> Do not turn to mediums or necromancers; do not seek them out, and so make yourselves unclean by them: I am the LORD your God (Leviticus 19:31 ESV).

---

7. Joseph H. Peterson, *Elucidation of Necromancy* (Lake Worth, Florida: Ibis Press, 2021).

Commenting on this John E. Hartley comments that:

> The Israelites are not to turn to אבת, "ghosts," and ידענים, "departed spirits," for conversation and divination. In many places in the Ancient Near East, communication with the dead was sought through mediums and spiritists. פנה, "turn," is sometimes used of turning to God but more often of turning to other gods in worship (v 4; Deut 31:18, 20; Hos 3:1). The second term, בקשׁ, "seek," in its religious usage expresses making significant effort in the worship of God (2 Sam 21:1; Hos 5:6, 15; Zech 8:21–22; but in Isa 8:19; 19:3 with אבות and ידענים). *Noordtzij* (207) *observes that this is its only use in reference to spirits of the dead. This language then intimates that these seekers are endeavoring to inquire of Yahweh through contact with departed spirits* (cf. S. Wagner, "בקשׁ biqqēsh," TDOT 2:238). The practice of turning to departed spirits in order to find special knowledge is witnessed to in the account of Saul's seeking out a witch in order that he might speak with the deceased Samuel (1 Sam 28). Yahweh abhors such practices, for death is directly opposed to his very being as the living God. (italics mine)[8]

So, the condemnation of communicating with the dead to inquire of Yahweh, also falls under "necromancy." This sounds exactly like what the Roman Catholics are arguing for.

Mark F. Rooker in his Leviticus commentary comments that:

> The Israelites were not to turn to mediums or spiritists who sought communication with the dead. This was a common Canaanite practice (19:31; see Lev 20:6, 27; Deut 18:11; 1 Sam 28:3, 9; 2 Kgs 21:6; 23:24; Isa 8:19; 19:3). The word "medium" ('ōbōt) is used of the pit from which the spirits are called up, the spirit of the dead, or as here the necromancer. The Septuagint nearly always translates 'ôb with the Greek word eggastrimuthos, "ventriloquist." This translation may indicate a deception used on the part of the necromancer to deceive others into thinking he was actually calling up the dead. This command was violated by King Saul in 1 Sam 28:3–25.[9]

While not showing that the same point as Hartley, Rooker is still showing that attempting to communicate with the dead are in fact committing a sin punishable by death under Torah law.

Exegeting Deuteronomy 18:9-14

When you come into the land that the LORD your God is giving you, you shall not learn to follow the abominable practices of those nations. *There shall not be found among you anyone who burns his son or his daughter as an offering, anyone who practices divination or tells for-*

---

8. John E. Hartley, *Leviticus, vol. 4, Word Biblical Commentary* (Dallas: Word, Incorporated, 1992), p. 321, Logos Edition.

9. Mark F. Rooker, *Leviticus, vol. 3A, The New American Commentary* (Nashville, Tennessee: Broadman & Holman Publishers, 2000), p. 263, Logos Edition.

tunes or interprets omens, or a sorcerer or a charmer or a medium or a necromancer or one who inquires of the dead, for whoever does these things is an abomination to the LORD. And because of these abominations the LORD your God is driving them out before you. You shall be blameless before the LORD your God, for these nations, which you are about to dispossess, listen to fortune-tellers and to diviners. But as for you, the LORD your God has not allowed you to do this (italics mine) (Deuteronomy 18:9-14 ESV).

Commenting on these passages J. A. Thompson says that:

All occult, superstitions, divination, sorcery, spiritualism, etc., were abominations (9, 12) to Yahweh and invited his judgment (cf. 7:1ff.). The practice of consulting unseen powers by these devices was tantamount to acknowledging a power other than Yahweh, and this was rebellion. [...] The last three terms relate to various forms of consulting the spirit world. The first two refer to those who consult or inquire of the spirits, while the third may be a summarizing term. The three terms occur together quite often but remain somewhat obscure. The first is the Hebrew 'ôb, translated medium in RSV. The 'ôb spoke from within a person (Lev. 20:27) with a twittering voice (Isa. 29:4). *Those who practised this art called up the departed from the realm of the dead, or rather, professed to do so*. Greek versions translate the term by engastrimuthoi, i.e. ventriloquists, while Syriac has zakkuro, 'ghost'. The second term (yidde'ōnî), wizard, is related to the verb yāda', 'know'. Possibly this was some kind of familiar spirit. The difference between the two may have been that those who divine by the former, call up any spirit (1 Sam. 28:11), while those who divine by the latter consult only a familiar spirit. [...] *The third term denotes 'one who enquires of the dead'. In Isaiah 8:19 the term seems to be synonymous with the first two terms in the present passage*, so that it may be a typical summing up phrase so characteristic of Deuteronomy. *Otherwise it seems to denote a necromancer.* [...] 12–14. *Not only are these practices an abomination to Yahweh, but anyone who practises them is likewise an abomination. Because of such practices Yahweh would dispossess the people of Canaan.* Israel, however, must be blameless (tāmîm) in regard to every form of divination, magic or spiritism. [...] It may be pertinent to comment that in our own day, when spiritualism, astrology, teacup reading and the like are widely practised, these injunctions given to ancient Israel have a particular relevance. Not only is it impossible to discover the future by such practices, but the practices themselves are forbidden by God to men who count themselves members of the covenant family. (italics mine)[10]

Further comments by Eugene H. Merrill:

---

10. J. A. Thompson, *Deuteronomy: An Introduction and Commentary*, vol. 5, *Tyndale Old Testament Commentaries* (Downers Grove, Illinois: InterVarsity Press, 1974), pp. 231–233, Logos Edition.

> The phrase 'practicers of divination' (qōsēm qĕsāmîm) refers generically to the *whole complex of means of gaining insight from the gods regardless of any particular technique*. Sorcerers (mĕʽônēn, lit., 'those who cause to appear') were diviners whose specialty lay in their ability to create apparitions (cf. Judg 9:36–37). The interpreter of omens (mĕnaḥēš) divined through the use of certain revelatory objects or devices such as a cup (cf. Gen 44:5) or through the actions or words of others (1 Kgs 20:32–33). He or she who engaged in witchcraft (mĕkaššēp) was adept at performing signs (cf. Exod 7:11) to ward off evil (Isa 47:9, 12) or to mislead God's people (Mal 3:5). The 'spell caster' (ḥōbēr ḥeber, v. 11), literally, 'the binder with a band,' was thought capable of invoking powerful curses that would bring their intended targets under control (cf. Ps 58:5; Isa 47:9). *The 'medium' (šō'ēl 'ôb, 'asker of the pit') was a necromancer, one who sought to communicate with the dead and thereby gain secret information.* The best known such practitioner in the Old Testament was the witch of Endor (1 Sam 28:3, 9; cf. Isa 8:19). In the same category is the spiritist (yiddĕʽōnî, from yādaʽ, 'to know'). This does not appear to be a different kind of false prophet from the medium, for both are associated with necromancy and the pit (cf. Lev 20:6, 27; 1 Sam 28:3, 9; 2 Kgs 21:6; Isa 8:19). *Finally, he 'who consults the dead' (dōrēs 'el hammētîm) is listed, no doubt as a general and summary term for necromancy* (cf. Isa 8:19; 11:10; 19:3). [...]
> Regardless of the precision with which the foregoing can be identified, the most important point to be made is that any means employed by the heathen to gain information from their gods or even *to manipulate them to a certain course of action had to be strictly avoided by God's elect people. Such practices were detestable* (tōʽēbâ) as were those who engaged in them. Indeed, *it was because the nations of Canaan were involved in such nefarious behavior that they would be expelled from the land* (v. 12). In contrast to such wicked behavior, the servants of the Lord were to be blameless (tāmîm, 'upright') in all their relationship and association with him (v. 13) (italics mine).[11]

The interesting reference here by Merrill is that a medium is an "asker of the pit." The pit is not necessarily a reference to Hell/Hades but Sheol, the ancient Hebrew realm of the dead. Likewise, in the same line of thinking, a medium is "someone that consults the dead." These practices were to be avoided by the people of God and would cause them to be expelled from the land just like the people of Canaan were for doing the same things.

All these comments make it quite clear that inquiring or communicating with the dead, or in Satanist church practice: angels, would bring the wrath of Yahweh and expel the people from the land.

---

11. Eugene H. Merrill, *Deuteronomy, vol. 4, The New American Commentary* (Nashville, Tennessee: Broadman & Holman Publishers, 1994), p. 271–272, Logos Edition

Exegesis of Isaiah 8:16-22

> Bind up the testimony; seal the teaching among my disciples. I will wait for the LORD, who is hiding his face from the house of Jacob, and I will hope in him. Behold, I and the children whom the LORD has given me are signs and portents in Israel from the LORD of hosts, who dwells on Mount Zion. And when they say to you, 'Inquire of the mediums and the necromancers who chirp and mutter,' should not a people inquire of their God? Should they inquire of the dead on behalf of the living? To the teaching and to the testimony! If they will not speak according to this word, it is because they have no dawn. They will pass through the land, greatly distressed and hungry. And when they are hungry, they will be enraged and will speak contemptuously against their king and their God, and turn their faces upward. And they will look to the earth, but behold, distress and darkness, the gloom of anguish. And they will be thrust into thick darkness (Isaiah 8:16–22 ESV).

Note verse 19b: "should not a people inquire of their God? Should they inquire of the dead on behalf of the living?" That is a pretty harsh condemnation. Should we be petitioning the dead, on behalf of the living (ourselves) to ask God for something? Well, the passages exegeted above, and Isaiah 8 specifically say no. And that condemnation will fall for it.

Commenting on this John N. Oswalt says that:

> At the same time, there is in the traditional reading an irony implicit in the very ellipses that corresponds well with *the Isaianic attitude toward idolatry. It is ridiculous to consult the dead on behalf of the living*, yet how easily those who reject life turn to the dead to discover the meaning of life (italics mine).[12]

So, interestingly, Oswalt makes the connection here that necromancy, consulting spirits/the dead is equivalent to *idolatry*. Not only does this fall under the condemnation of magic and necromancy, but also complete apostasy in committing idolatry. To consult the dead, now including angels, on behalf of the living, is ridiculous. As the other Torah passages above have shown, it is strictly forbidden and as the history of Israel and Judah show, is one of the reasons that they were sent into exile. The northern kingdom of Israel never officially returned. Judah however was released from exile after seventy years. This is a very harsh condemnation for necromancy. Seeing the state of the Roman Catholic Church and the Prosperity, WoF and NAR churches that actively practice the praying for angels, petitioning dead saints and Mary, and believing that the Holy Spirit cannot be around until they invite him in, are we really surprised the church is in such moral

---

12. John N. Oswalt, *The Book of Isaiah Chapters 1–39* (Grand Rapids, Michigan: Wm. B. Eerdmans Publishing Company, 1986), p. 237.

and biblical decline?

J. Alec Moyer comments on this section to say that

> Why consult...? Is just a biting exclamation, 'On behalf of the living, to the dead?' *It is commonly claimed that the dead are in possession of greater powers and superior knowledge to the living.* In the Bible it is not so. The Old Testament knows that, leaving their bodies behind, the dead can only be shadows of what they were (Isa 14:10); the dead Samuel knows no more after death than he proclaimed when alive (1 Sam. 28:16ff). [...] Enduring privation they go into exile (roam through...), exasperated with their lot politically (king) and spiritually (God). *They are left without hope form God*, from earth or from the future (utter darkness) (italics mine).[13]

Again, we have Moyer here confirming what inquiring, or petitioning the dead will result in. The Catholic Church churches seems to believe that because the saints are dead that they have more direct access to God. The Satanist churches seem to believe that angels have more direct access to their Satanic form of God as well. So, Moyer's comments about "greater powers and superior knowledge" are applicable here. Anyone that believes in the legitimacy of petitioning the saints, and Mary, or angels are committing the sin of necromancy, and the condemnation of such will lead them into exile (spiritually) and "without hope from God."

Exegeting Isaiah 19:1-4

> An oracle concerning Egypt. Behold, the LORD is riding on a swift cloud and comes to Egypt; and the idols of Egypt will tremble at his presence, and the heart of the Egyptians will melt within them. And I will stir up Egyptians against Egyptians, and they will fight, each against another and each against his neighbor, city against city, kingdom against kingdom; and the spirit of the Egyptians within them will be emptied out, *and I will confound their counsel; and they will inquire of the idols and the sorcerers, and the mediums and the necromancers; and I will give over the Egyptians into the hand of a hard master, and a fierce king will rule over them*, declares the Lord GOD of hosts (italics mine, Isaiah 19:1–4 ESV).

Just quickly noting the italicized text. The confounding of apostolic counsel (relying on the pope or the Satanist apostles) causes them to consult the dead (the saints, Mary, and angels) and will result in a fierce king ruling over them (probably meaning Satan today).

Turning to Oswalt again, he notes that:

> Egyptian religion, especially during the Middle Kingdom (1990-1785

---

13. J. Alec Moyer, *Isaiah* (Downers Grove, Illinois: IVP Academic, 1999), pp. 98–99.

BC) and the New Kingdom (1550–1221 BC), *exhibited a number of universalistic and monolatrous trends. But after this time the ancient polytheisms and spiritualist tendencies began to reassert themselves. That is the picture here. As the more intellectualized and conceptualized polytheism break down under the stress of the times, the more magical, subliminal spiritism reasserts itself.* This situation is not restricted to polytheistic lands. *It can also happen to a land where a paganized, manipulative Yahwism is practiced* (8:19–22). Only a robust, pure faith in the God of the Bible can stand the shocks which must eventually come to every person and nation (italics mine).[14]

The italicized words are a pretty big condemnation of our world, and any church that adopts pagan and secular ideology into it. The Roman Catholic Church since Vatican II has in fact made universalism a part of their theology. Since Pope Francis has called Muslims and other pagan religions as worshipping the same God and so also inheritors of the salvation of Christ, universalism is part of their official doctrine. Because this has happened, it is no surprise that the petitioning of the dead (saints and Mary) has become even more pronounced in the last few years, it should be no surprise that Isaiah shows what will happen in such circumstances. Isaiah also shows that this can happen to a nation (or church) that believes in a paganized version of God. Since the Catholic church is promoting such ideology, it should be no surprise that the true God has condemned the Catholic worship of this paganized God and necromancy even though it is a common practice. The same is true of the Satanist church. Since the Satanist church has admitted that their prosperity gospel is the true gospel, we should not be surprised that necromancy is a common practice in their churches.

How does necromancy or, goetic/demon practice, relate to Satanism directly? Ford has an answer for us

> [a] Deific Mask within the Luciferian tradition is like a God-form; a magickian invokes a specific deity or demon to attain the knowledge and energies of the Spirit. [...] assume the God-form and compel the power which is given in turn from the Names of Power.[15]

Flowers continues the thought saying that

> black magicians would call on "demonic" entities. [...] demonic forces are coerced by the power of the names of God to do the magician's bidding, which could be virtually anything. Angels could be used to seduce or kill demons to gain wisdom and discover truth. [...]The black magician refuses to be limited in his use of magic just because this activity belongs to a class of behavior usually condemned by orthodox religion.

---

14. Oswalt, *Isaiah*, p. 368.
15. Ford, *Adversary*, p. 56, Kindle Edition.

> If a goal is worth attaining by any means, it is perfectly acceptable to use magic if necessary to attain it.[16]

If this makes you feel uncomfortable considering the context of this section, that is the entire point. Since there are absolutely zero examples of any human person, not including Christ who in fact still did not "pray" for angels but as God could command them to come (Matthew 26:53), in the Bible calling on God to send angels, or any other spirit at all, the practice of praying for angels, or interceding to saints or Mary, is not just an act of necromancy, but a practice rooted in Satanism.

John Eckhardt falsely claims that

> [b]inding is done by legal authority. We have legal authority in the name of Jesus to bind the works of darkness. The works of darkness encompass sin, iniquity, perversion, sickness, disease, infirmity, death, destruction, curses, witchcraft, sorcery, divination, poverty, lack, divorce, strife, lust, pride, rebellion, fear, torment, and confusion. We have legal authority to put a stop to these things in our lives and in the lives of those we minister to.
>
> Loose means to untie, to free from restraint, to detach. It also means to disjoin, divorce, separate, unhitch, get free, get loose, escape, break away, unbind, unchain, unfetter, free, release, unlock, liberate, disconnect, and forgive.[17]

This is a misinterpretation of the following verse

> [i]f your brother sins against you, go and tell him his fault, between you and him alone. If he listens to you, you have gained your brother. But if he does not listen, take one or two others along with you, that every charge may be established by the evidence of two or three witnesses. If he refuses to listen to them, tell it to the church. And if he refuses to listen even to the church, let him be to you as a Gentile and a tax collector. Truly, I say to you, whatever you bind on earth shall be bound in heaven, and whatever you loose on earth shall be loosed in heaven. (Matthew 18:15–18 ESV)

This verse, with the preceding context has absolutely nothing to do with demons, angels, or any "powers of darkness" at all. Eckhardt here is using his own biased beliefs about what this out of context verse means to force a goetic point, rather than a biblical one.

R. T. France gives an accurate description of what is happening here

> the meaning of "tying" and "untying," where I argued that they do not refer to condemning or forgiving a person but to making decisions about

---

16. Flowers, *Left-Hand*, p. 25.
17. John Eckhardt, *Deliverance and Spiritual Warfare Manual* (Lake Mary, Florida: Charisma House, 2014), p. 99.

what is right and wrong. In this context, where the "sin" of a member of the community has been under consideration, the rabbinic use of these terms for "declaring what is or is not permitted" seems particularly relevant. Here, as in 16:19, the object of the "tying" is expressed in the neuter, not the masculine: it is things, issues, actions that are tied or untied, not people—though of course, as v. 17b has made clear, the decision made in principle will have practical implications for the person involved. The individual who was at first concerned over the offender's action has, in v. 17, found it necessary to appeal to the gathered community, and the community has endorsed that individual's assessment that this was "sin."[18]

Realizing what France has said, pick whatever term you want for the way Eckhardt has interpreted Matthew 18:18, goetic and/or necromantic, it is a teaching drawn right out of Satanism, or as Flowers puts it "black magic", and has nothing to do with the Bible at all.

Conclusion

Remember that the Bible is very clear on the issue of necromancy and the occult. While scripture can be twisted in many different ways by tradition and even by "Protestants" that refuse to see the inherent error in the argument, we now have entire groups of Christians who will not condemn other "Christians" for committing one of the most heinous sins in the Bible.

Are we really surprised at the rise of New Age and LHP ideology in the church? Even our own Protestant apologists cannot recognize necromancy and magic when it is staring them right in the face.

No other spirit, than God alone is to be prayed to or petitioned in anyway. Other spirits, really demons which includes any versions of saints, Mary, and angels are not able to do what these churches have taught. Nor do these spirits, and the churches teaching this necromancy, even have the biblical authority to do so.

---

18. R. T. France, *The Gospel of Matthew, The New International Commentary on the New Testament* (Grand Rapids, Michigan: Wm. B. Eerdmans Publication Co., 2007), pp. 696–697.

Chapter VIII: Lilith

Before we go any further, I need to define exactly who Lilith is. Within occult circles the generally accepted "truth" about Lilith is that she was Adam's first wife that refused to submit to Adam by laying under him during sex, and in an act of defiance called on Samael to carry her out of the Garden of Eden. Samael (Satan in Jewish mythology, this will be proven later), then took Lilith to the Euphrates River where he had sexual intercourse with her and impregnated her. As a part of her judgement, Gabriel came to make sure hundreds of her demon children died that she was bearing each day. This form of the Lilith myth is found in the *Alphabet of Ben-Sirach* which has been concluded to be a parody of the creation story, but many people, not just in the occult, take it as fact. This version of Lilith is what I will call the "Adamic-Lilith".

There is within history another Lilith that is often mixed with the Adamic-Lilith. This second Lilith I will refer to as the "Assyrian-Lilith". Despite similarities, they are two different "persons". The Adamic-Lilith is fictional fantasy. The Assyrian-Lilith, however, is in the Bible.

I will quote several Bible versions of Isaiah 34:14 to show what is going on. The italics in the following verses were all inserted by me.

> And wild animals shall meet with hyenas; the wild goat shall cry to his fellow; indeed, there the *night bird* settles and finds for herself a resting place. (ESV)

> Desert creatures will meet with hyenas, and wild goats will bleat to each other; there the *night creatures* will also repose and find for themselves places of rest. (NIV1984)

> The desert creatures will meet with the wolves, The hairy goat also will cry to its kind; Yes, the *night monster* will settle there And will find herself a resting place. (NASB1995)

> The wild beasts of the desert shall also meet with the wild beasts of the island, And the satyr shall cry to his fellow; The *screech owl* also shall rest there, And find for herself a place of rest. (KJV)

And the desert creatures will meet with the wolves; The hairy goat also will cry to its kind; Surely, the *night creature* will obtain relief there And will find itself a resting place. (LSB)

For one more reference, take a look at the Clementine Latin Vulgate

Et occurrent dæmonia onocentauris, et pilosus clamabit alter ad alterum; ibi cubavit *lamia*, et invenit sibi requiem. (CV)

Lamia here is defined as: "witch; bogey/demon; female monster (eats children/child's blood); vampire".[1] Another Latin language lexicon holds a similar translation "a witch, sorceress, vampire".[2] This is interesting, since the Latin Vulgate was one of the first versions of the Bible translated into a "western" tongue. Before this, all the versions of the Old Testament are either languages of the Ancient Near East, or Koine Green in the Septuagint (LXX). Greek is a "western" language however since it was the trade language of the Roman Empire, it does not exactly fit the definition that we need here. However, even in the Koine Greek, a lamia is defined as "Λάμιᾰ [ᾰ], ἡ, a fabulous monster said to feed on man's flesh, a bugbear to frighten children with".[3] So this definition of lamia/Lilith is still appropriate, as a non-western language, to the use that will be shown below.

Some lay person commentators have attempted to claim that "Lilith" in this context is being read into the text.

> I find this to be an occultic interpretation of Isaiah 34:14 and could not find the original source from which it came from. This verse has mostly dominated the internet as a suggested authority. However, anyone can put anything up on the internet and call it fact. Anything placed online and presented as fact without scholar or theologian approval should never be accepted as genuine material; there needs to be an authority. The Bible does not specifically say the name of Lilith when referring to the above verses. In the many translations of the Holy Bible there is not one mention of Lilith anywhere by name.[4]

Is this claim by Haggart true? Looking at the Hebrew text, it seems that Haggart is misinformed.

וּפָגְשׁ֤וּ צִיִּים֙ אֶת־אִיִּ֔ים וְשָׂעִ֖יר עַל־רֵעֵ֣הוּ יִקְרָ֑א אַךְ־שָׁ֣ם הִרְגִּ֔יעָה [לִילִית֙] וּמָצְאָ֥ה לָ֖הּ מָנֽוֹחַ׃

---

1. William Whitaker, *Dictionary of Latin Forms* (Bellingham, Washington: Logos Bible Software, 2012), Logos Edition.

2. Charlton T. Lewis, *An Elementary Latin Dictionary* (Medford, Massachusetts: American Book Company, 1890), Logos Edition.

3. Henry George Liddell et al., *A Greek-English Lexicon* (Oxford, England: Clarendon Press, 1996), p. 1027, Logos Edition.

4. G. P. Haggart, *Screech Owl: The Lie Behind Lilith* (Morrisville, North Carolina: Lulu Press, Inc., 2009), p. 7, Kindle Edition.

(brackets around לילית mine) (BHS4)

The word that is of notice in the square brackets is לילית or lî·lît. Take a look at several lexical definitions of lî·lît.

> Lilith (Milton Che nighthag), name of a female night-demon haunting desolate Edom; prob. borrowed from Bab., Is 34:14 (NH id.; Assyrian lilîtu, Dl 377; Syriac [...] (lelito) PS1951; on the development of legends of Lilith in later Judaism, v. Bux Lex. Talmud., s.v. Chead loc. Grünbaum xxxi. 1877, 250 f.—Connexion with לילה perhaps only apparent, a popular etymology).[5]

> [לילית] f. prop. nocturna (from [ליל], with the adj. term. fem. [ית-]), a nocturnal spectre, which had, according to the rabbins, the form of a beautiful woman, and lay wait for children by night. [All this is utterly absurd when thus connected with the nature of something real mentioned in Scripture; what it is, may be doubtful.] Like this are the Greek and Roman fables about the woman Ἔμπουσα, about the ὀνοκένταυροι (see Arist. Ran. 293; Creuzer, Comment. Herod. page 267), the Lamiæ, the Striges, and the Arabian fables about the Ghûles [...], i.e. female monsters inhabiting deserts, and tearing men in pieces. Compare other names of spectres, [עלוקה שעירים]. Isa. 34:14. More may be seen in Bochart, in Hieroz. vol. ii. page 831; Buxtorf, in Lexicon Ch., and Talmud. page 1140, and in my Comment. on Isa. 13:22; 34:14. [It is really lamentable that any one could connect the word of God with such utter absurdity; many understand the nocturnal creature spoken of to be simply the screech owl.][6]

> [לילית]: Lilith, (female) demon relating to sexual life (oth.: nightmare, or wood-owl) Is 34:14, cj. Jb 18:15 (for mibbelî-lô).[7]

> [לילית] (lî·lît): n.fem.; ≡ Str 3917; TWOT 1112—1. LN 4.1–4.37 (NIV, NKJV, NASB, KJV, NEB, REB) night creature, i.e., any of several nocturnal natural animals that roams at night, like an owl, or nightjar bird (Isa 34:14+), note: for another interp, see next; 2. LN 12.1–12.42 (NRSV, RSV, ASV, NAB, NJB, Tanakh) Lilith, the Night Hag, i.e., a supernatural female demon, night creature considered a monster (Isa 34:14+), note: in context, the goat just prior may be a "goat-demon."[8]

---

5. Brown, *Lexicon*, , p. 539.

6. Wilhelm Gesenius and Samuel Prideaux Tregelles, *Gesenius' Hebrew and Chaldee Lexicon to the Old Testament Scriptures* (Bellingham, Washington: Logos Bible Software, 2003), p. 438, Logos Edition.

7. William Lee Holladay and Ludwig Köhler, *A Concise Hebrew and Aramaic Lexicon of the Old Testament* (Leiden, Netherlands: Brill, 2000), p. 176, Logos Edition.

8. James Swanson, *Dictionary of Biblical Languages with Semantic Domains: Hebrew (Old Testament)* (Oak Harbor, Washington: Logos Research Systems, Inc., 1997), Logos Edition.

116 Chapter VIII: Lilith

Despite Haggart's claim, and Gesenius et. al's claim to "absurdity", the running consensus here is that there is some demonic connection here. Just because we think it is absurd for this assumingly singled out section of the Bible to be talking about the demonic, there are many different demonic references in the Bible that have been turned into a more "natural world" reading in order to adapt it to the thinking of post-renaissance science. However, the ancient Israelites, and Jews of Jesus' day did not think this way and thought of the world as an extremely spiritual place. Just as it is today.

> The Heb term lîlît as a →demon in Isa 34:14 is connected by popular etymology with the word laylâ 'night'. But it is certainly to be considered a loan from Akk lilītu, which is ultimately derived from Sum líl. [...] In Akk texts lilû, lilītu and (w)ardat lilî often occur together as three closely related demons whose dominion are the stormy winds. [...] In this aspect we can compare these demons with Ishtar who stands at the window looking for a man in order to seduce him, love him and kill him. [...] The only reference to this demon in the OT occurs in Isa 34:14. The whole chapter describes the prophetic judgement on →Edom which will become waste land. Then all kinds of demons will dwell there: among them hyenas, tawny owls, vultures and also Lilith. [...] Well known is also the legend of Lilith who was →Adam's first wife but flew away from him after a quarrel; since then she has been a danger to little children and people have to protect themselves against her by means of amulets. Solomon in his great wisdom also possessed might over demons and the Liliths; in later Jewish legends one of the two wives from 1 Kgs 3:16–28 was identified with Lilith; so was the Queen of Sheba (1 Kgs 10). Such legends spread until the Middle Ages. In popular belief Lilith became not only the grandmother of the →devil or the devil himself, but also the arch-mother of witchcraft and witches.[9]

The claim that Solomon had control of demons and Lilith's is derived from ancient pagan and even medieval goetic texts such as *The Lesser Key of Solomon*, *The Lesser Key of Solomon* does not refer to Solomon controlling Lilith's but other demons, however the reference still stands. Isaiah 34:14 is speaking of a lilit or Lilith and the ancient world, including the Israelites, were very aware that this demon was real.

The quoted section by Hutter above mentions that the Lilith's are like Ishtar in their search for a sexual partner. In looking at the associations that the Assyrian-Lilith had we find an interesting chain

אנתי הי איפרודיטי שהכל נשים ושהכל מו[ראות] ל[]יך

---

9. M. Hutter, "Lilith," ed. Karel van der Toorn, Bob Becking, and Pieter W. van der Horst, *Dictionary of Deities and Demons in the Bible* (Leiden; Netherlands: Brill, 1999), pp. 520–521, Logos Edition.

מ[ש]בדות ליך ושהכל ברושו[ת] ש[פ]חות [משבדות ליך
א[שב[עי[ת על[י]כי[ליליתא [---] ב[ק]לע פשוטא ובחרב

> You are Aphrodite, (to) whom all women and to whom all are dis[played ---] to [--- are] enslaved, and [to] whom all are legitimate[ly enslaved] (as) maid[ser]vants. I [be]swea[r you], lilith [---] with a straight [s]ling and with a sword[10]

Before someone tries to point out the alef (א) at the end of the word "lilit" to say they are different demons, the fact is they are the same:

> בר פרח[י]א ליליתא [לילית] דכר וניקבא שלנ[ית]א וחטפיתא
> (brackets around לילית mine)
>
> bar Peraḥ[i]a. Liliths, male and female *lilith*, the grabb[er] and the snatcher (italics mine)[11]

It is the same Lilith, whether in Hebrew or Aramaic.

Lilith here is being associated with Aphrodite. In the ancient world, they were recognized as either the same or closely related gods/demons. However, the associations with Aphrodite do not end there.

> 'Isle of Astarte' or [...] loan translations in the sense of an *interpretatio Graeca* or *Romana* by which Astarte was equated with Aphrodite. (italics in original)[12]

> is accompanied by Astarte/Aphrodite/Venus, under the different names of Melqart, Bes, Eshmun and Adonis. The association of these deities, even in the context of the probable duality of the cult within the temple, characterised by a bipartite adyton, would be justified by their common nature as divine entities linked to the marine world, without forgetting their shared function as deities with curative powers.[13]

Now that we see that Lilith is associated to Astarte, some interesting new arguments open up.

The divine name Astarte is found in the following forms: [...] Heb

---

10. Shaul Shaked, James Nathan Ford, and Siam Bhayro, *Aramaic Bowl Spells* (Leiden, Netherlands: Brill, 2013), p. 140.

11. Shaked, *Aramaic*, p. 139.

12. Theo Vennemann gen. Nierfeld, *Germania Semitica* (Berlin, Germany: De Gruyter, 2013), p. 398.

13. Romina Carboni, "Between Astarte, Isis and Aphrodite/Venus. Cultural Dynamics in the Coastal Cities of Sardinia in the Roman Age: The Case Study of Nora," in *Naming and Mapping the Gods in the Ancient Mediterranean*, ed. Thomas Galoppin, Elodie Guillon, Max Luaces, Asuman Lätzer-Lasar, Sylvain Lebreton, Fabio Porzia, Jörg Rüpke, Emiliano Rubens Urciuoli and Corinne Bonnet (Berlin, Germany: De Gruyter, 2022), pp. 568–569.

'Aštōret (singular); 'Aštārôt (generally construed as plural); [...] this in turn occurs, though as the name of a goddess, as Akkadian →Ishtar. The Akkadian [...] is probably, in the masculine form, the name of the planet Venus [...[Both god and goddess are probably, but not certainly, to be seen as the deified Venus [...] This is indeed the case, since if the morning star is the male deity [...] then the goddess would be the evening star. [...][14]

It is probably Ashtart who was denoted by the title →'Queen of heaven', referred to in cults of the end of the monarchy (Jer 7:18; 44:17–19, 25).[15]

Astarte, being the "queen of heaven" and the wife of the Canaanite El, who was later associated with the biblical Yahweh, is put onto a very high podium. Following the chain-links here: Lilith is Aphrodite, Aphrodite is Astarte, and Astarte is Ishtar. The ancient world believed that there was some kind of divine royalty associated with Lilith, something that is reflected in the Christian Satanist movements today.

Some other interesting notes about the Lilith comes up in these Aramaic bowl spells

בפומה בקלע בפומה ובחרב פשוטא {ב} אשבע[ית על]יכ[י]
לילתא דיכרא וניקבתא ב[צ]דקי [---] ושלא [ת]יראי ליה
לבהמנד[ד] בר מגיתא ול[---]תא ב[ת]

in her mouth, with a sling in her mouth, and with a straight sword. [I] beswear yo[u], lilith, male and female, by [Ṣi]dqi [---] and that [you should] not show yourself to Bahmanda[d] son of Magita and to [---]ta daug[hter of][16]

Note that the demon Lilith here is being referred to in the singular, in other words one demon that is male and female.

[---] ולאחתין ביסר בנין וכולה[ו]ן קטילי ביתהון [---] סוסני
ססוני וסניגרי וארדקי עלאיסור בגדנה מלכה מלכיהון דשידי
[ודיוי ושליטא]

[---] and they boil (?) the flesh of children, and all of th[e]m, the dead ones of their house [---] nomina barbara Elisur Bagdana, the king, the king of demons [and dēvs and] the great[17]

[ביש]תא עזיזתא תקיפתא מן חרשי מעבדי מן חרשי דז[נ]י

---

14. N. Wyatt, "Astarte," ed. Karel van der Toorn, Bob Becking, and Pieter W. van der Horst, *Dictionary of Deities and Demons in the Bible* (Leiden, Netherlands: Brill, 1999), pp. 109–110, Logos Edition.

15. Wyatt, *Astarte*, p. 113.

16. Shaked, *Aramaic*, p. 140.

17. Shaked, *Aramaic*, p. 193.

Chapter VIII: Lilith

ז[מ]ר[ת]א [זנית]א ליליתא
{דשריה} דמקטלא בני דיליה בני דחיברתיה דאם {י} תיהון
ראשאה ושליט[א ב]נפשיכי לכל
איניש דיתצבין דיכתבית ליכי גיטא גיט פיטורין מן אימי בת
קאקי כל שום דאית ליכי מומנא משבענא

strong (and) severe spirit, from sorcery (and) magical acts, from the sorcery of Za[nay, the fornicat]ing [sin]gi[ng]-girl, the lilith who massacres her own children (and) the children of her companions. In order that if you may have authority and powe[r over] yourself to any man that you wish, for I have written to you a deed of divorce (and) a deed of release from Immi daughter of Qaqay, (and) any name that you have. I adjure (and) beswear[18]

The text shows here that Lilith massacres her own children to gain "authority and power over any man that you wish."

ליכי אנתי זני זמרתא זניתא ליליתא דשריה בביתיה דאימי בת
קאק[י] אם [ד]כר אם ניקבה בשמיה דגבריאל

you, you, Zanay, the fornicating singing-girl, the lilith who resides in the house of Immi daughter of Qaqa[y], whether [m]ale or female. By the name of the angel[19]

לגיסתא בת איפרה הורמיץ לא בליליה ולא ביממא ולא
בדיכרא ולא בניקבתא מנקודם דהדין קמיעא י[ה]וי לכון
גיטיכון ופיטוריכון כמא דנסבין שידי גיטי
לנשיהון ותוב לא הדרין עלאהין רוחי בישתא ליליתא בישתא
דיכרי וניקבתא תוב לא ת[י]הדרון [ו]לא תיתחזון לה לגיסתא
בת איפרה הורמיץ מן יומא דין ולעלם

Gista daughter of Ifra-Hormiṣ, neither by night nor by day, and neither as male nor as female, because this amulet shall [b]e for you your deeds of divorce and your (writs of) release, just as demons take deeds of divorce to their wives and they do not come back again unto them. Evil spirits, evil liliths, male and female, you [shall] not come back again [n]or appear to Gista daughter of Ifra-Hormiṣ from this day and for ever.[20]

There is a definite theme here between the murder of children, and the confusion of male and female when it comes to the Assyrian-Lilith demon. Which is extremely important to the argument.

In commenting further in what Lilith may really be, J. D. Douglas suggests

---

18. Shaked, *Aramaic*, p. 226.
19. Shaked, *Aramaic*, p. 229.
20. Shaked, *Aramaic*, p. 274.

It may, however, be misleading to regard the creature as necessarily associated with the night: the darkness which some demons were said to love was that caused by desert storms (cf. Sumerian LIL.LÁ, 'storm-wind'; and also a possible conclusion from Jerome's translation cited above). Some scholars regard it as the equivalent of the English vampire. Later Jewish literature speaks variously of Lilith as the first wife of Adam, but she flew away and became a demon; as a fabulous monster which stole and destroyed newly-born infants; and as a demon against which charms were used to keep it from the haunts of men, lest it enter and bring disease.[21]

While Douglas doubts the supernatural rendering of the Lilith, Wesley Callahan says that "[a]lthough there may be a touch of sarcasm in the phrase [meaning Douglas's above], the analogy may be very accurate."[22] Since the Latin, "lamia", was a creature that feasted on human flesh, and was associated with the vampire, as well as the very Hebrew word לילית meaning a vampire of some sort as well, it should not be absurd to consider that the Lilith is in some way the earliest source of the vampire myth. The vampire myth is one of those stories that seems to go into every culture across the world. Janet Carsten in her book *Blood Work* mentions that "[v]ampire spirits are quite commonly reported in Malaysia".[23] Carsten continues that

> Stories about vampire spirits in Malaysia are often told with a kind of relish that is also palpable in newspaper accounts. Here the spectral register is part of the everyday and may be experienced in the most modern and technologically advanced contexts—including hospitals, factories, and universities. In these stories, which connect criminality, ghosts, and blood's nefarious potential, spirits are attracted by blood's animating powers. Such spirits may have murderous intentions and may also as the victims of murderers.[24]

In another academic work by James B. Twitchell *The Living Dead: A Study of the Vampire* in Romantic Literature, the Adamic-Lilith is connected directly to the Assyrian-Lilith

> There was another mythic precedent: Lilith was the Hebraic temptress that supposedly turned to blood-sucking after being spurned by Adam, and Lamia was her classical counterpart, who, when found by Hera to be Zeus's lover, was transformed into a child-eater.[25]

---

21. J. D. Douglas, "Lilith," ed. D. R. W. Wood et al., *New Bible Dictionary* (Downers Grove, Illinois: InterVarsity Press, 1996), p. 691, Logos Edition.

22. Wesley Callahan, "Satyrs, Liliths & Lunatics," in *The Forgotten Heavens*, ed. Douglas Wilson (Moscow, Idaho: Canon Press, 2010), p. 119.

23. June Carsten, *Blood Work: Life and Labratories In Penang* (London, England: Duke University Press, 2019), p. 158.

24. Carsten, *Blood*, p. 159.

25. James B. Twitchell, *The Living Dead: A Study of the Vampire in Romantic*

The comment about the "spurning by Adam" is not exactly accurate to the myth of the Adamic-Lilith in the *Alphabet of Ben-Sirach*, but the connection is still made between the Adamic-Lilith and the Assyrian Lilith to the vampire myth even though they are distinctly different "persons". The importance of this will be returned to later.

In tying Lilith to the LHP, note Ford as saying that the

> Feminine "Lilith" represents the emotional fiery instincts which give expressions emanating from the primal unconscious mind, the oldest reptilian part of the human brain. Samael is the Black Serpent and Lilith the Red; without Lilith, Samael is incomplete and ineffective. Without Samael, Lilith is only primal expression and destructive impulses. Leviathan the Crooked Serpent and Coiling Dragon is the Ouroboros which is the circle in which Samael and Lilith are joined in Infernal Union.[26]

Ford also says that the

> Infernal Union of Samael and Lilith within the Luciferian is not a gender-related concept; rather it is gaining awareness of balanced opposites which have different traits yet compliment and motivate the Black Adept.[27]

Gershom Scholem in his translation of *Treatise of the Left Emanation* an early Kabbalistic text shows that

> A form destined for Samael stirs up enmity and jealousy between the heavenly delegation and the forces of the supernal army. This form is Lilith, and she is in the image of a feminine form. Samael takes on the form of Adam and Lilith the form of Eve. They were both born in a spiritual birth as one, as a parallel to the forms of Adam and Eve above and below: two twinlike forms. Both Samael and [Lilith, called] Even the Matron—also known as the Northern One—are emanated from beneath the Throne of Glory.[28]

Also

> Samael, the great prince and great king over all the demons, cohabits with the great Matron Lilith. Asmodeus, the kind of the demons, cohabits with the Lesser [Younger] Lilith. The scholars of this tradition admit to many horrendous details concerning the forms of Samael and Asmodeus and the images of Lilith the bride of Samael and Lilith the bride of Asmodeus.[29]

Literature (Durham, North Carolina: Duke University Press, 1997), p. 40.
    26. Ford, *Adversary*, p. 52.
    27. Ford, *Adversary*, p. 73.
    28. Gershom Scholem, *The Early Kabbalah* (Mahwah, New Jersey: Paulist Press, 1986), p. 173.
    29. Scholem, *Kabbalah*, p. 175.

As can be seen, Samael and Lilith are recognized as husband and wife. I had mentioned earlier that Samael and Satan were recognized as the same demon. In the introduction to *Abraham Abulafia's Esotericism* Warren Zev Harvey makes the connection that "(Samael = Satan)" in footnote 11.[30] Recognizing that Satan and Lilith are married, that the Satanists that call themselves Christians are theistic worshippers of Satan, who they call "God", and that Lilith is associated with the "queen of heaven", it should not surprise us that Lilith ideology has made its way into Hillsong, and Prosperity, WoF, and NAR movements.

Within the RHP is the concept of the Kabbalistic Tree of Life which consists of ten sephirot that must be ascended to attain unity with "God". While the full concepts of the RHP are beyond the scope of this book, it is notable that there is also a "dark sephirot" in a form of the LHP that exists in Sweden known as the Dragon Rouge. In the Dragon Rouge, Kennet Granholm ironically notes that the ten sephirot exist in a

> Sephiroth of Darkness or Evil which mirrors the Sephiroth of Good [...]. The qliphoth consist of the ten worlds, from the world closest to our own to the world farthest away, *Lilith*, Gamaliel, *Samael*, A'arab Zaraq, Thagirion, Golachab, Gha'agsheblah, Satariel, Ghagiel and Thaumiel. (italics mine)[31]

Again, we can see here that Lilith and Satan/Samael are intimately linked. In the greater sephirot it is interesting where the Dragon Rouge place Lilith.

> Lilith represents the dark side of the normal world. Lilith's sephirotic counterpart is Malkuth, which in qabalah represents the material world.[32]

As was shown in the chapter three, Malkuth is the very first, or last, of the sephirot. There is no way to get through the Tree of Life without starting or ending with Malkuth. Like other LHP movements that emphasize the importance of Lilith, the Dragon Rouge have placed Lilith as the start of their Tree of Life. Lilith is the base starting point. Lilith is the starting line and defining what role she has played in world history is important when speaking of the LHP. Within the Dragon Rouge, Lilith holds an interesting place in their, for lack of a better way to describe it, "salvific" journey.

---

30. Warren Zev Harvey, "Foreword: A Maimonidean Kabbalist," in *Abraham Abulafia's Esotericism* (Berlin: German: De Gruyter, 2020), p. xiii.
31. Granholm, *Dragon*, p. 23.
32. Granholm, *Dragon*, p. 225.

> Lilith, you hold the sceptre and you hold the domination. Give us dominance and the fulfilment of dreams![33]

Realizing who Lilith is it is not surprising that this particular LHP group sees that the

> women's rights discourse is most prominent among the female members of the order, but is also more indirectly produced in the teachings of the order. Female deities and demonesses, such as Kali, Hel and Lilith, are of special importance in rituals and texts. Male deities play a much less visible role.[34]

As I have shown about Lilith and her association with the LHP, her association with Satan is inseparable. If a group adheres to the LHP in any kind of way, Lilith is part of the discussion and cannot be kept outside of the doctrine of that order. It should be no surprise then, that Lilith has found her way into the Satanist churches of the Hillsong, and Prosperity, WoF, and NAR movements. The connections to Lilith may not seem to be obvious, but they are there. Because of the subtleness of the way many of these Satanist preachers have manipulated the "divine feminine" into their ideology, picking out what is "Lilithian" and what is not will be a difficult task. However, Satanist churches are not the only ones to have brought in Assyrian-Lilith ideology into their churches. The entirety of the Progressive, Exvangelical, and Deconstructionist movement have done so as well (from here on in, all these terms will be put under the umbrella of "Progressive").

The Progressive movement in their wild acceptance of homosexuality, the trans movement and other deviant forms of sexuality have incorporated the idea that the Assyrian-Lilith is both male and female, that as the *Treatise of the Left Emanation* that both Lilith and Satan (Samael) "were both born in a spiritual birth as one". But it has not stopped there unfortunately. The Progressive movement has also imparted the Lilith gender ethic, being both male and female, and as Satan and Lilith originally being "one", onto the person of who the Progressives claim is the biblical God. This imparting of Lilith is highly in error by the Progressives. This de-gendering of God has roots in Kabbalistic and LHP ideology, however, the Progressive movement is stuck on the idea that God is they/them instead of using the identifier the Bible gives us for God as Father and He/Him.

Showing what the Lilith and Satan relation is and where it has come from, this next statement will also be quite shocking: modern Bible versions that have removed God as "Father" or "He" and "Him"

---

33. Granholm, *Dragon*, p. 222.
34. Granholm, *Dragon*, p. 285.

have incorporated a Satanist form of a "god" into the Bible. At its core, Satanism, via Lilith and Satan's union, need to de-gender God and all his image bearers.

What is also shocking with the Progressive movement is their support of abortion. Looking through the *Aramaic Bowl Spells* quoted above, two shocking rituals are shown that "they boil [...] the flesh of children" and also that Lilith would "massacre her children" for the goal of controlling any man. Looking at the two most common forms of abortion procedures today, the use of a uterus acid to boil the fetus or to rip the child apart and removed from the uterus bit by bit, or massacring children, the connection is not hard to make to the *Aramaic Bowl Spells*. The goal of women to abort babies when it comes to keeping men with them or to keep drawing sexual interest towards them from men, it is not surprising that abortion and this form of Satanism are also, once again connected. Since the Progressive movement has argued for the legitimacy of abortion, again, it should not be surprised that Lilith ideology is embedded in their doctrine. While the Progressive movement is not identified as LHP in the same way that the Satanist churches are, it is not hard to believe that they would have no problem partnering with Satanist churches to push their "gospel". Remember that Progressive churches deny the humanity or "personhood" of the human fetus.[35] That ideology is a Christological heresy. If Christ was not human from the point of conception, then he was never the appropriate replacement for us in penal substitutionary atonement, therefore it is a different gospel.

So, now connections need to start being made between Lilith, LHP and the Satanist church. Some may have been wondering why I was emphasizing the vampire connection so much. I have no doubt that a few readers were thinking that this is just too weird to be serious. However, at the 2020 Southwest Believers Convention, Kenneth Copeland, a false teacher embedded with the entire Prosperity, WoF, and NAR movement, showed a video where in taking communion, Copeland and another teacher pretended to cut their hands open, mix the "blood" into the fruit juice they poured into a cup, then Copeland drank the cup as a true sign of communion.[36]

Before criticisms come, watching the video closely, it is obvious that no actual blood was put into the cup. People in the audience at the time, may or may not have realized this, it is hard to say. The problem

---

35. Allie Beth Stuckey, "Pro-Life Christian vs Pro-Choice Leftist on Roe & Abortion | Guest: Brandan Robertson | Ep 612," *YouTube*, July 13, 2023, https://www.youtube.com/watch?v=HbxF6SRxJyk.

36. Revealing Truth, "Kenneth Copeland Takes Creepy to a Whole New Level," *YouTube*, July 13, 2023, https://www.youtube.com/watch?v=-At56s393Ko.

is the implied and inherent association with literal human blood that Copeland is suggesting being part of communion and the Lord's Supper. This is not even close to being the same as the Roman Catholic Churches belief in trans-substantiation. What Copeland showed is a blood ritual that is reflective of LHP ideology that comes from ancient Lilith teaching. Copeland in this video is promoting a form of vampirism for the liturgy of the "Christian" church. To say that Copeland is not a Satanist at this point would be absurd.

> My hope is that as each of us matures in revelation about our own personhood and that of feminine humankind, we will see a new day dawn for countless thousands of women across the earth—a new day not only for those captive to an unhappy or impoverished soul, but a new day for multitudes who are literally captive to forces beyond their control. The sanity, freedom, well-being, and hope of these women hinge on our—yes, you and me—collective awakening.[37]

Remember what Flowers said about consciousness "The first form or general principle of isolate intelligence from which all the particular manifestations of individual consciousness". Flowers made this comment about the idea of the "Prince of Darkness". A collective awakening is pointing at the idea of a collective conscience that exists in some larger form, or Flowers' "Prince of Darkness". Some pro-Hillsong/Satanist advocates would most likely say that Bobbie Houston is not referring to some "greater consciousness" but the wording she has chosen is unmistakable. Bobbie Houston is talking about her women, in a Satanist mindset, waking up other women's "conscience" in an attempt to gain a "collective awakening". Whether we as individuals in the church decide to "awaken" will have no effect on other people minds. The gospel is Jesus crucified, resurrected and nothing more. There is no need for a "collective awakening" in the sense that Bobbie Houston is arguing. That ideology is rooted directly to the LHP.

In her book of a collection of essays, Judith Plaskow brings the reality of what Bobbie Houston is saying back to Adamic-Lilith ideology. In her essay *The Coming of Lilith: A Feminist Theology* Plaskow says

> [s]ince the felt need for such theology arises through the conscience-raising experience, this theology constantly needs to measure itself against and recapture the richness of feeling and insight through conscience-raising.[38]

---

37. Bobbie Houston, *The Sisterhood* (New York, New York: FaithWords, 2016), pp. 5-6, Kindle Edition.
38. Judith Plaskow, *The Coming of Lilith: A Feminist Theology* (Boston, Massachusetts: Beacon Press, 2005), p. 23.

> In affirming my own womanhood—or personhood as a woman—I affirm it in all women. But I also and particularly affirm those women with whom I share my experience of affirmation.[39]

> We also felt the need for using older materials that would carry their own reverberations and significance, even if we departed freely from them. We choose, therefore, to begin with the story of Lilith, demon of the night, who, according to rabbinic legend, was Adam's first wife. Created equal to him, for some reason she found that she could not live with him and flew away. Through her story, we could express not only our new image of ourselves, but our relation to certain of the elements of our religious traditions.[40]

Is this what Bobbie Houston is doing here? Bobbie Houston is definitely using a Lilith-based theological basis to affirm the "freedom" of women and to redefine "religious traditions." Most, if not all, of the Satanic churches have cast away "religious traditional" gender roles that are shown in the Bible. When people within the Christian theological framework start to promote the idea of women pastors and elders, they are very directly violating 1 Timothy 2:12 and 1 Timothy 3:2

> I do not permit a woman to teach or to exercise authority over a man; rather, she is to remain quiet. (1 Timothy 2:12 ESV)

> Therefore an overseer must be above reproach, the husband of one wife (1 Timothy 3:2 ESV)

In calling herself a "pastor", Bobbie Houston is violating these two biblical commands. Commenting on 1 Timothy 2:12, Donald Guthrie shows

> If the present prohibition is restricted to public teaching (as seems most probable) it accords perfectly with the 1 Corinthians passage. Paul cannot be accused of being a woman-hater, as is sometimes alleged, on the strength of this evidence, since he acknowledges some women among his own fellow-workers, such as Priscilla (Rom. 16:3–5) and Euodias and Syntyche (Phil. 4:2–3). The prohibition may have been due to the greater facility with which contemporary women were falling under the influence of imposters (cf. Falconer). A similar idea is that the tendency among later Gnostics to ignore the differences between men and women is being combated (cf. Brox), but this tendency may have had much earlier roots in the first century.[41]

Guthrie shows that there is a prohibition on women as pastors and

---

39. Plaskow, *Lilith*, p. 26.
40. Plaskow, *Lilith*, p. 30.
41. Donald Guthrie, *Pastoral Epistles: An Introduction and Commentary, vol. 14, Tyndale New Testament Commentaries* (Downers Grove, Illinoios: InterVarsity Press, 1990), p. 90, Logos Edition.

elders including not publicly teaching, despite the way other commentators have tried to work around this. The text is clear. Not only that, but Guthrie also points out that this the same issue with Gnostics who would frequently ignore the differences between men and women. Gnosticism had a great influence on both modern occultism and the LHP. It was Gnosticism that affirmed Satan/Lucifer as "the Light Bringer" that came to free Eve from the deception of, in Gnostic thought, the evil Yaldabaoth, or the biblical Yahweh. Bobbie Houston in affirming her "collective conscience" in order to free women and to believe that she is a "pastor/elder" goes right along with the teaching about Lilith and her "queen of heaven" thinking from the ancient world. Lilith stands for freedom from "traditional religion" as Plaskow argued, and Bobbie Houston has taken that ideology and affirmed her own Assyrian-Lilith given freedoms, that are really LHP and slavery.

Bobbie Houston continues that

> I pray that you are inspired to step back a little and appreciate anew the divine (people) connections at work in your life.[42]

Within the context of Bobbie Houston's book *The Sisterhood*, Houston is speaking of divine women. Which points us back to the fact that human beings are in no way divine, that is LHP. And since Bobbie Houston is pushing the idea of the divine feminine, we are once again dealing with the Assyrian-Lilith, once again a demon that cannot be separated from LHP thought.

> The Sisterhood cannot be reduced to an event or conference, or even a new wineskin within the church. It's all of these and a whole lot more. The true spirit of Sisterhood relates to the feminine heart realizing that she is truthfully a daughter of the Most High God, fashioned perfectly in His image and invited into intimate relationship with Him. When a woman awakens to that, she lives and walks differently, and everything about her life affects others.[43]

Again, there is a theological conundrum here in Bobbie Houston's thinking. We are not formed perfectly in God's image any longer. With sin still in us, but as these Satanists believe we no longer have sin in us which makes us divine, we are not perfect bearers of God's image. Likewise, Bobbie Houston, again commenting that "when a woman awakens to that", while she may not be intending to directly say this: it is clear that by the theological position that Hillsong and their allied Satanist churches have taken, that Bobbie Houston is arguing that

---

42. Houston, *Sisterhood*, p. 125.
43. Houston, *Sisterhood*, p. 251.

once a woman "awakens" to her divine femininity, or Lilith-like nature, she can change other people around her which is again, occultism. Christian's themselves do not change people, only God can do that.

Like Bobbie Houston, a quote from the section about defining Satanism, Bill Johnson said that "[t]he renewed mind is necessary to more consistently taste the supernatural life." Again, we are dealing with a Lilith-influenced ideology since Bethel Church, before Benni Johnson passed away, had Johnson's wife, Benni, as a full-time pastor as well who was equally "empowering" women spiritually.

Brian Houston, Bobbie's husband pushes the idea of freeing the conscience as well

> I shrank my whole consciousness down to me when the realm of Christ is so much bigger. Being self-conscious means you are far too aware of self. If I had allowed my discomfort to confine me, I might not have persisted, and you would not be reading this book. Today, by God's grace, I regularly travel the globe and speak to tens of thousands of people. This would not be possible if I were still imprisoned by self-consciousness.[44]

Are we seeing here what both Houston's and what they have been teaching and pushing in Hillsong? As the proof, the evidence has all been laid out, it should be abundantly clear. Both Houston's are pushing Satanism and Assyrian-Lilith ideology along with it. Similarly to what other LHP members like LaVey, Ford and Flowers have said, Ed Russo comments that

> [w]ithin our self our own self-centeredness will do this. If one tends to be judgmental, our ego will push us to forgo our judgment. Every test is designed perfectly for us to learn. Sometimes others may give a nudge. Each test is aligned perfectly with who we are today. Lilith and her Emissaries are here to bring Light. They are the Light-bringers and they do that by revealing the covering over the lampshade so that you can remove it in the room that is already lit inside you.[45]

This sounds eerily familiar to what both Houston's have said. Freeing the "collective conscience" not being held down so that your conscience can realize that "the realm of Christ is so much bigger." Again, it is boiling over with not just New Age, but LHP thought. Russo comments at the beginning of his book:

> We are entering the Age of Aquarius. For 6000 years we have been under patriarchal rule in this Age of Pisces that is coming towards its end.

---

44. Houston, *Born*, pp. 139-140.
45. Ed Russo, *Lilith: The Power of the Woman's Spirit in the Age of Aquarius* (Morrisville, North Carolina: Lulu Press, Inc., 2014), p. 55, Kindle Edition.

> It is now time to balance the male and female energies in this New Age if we are going to have balance on this ball of dirt we call earth.[46]

Balancing "male and female energies" sounds exactly like what Brian and Bobbie Houston are attempting at their church. Not only is Hillsong doing this, but many examples of male and female "spiritual balancing" is happening in the Satanist church as a whole. Bethel, Elevation, Joyce Meyer, the International House of Prayer, Kimberly Daniels, all of these organizations and people are pushing this ideology. All this ideology is LHP.

What also must be noted in this chapter about the Assyrian-Lilith is the idea of the Satanist women "apostles" like Paula White, Joyce Meyer, Kimberly Daniels, and others. Let me be very clear here: I personally do not have an issue with women taking up roles of leadership in politics or business. When it comes to the role of primary religious and family leadership however, the Bible is clear that these roles are to be taken by men alone. That being said: these apostolic roles that these Satanists are claiming for themselves are not political appointments alone. These apostles are religious tyrants/Satanists that believe as "God's" chosen, they have a right to rule the world, much like King James did in chapter one. This claim to apostleship is not merely political but a use of the religious to control and rule the political. As a result, these seven-mountain mandate, apostolic Satanists are using an Assyrian-Lilith ideology to attempt to claim a self-divinized right to rule the world. This being said: I also have no issue with women running online commentary platforms that are helped to teach about real world issues either politically, or even in the religious. The restriction that scripture gives is that they are not to lead the church, be in pastoral positions, or as the heads of households. Any other position or platform that a woman wants to take to help, by all means, please do so. However, the positions that these self-proclaimed "apostles" have taken violate every command of scripture and introduce the Assyrian-Lilith as the leading ideology of that church.

You also will have noticed an interesting term in the last quote by Russo, the "Age of Aquarius", it is to that and to the eschatology of these Satanist churches that we will now turn.

---

46. Russo, *Lilith*, p. 1.

Chapter IX: The Age of Aquarius, Klaus Schwab, the Order of Nine Angles, and the Eschatology of Prosperity, Word of Faith, and the New Apostolic Reformation Movements

In the last chapter I left off with the idea of the "Age of Aquarius." While many websites and articles exist to try and explain what the concept of the Aquarian Age is, like with all the other evidence I have given about direct LHP beliefs, it is easier to explain the beliefs from people that exist within New Age movements themselves. What is important to remember is that while the New Age movement is distinctly different in theory from the LHP, since the New Age is technically RHP, the two paths have merged the idea of the Age of Aquarius in different ways and with different terminology. Being able to classify what is meant by the Age of Aquarius is critical to explaining what is happening within the Satanist church, otherwise known as Hillsong, and the Prosperity, Word-of-Faith, and New Apostolic Reformation movements.

The Age of Aquarius

The Age of Aquarius to briefly define what it is, is difficult. In a general sense, the Age of Aquarius means it is a time that humanity, as a whole, will recognize their divinity and start to rule the earth as the divine light that will bring restoration and peace. In order to do this restoration however, the old systems and structures of, specifically religion, need to be torn down and replaced. The beginning stages of the new Aquarian Age are identified in this way by Pauline Edward:

> As we will see, concepts, terminology and language that may have been suitable in the past, as is commonly found in traditional spiritual, metaphysical or religious teachings, may need a little updating in the new climate of Aquarius. Long-standing beliefs, as well as language, will be examined to ensure that they facilitate our growth and learning so we can experience this much-anticipated, and above all, much-needed, shift of consciousness.[1]

The identification that "long-standing beliefs...will be examined to ensure they facilitate our growth" in order to "experience this... much-needed, shift of consciousness" is a startling statement. Whether Edward realizes what she is saying or not, the statement in a very basic way states that: we will have to determine if what you believe is okay, and if it is not, it will be discarded, and you will be required to believe what we believe. This is obvious in our current culture with the sexual and gender movements that are active today. We as human beings, and Christians, are being required to believe what these social movements believe, and the Progressive churches, as shown previously, are going along with that thinking.

Another New Age advocate, Russo who wrote the book *Lilith: The Power of the Woman's Spirit in the Age of Aquarius* an unironic title considering how much the idea of the Assyrian-Lilith has indeed consumed western culture and the Progressive and Satanist church, identifies when the Age of Aquarius first started to move in the world. Russo says that

> [w]e are now entering the New Age. The Age of Aquarius refers to the advent of the New Age movement in the 1960s and 1970s. Astrologers maintain that an astrological age is a product of the earth's slow processional rotation and lasts for 2,160 years, on average. The Age of Aquarius follows the Age of Pisces which is the time where the patriarch has ruled.[2]

While Russo does not say directly what is meant by "the patriarch" there is a definite hint in the talk of New Age advocates that "the patriarch" is at least speaking about the Christian Church, regardless of whether it is the Roman Catholic Church, Eastern Orthodox Church, or Protestant Church, and at most "the patriarch" means the person of Jesus. Remember that the RHP does believe in a form of "God" in

---

1. Pauline Edward, *Aquarius: The Age of Revelation, Choice and Transformation* (Montreal, Quebec, Canada: Desert Lily Publications, 2021), pp. 5–6. Kindle Edition.
2. Russo, *Lilith*, p. 117.

whatever way the New Age advocate defines their "god".

Realize what the new Age of Aquarius means within the grander scope of thinking, Edward again gives us an understanding of how confusing their ideology really is:

> [c]ontrary to Pisces, which is faith- or belief-based, Aquarius is science-minded and fact-based. Yet, despite an affinity for science and cold, hard logic, Aquarians are humanitarian at heart. They hold a strong sense of community and recognize the need for more equality in the world. They can also express great intuition and creativity, indicating that they may be more in tune with pure Source or higher consciousness than they realize.[3]

What Edward is inadvertently saying here is that, yes, the "Aquarian" puts valuable stock in science, if in the end the science does not work for the "Aquarian" community, then they will push for a new definition without "science" in order to create "more equality in the world." Again, we as Christians, can see this happening all over the world right now. Science does not matter when it comes to defining what gender or sexuality is. To Edward, the definition that creates more "equality" is what matters.

Flowers, again confirms Russo's timeline as to when the Age of Aquarius first started being taught and making a movement in western culture. In speaking of the Age of Aquarius, from a LHP perspective, Flowers has this to say

> [o]nly in more modern times, with the discovery of the planets outside the orbit of Saturn, was Aquarius assigned to the planet Uranus. This Aquarian-Uranian Age, ruled by Saturn, will be one in which a spiritual elite will be increasingly powerful.[4]

The point can be fully understood here about the Age of Aquarius. The spiritually elite individuals will be the ones with more power and influence. These "elite" will in a sense dominate with their superior divinity to guide, or "rule" those below them. For those aware of what has been said and shown in earlier chapters, this is starting to sound very familiar with the Satanist church.

If you remember in chapter six with *Andrew Denton and the Occult* when I made the claim that the idea of "Source" or, "the Source" as a proper noun is a term rooted in occult ideology, now is the time, when talking about the Age of Aquarius to properly define where exactly that word comes from.

Edward again helps us to understand exactly where the proper

---

3. Edward, *Aquarius*, p. 29.
4. Flowers, *Left-Hand*, p. 197.

noun of "Source" comes from, "[a]s an expression of Source, Being is in constant movement, and learning is a natural by-product of this movement."[5] Later Edward expands on this definition to say that, "[s]pirituality is effectively a quest for a direct experience of the Source of Life, a knowing of the true Self as an expression of Source Energy or God."[6] Again, there is a clear distinction here where calling God, as a proper noun, "the Source" comes from. Since the Bible never refers to God as "the Source" as a proper name, but rather "God is the source of all things" (paraphrased), there is a direct bastardization here of biblical truth to insert occult ideology into the Bible.

Not stopping there, Edward again helps us to understand how she believes it is crucial we start to reinterpret not only the Christian faith, but the person of Jesus.

> Those familiar with my earlier books are aware that this quest was ignited long ago by a desire to uncover the truth of who and what we are, to know the true meaning of life. There was always a sense that what was taught in school and in church somehow didn't add up.[7]

There is a clear indication here that Edward, by her own human limitations, believes that what school and church taught her was not making sense to her. In another book by David Hart called *The Age of Aquarius: The Golden Age of Mankind* we get a definition of what many in the New Age and Age of Aquarius movements believe about history.

> It was Romans who gave Jesus divinity, they always defied their rulers, and Caesar was officially a GOD. Catholic orthodoxy was spread principally by Irenaeus Bishop of Lyons, around 180 AD, he was totally opposed to any deviation and in particular Gnosticism, which was based on PERSONAL EXPERIENCE, PERSONAL UNION WITH THE DIVINE, because it undermined the supreme authority of the church and the priesthood.[8]

Remember that Edward made the claim that when science does not work in the desire for equality, and that those that do are more in tune with "Source", we start to understand how Hart could not only reject science, but history as well. There is not space in this book to show how Hart is wrong here, however, the facts of history speak for themselves. Needing to redefine history to push the idea of the Age of Aquarius is fallacious to the core. However, seeing how culture is accepting redefining scientific and historic facts for the sake of equality,

---

5. Edward, *Aquarius*, p. 12.
6. Edward, *Aquarius*, p. 37.
7. Edward, *Aquarius*, p. 70.
8. David Hart, *The Age of Aquarius: The Golden Age of Mankind* (London, England: Austin Macauley Publishers Ltd., 2018), pp. 30–31, Kindle Edition.

we as Christians really should not be surprised. Hart does make a correct claim about the beliefs of Gnostic heresies, but the implied claim that it was a "truth" the church suppressed is absurd in every way since it was in fact heresy. Hart defends the need to make his absurd claim because to him the reality is that "[o]ccultism is necessary in the presence of the temporal power of the church. The spirit of prophecy protests at the insolence of the rich corrupt prelates."[9]

Looking back again at what the end goals of the Age of Aquarius are, Russo gives us a picture of that. While at the beginning of this chapter I said that the Age of Aquarius meant that humans recognized their own divinity and ruled the earth with that knowledge there is a much more nefarious purpose in mind.

> When General Washington had his unearthly encounter at Valley Forge the being laid out the plans for America's future as the New Atlantis. This country is founded by the Bill of Rights that endorses individual rights and that we as the individual is more important than anything else. These principles are in synch with the teachings that each of us is god which is the teachings that most receive who had extraterrestrial encounters.[10]

Again, just like with Hart needing to redefine history, Russo is doing the same to push the Age of Aquarius mandate. Russo is doing this to set up America as some new enlightened nation that will essentially "conquer the world with enlightenment". Again, this sounds eerily familiar to the Satanist church. Russo also shows that the Age of Aquarius advocates believe that despite facts, and laws, human rights are more important than anything. In Russo's thinking, occult rights which to him are individual rights, are more important than any "human" thing, including what Russo would say is the "fake Christian God."

Russo shows that the intention for this New Atlantis to conquer the world through "enlightenment' is embedded in Age of Aquarius thinking.

> It seems that for us to have world unity it first had to begin with the New Atlantis which is America. America gives us freedom and allows technology that progress society which cannot happen under a theocracy.[11]

Putting aside the current controversy over the idea of theonomy, which is different than a theocracy, Russo believes that humanity, via this New Atlantis cannot move forward under the biblical version of God's

---

9. Hart, *Golden Age*, pp. 110–111.
10. Russo, *Lilith*, p. 119.
11. Russo, *Lilith*, p. 119.

law and rule. He furthers this argument by saying that

> in distant times it will be, when the Fourth Millennium after Jmmanuel's (Christian) time reckoning comes, that the Earth and its humanity will have its creational order again, and there will be true love and unity, true freedom and harmony, as well as true worldwide peace.[12]

Russo could not have spit into the face of God himself with anymore violence than he has here. The Age of Aquarius, in every way, is an attempt to replace what the Bible says about God, Jesus and this world and replace it with a fantasy version of both history and science.

When considering why there is not more acceptance of the Age of Aquarius in all societies, cultures and communities in the world, Edward again gives a criticizing rebuke.

> For a student of A Course in Miracles, an initial response might be to chalk up the resistance to the ego, that aspect of self that will not support what will ultimately lead to its undoing. Those familiar with this journey are aware of how fiercely this small self will resist the shift toward awakening, something it will do with surprising cleverness and creativity.[13]

For those unaware, the book *A Course in Miracles* claims to have come from the teachings of Edgar Cayce, a clairvoyant who lived in the United States and was born in 1877 and died in 1945. This book, supposedly written by a descendent of Cayce's, is in the simplest explanation, the "handbook of the New Age", and much of what is being taught in this book, which contradicts scripture, is finding its way into evangelical Christianity.

When asking the final question in concern about when the Age of Aquarius is supposed to begin, no one within the larger New Age movement can really agree on a starting date. Once again, Hart gives us some startling information.

> At various times Master initiates have tried to lead the way back to the One Truth and it is appropriate that in the age of man (Aquarius) which commences towards the end of 1992 and starts to really show in 2011—2023 that it should be man himself who leads the way back.[14]

Looking at that time bracket, it is not surprising that since the occult is moving so much in western culture right now, with Hart publishing his book back in 2018, it is evident that much of what is happening with redefining gender and sexuality, in the way that it is being done today,

---

12. Russo, *Lilith*, p. 129.
13. Edward, *Aquarius*, p. 12.
14. Hart, *The Golden Age*, pp. 89–90.

is happening in such a massive scale at the time of writing (2023). What is troubling, however, are the number of Progressive churches that are accepting this new Age of Aquarius doctrine as some new revelation or forgotten truth and redefining biblical history to do it. If you want to see a very real example of the Progressive church needing to redefine historical facts, and insulting those that are holding to the truth look up *Debate With LGBT Theologian Brandan Robertson* by Apologia Studios on YouTube.[15]

I will return to how this all applies to the Satanist Church in Christianity later.

Klaus Schwab

The name Klaus Schwab has been going around some Christian churches with notoriety in recent years. While some churches praise him as the leader of the World Economic Forum (WEF), many other churches are not so sure of Schwab's intentions. While the purpose of this section of this book is not to associate Schwab with any worldwide takeover plans, I want to point to some simple things that Schwab has said that will help us to understand the link between Schwab's thinking, the thinking of the Satanist churches, the New Atlantis of the Age of Aquarius, and lastly the thinking of the Order of Nine Angles that is to be detailed after this section.

The criticism that has come to Schwab and other political leaders that have joined the WEF is what is commonly referred to as Agenda 2030. While many may not be familiar with this term, it is a reference to what Schwab, via the WEF is attempting to accomplish by or at the year 2030. Schwab describes the 2030 Agenda as a way forward because as

> economies restart, there is an opportunity to embed greater societal equality and sustainability into the recovery, accelerating rather than delaying progress towards the 2030 Sustainable Development Goals and unleashing a new era of prosperity. What could make this possible and raise the probability odds in favour of such an outcome?[16]

This sounds like a noble goal from Schwab. The reason that Schwab says that the 2030 plan is needed is because "[w]e are now at a crossroads. One path will take us to a better world: more inclusive, more equitable and more respectful of Mother Nature."[17] Inclusiveness and

---

15. Apologia Studies, "Debate With LGBT Theologian Brandan Robertson," *YouTube*, July 15, 2023, https://www.youtube.com/watch?v=ti0FzdOHW_8.

16. Klaus Schwab, Thierry Malleret, *COVID-19: The Great Reset* (Geneva, Switzerland: Forum Publishing, 2020), pp. 248–249, Kindle Edition.

17. Schwab, *The Great Reset*, p. 250.

equality are catch words these days. Catch words are words that can easily be stated that will have people quickly "catch on" to your argument and support you. Schwab's use of catch words seems genuine but looking at other parts of his book *COVID-19: The Great Reset* something does not seem right. Looking at how occultists of our day have defined the Age of Aquarius, Schwab's definition of why Agenda 2030 is *needed* seems quite clear. Schwab's Agenda 2030 is leading into a very Age of Aquarius type manner.

In commenting about how epidemics have assisted in this process in the past, Schwab notes that

> in 1665, over the space of 18 months, the last bubonic plague had eradicated a quarter of London's population, Daniel Defoe wrote in A Journal of the Plague Year (published in 1722): "All trades being stopped, employment ceased: the labour, and by that the bread, of the poor were cut off; and at first indeed the cries of the poor were most lamentable to hear ... thousands of them having stayed in London till nothing but desperation sent them away, death overtook them on the road, and they served for no better than the messengers of death." Defoe's book is full of anecdotes that resonate with today's situation, telling us how the rich were escaping to the country, "taking death with them", and observing how the poor were much more exposed to the outbreak, or describing how "quacks and mountebanks" sold false cures.[18]

Schwab is mentioning "quacks and mountebanks" who "sold false cures" is definitely supporting the actions of platforms such as YouTube that pulled down videos of Christians offering prayer for those afflicted with the Covid-19 virus and also of videos claiming that Jesus was the answer to curing the world of Covid-19. Neither of these last two statements are theologically bad. These statements and videos that YouTube pulled down, was the Christian community reaching out in a digital world to offer hope to people that were forced to stay in their homes, most times, against their wills.

In continuing to comment about how *good* epidemics are for economies and social structures, Schwab states that. "[h]istory shows that epidemics have been the great resetter of countries' economy and social fabric."[19] This is a bit of a troubling statement but needs to be substantiated. Schwab claims that going as

> far back as the Black Death that ravaged Europe from 1347 to 1351 (and that suppressed 40% of Europe's population in just a few years), workers discovered for the first time in their life that the power to change things was in their hands. Barely a year after the epidemic had subsided, textile workers in Saint-Omer (a small city in northern France) demand-

---

18. Schwab, *The Great Reset*, p. 37.
19. Schwab, *The Great Reset*, p. 38.

ed and received successive wage rises.[20]

This is a troubling statement by Schwab. Likewise, to support his claims, Schwab says that history

> shows that a shrinking population doesn't have to lead to economic oblivion. Japan's high living standards and well-being indicators offer a salutary lesson that there is hope in the face of economic hardship.[21]

This is an interesting and disturbing statement by Schwab. In saying that, Schwab has stated that mass deaths from epidemics can be a good thing that brings economic and social reforms. Continuing with his idea that a mass worldwide death would be a good thing, Schwab needs to try and convince us that more people is inevitably bad. Schwab tries to say that

> most scientists would agree that the greater population growth is, the more we disturb the environment, the more intensive farming becomes without adequate biosecurity, the higher the risk of new epidemics.[22]

For Schwab, the value of human life here is minimized. In his claim above, Schwab wants us to believe that people need to die, via epidemics, so that we will no longer "disturb the environment", because large populations will lead to "intensive farming", that he claims is damaging to the earth when it is in fact not at all like Schwab claims. Lastly, if the population does not go down in massive numbers, new epidemics will likely come at a higher risk. Note that in his book, Schwab does not back up these claims in any way. Schwab simply states it, again as catch words, to get people needlessly worried.

To push the narrative further Schwab once again states that we need to be

> spurred by a different narrative, in which businesses and governments are emboldened by a new social conscience among large segments of the general population that life can be different, and is pushed by activists: the moment must be seized to take advantage of this unique window of opportunity to redesign a more sustainable economy for the greater good of our societies.[23]

Someone may look at this and not see what I am trying to get at. In 2021, Yuval Norah Harari, a top WEF advisor stated that "we will become gods".[24] In connecting what I have shown about Satanism and

---

20. Schwab, *The Great Reset*, p. 39.
21. *Schwab, The Great Reset*, pp. 71–72.
22. Schwab, *The Great Reset*, p. 139.
23. Schwab, *The Great Reset*, pp. 143–144.
24. Your Weekend Show, "'We will become gods...' Yuval Noah Harari- WEF

the end goals of the Satanist church, can we as Christians see a connection here?

Again, in his book *There is More* Brian Houston makes the following statement that

> in the twenty-first century, it seems that electronic "smart gates" are the new world order. You simply scan your passport, answer a few questions, press a couple of buttons, look up at an automated camera, and watch it flash. Then glass gates give you access and away you go! Now, that's my kind of speed.[25]

Someone can try to claim that this does not mean that Houston supports the WEF digital ID program, but the contrary does seem to be confirmed. Since Schwab has been pushing for a digital form of ID which will make everyone traceable and also make things "easier" essentially for those that Schwab approves of, Houston here is pushing something very dangerous. While there are no lists or membership roles with Brian Houston on the WEF membership, we still need to be asking questions here. Is Hillsong, because of Brian Houston, associated with the WEF? It is possible that Hillsong is. This one quote, however, is not enough to make the point. In order to show the mass death desire of the Hillsong, Prosperity, WoF, NAR and WEF movements as connected to Satanism, it is now time to look at one of the darkest groups of the LHP to exist in our modern day. That group of the LHP is the Order of Nine Angles.

The Order of Nine Angles

Author's Note: The information contained in this section is of an extremely dark and disturbing nature. Although I was able to track this information down, it was not by going to "safe" websites to do so. Although these websites were not on the so-called "darkweb", these websites are still unsettling places for a Christian to go to. I will as a faithful academic, provide the references to the source documents from where I am getting the information. If someone reading this book wants to confirm the sources, you are welcome to, but I would highly suggest having good, not just "okay", or "mediocre", internet security software on your device.

***

When dealing with the Order of Nine Angles (ONA), there has been

---

Advisor, *YouTube*, July 16, 2023, https://www.youtube.com/watch?v=XmS5rEKI-3eQ&t=9s.

25. Houston, *More*, p. 204.

critique from those in the occult community that claim the ONA do not exist and that all the texts are an elaborate scam. In a book by Nic Redfern called *Secret Societies: The Complete Guide to Histories, Rites and Rituals* Redfern quotes a person by the name of Sinister Moon that claims that

> the credibility, of the Order of Nine Angles, a group which never existed as a real functioning Occult order let alone a Satanist one. The ONA itself was never more than a myth, a marketing device, a honeytrap, and—latterly—just an Internet phenomenon.[26]

However, this claim seems to be unjustified. Despite the claims that the ONA never existed and are just a "myth", academic scholarship has confirmed the existence of the ONA. Going back to Introvigne, he says that "idiosyncratic exceptions such as [...] the Order of Nine Angles also existed."[27] In the face of academic scholarship, Sinister Moon, whomever that may be, seems to be trying to push the ONA into the realm of a "conspiracy theory" rather than to accept that such a vile group is working in the world. But the existence of the ONA has not only been confirmed but tracked back to the early 1970's by a neo-Nazi by the name of David Wyatt.[28] Most of the "core" texts of the ONA were written by a man by the name of Anton Long. While many assumed that Long was a pseudonym of Wyatt, the ONA until recently has denied this.[29] There is no question however that Wyatt did start a theistic-LHP group by the name of the Order of Nine Angles sometime around 1970. The reason that I believe that people like Sinister Moon within the LHP are denying that the ONA exist, is becuase the ONA ideology, as will be shown below, has been the most successful infiltrator of the "Christian" church. In order to make sure that it continues to destroy the lives of people around the world, the LHP has officially claimed, falsely, that the ONA do not exist so that the mission of infiltrating the church with ONA beliefs can continue.

Since other groups in the LHP have tried to deny the existence of the ONA, we need to ask the inevitable question of: why? What is so evil about them? How does this tie into the Satanist church of Hillsong, the Prosperity, WoF, and NAR movements? The last question we will return to later. The first two I will show you now.

You saw me say that the ONA is a theistic-LHP group, which by definition means that the ONA believe in a real, spiritual, and personal

---

26. Nic Redfern, *Secret Societies: The Complete Guide to Histories, Rites and Rituals* (Canton, Michigan: Visible Ink Press, 2017), pp. 227–228.
27. Introvigne, *Satanism*, p. 555.
28. Introvigne, *Satanism*, p. 555.
29. Introvigne, *Satanism*, p. 556.

being named "Satan." To address this question directly, I refer to a disturbing novel written by Anton Long with the following comments that concerning Satan

> [h]e exists, but not in the way most believe: e.g. a horned figure with cloven feet. Rather, He is not bound by our everyday spatial and temporal dimensions, but exists instead in what esoteric tradition calls 'the acausal'. We apprehend the acausal mostly in an archetypal way – i.e. we impose an image upon its acausal and non-spatial structure. reality is far more terrifying and evil – when viewed conventionally, of course! Further, terms like 'respect' depend on the opposites inherent in an un-initiated view. In reality, there is only a working with the acausal energies or forces or 'entities' as those things are: a becoming-like the Devil; an identity-with Him, if you wish. And this is an extension of one's own being or existence, rather than a negation, submergence. Expressed simply, one becomes one with Satan, and in the early stages strives to be like Him.[30]

In continuing Long's line of thought about the reality of the person of Satan, Coire Riabhaich explains to us that

> Satan is the very essence of the striving to become a god – Satan is the arrogance within that enables us to leave behind the archaic gods, and to find the courage to be the new gods. Satan is how we live, how we die, and how we shall be after causal life.[31]

After everything that has been written so far about the LHP and the Satanic church, this statement should not be all that surprising. The person of Satan is the example the ONA uses to achieve their own godhood. In every way, the real Satan, is the example of ultimate deity.

Another term that most likely caught your attention was the term "acausal", to explain this concept is strange but when you read through it and consider what it is saying, you can start to see parallels in certain Satanist churches. Long explains that

> [t]he spheres of the Septenary may be said to be the Nexus between causal and acausal (or 'Being' and 'non-being') and the paths linking the spheres may be regarded from a magickal point of view as zones of energy.[32]

Going onto further descriptions, Long explains from another book that

---

30. Anton Long, *The Temple of Satan—A Symphonic Allegory* (Gent, Belgium: Skull Press, 2003), p. 77.
31. Coire Riabhaich, "CIRA: A Satanic Guide to Future Magick," in *Codex Saerus: The Black Book of Satan III* ed. Anton Long (Houston, Texas: Vindex Press, 1998), p. 3.
32. Long, *The Temple of Satan*, p. 31.

> [a]ccording to tradition, the Dark Gods are waiting, in what may be described as a parallel universe, to return to Earth and thus our spatial, causal universe. Essentially, the universe of the Dark Gods is acausal and the two universes may be re-presented as being joined by various Star Gates (or more accurately 'nexions'). These 'Gates' are regions of space-time where passage from one universe to another is possible at certain times – that is, when the Gates are aligned according to their cosmic cycle. Traditionally, it is believed that these Gates open about once every 2,000 years. Because of the nature of the two connecting universes (that is, their difference in time and spatial geometry) not only is physical travel possible between them, but also to a limited extent, a special form of astral travel. This astral form is possible because our own consciousness, by its nature and evolution, is partly acausal and therefore already to an extent on a primal level part of this other universe. Thus, it is possible for an individual to journey into the other realms where the Dark Gods are waiting just as it is feasible – if the psychic Gates are opened – for those dreaded and negative entities who are seldom named to manifest on our level. Such travels are manifestly only feasible when a nexion is about to be opened, is open or is closing – that is, at the beginning and ending of an Aeon.[33]

To understand how this whole concept between the ONA and Satanist church all interacts, the idea of the acausal and the nexion is important. While we may not think of the word nexion when thinking within Christian circles, or in the terms of a "star gate", but we will often think in the terms of "portals" to the spiritual world. Since the Bible never refers to such a reality of "portals"[34] to another realm, even to heaven, we need to start asking serious questions about that terminology.

To further describe and explain what the nexion truly is within the thinking of the ONA, Riabhairch continues to show their belief

> that of a nexion being a point where the acausal intrudes into the causal universe (and vice versa) – the outer form that a nexion may take requires some further explanation. Firstly, a nexion can take many forms, and may even be a combination of forms. According to very rare conditions, an aeonic nexion may be an individual. Or it could be a revolutionary Religious form. Or, as stated, it could constitute several such forms co-existing in the world in order to bring forth the aeonic tran-

---

33. Anton Long, "H. P. Lovecraft & The Dark Gods," in *Codex Saerus: The Black Book of Satan III* ed. Anton Long (Houston, Texas: Vindex Press, 1998), p. 1–2.

34. I have seen people try to use the dream of Jacob in the place he renamed Bethel in Genesis 28:10–22, the "ladder" that was spoken of did not speak about transporting or opening a portal to another realm. Rather, the context is speaking that the ladder led to the "third heaven" which existed above the known skies of Jewish cosmology. In other words, this ladder simply went to a place that was higher in the "sky" than any human would be able to see if it that person was not given a dream or "vision" by God to see it.

sition.³⁵

We can see from the last two quotes that the ONA reasonably believe that the change from one Aeon (or "age") to the next is happening at any second. Looking at what Riabhairch said in the above quote, there is no doubt that this aeonic transition is the same as what was described at the beginning of this chapter as the Age of Aquarius. Although the ONA do not use that term for the aeonic age, the similarity between the aeonic age and the Age of Aquarius are too similar to deny.

> To open a Star Gate and return the Dark Gods to our causal universe a crystal tetrahedron made of quartz is required. This should be as large as possible – and made from a natural shape by a skilled operator. The Master lays the S.Knife on the womb of the Priestess while the Mistress places her hands on the crystal and joins the Master in chanting the Diabolus in fourths while visualizing the nexion opening. [...] The Guardian brings the Opfer forward. The Master gives the Opfer a chalice of wine, which he drinks. [...] The Priestess holds the Opfer in sexual union and visualizes the nexion opening as she draws by movement the secret fire from the Opfer.³⁶

Now there is yet another term that is important to this study that needs to be defined, that of the "opfer". And this is where things start to get really disturbing about what the ONA believe and practice if it was not already disturbing to begin with. To define what an opfer is, Long continues his disturbing narrative.

> According to Tradition, the Priest was sacrificed after the sexual union, [...] the sacrificial aspect being regarded as necessary to retain the "Cosmic Balance" – in modern terms, to keep a Nexion open (and thus preserve the associated higher civilisation, etc.). The Chosen One, or 'Opfer', was able – because of the sacrifice – to partake of an 'acausal existence' – becoming thus an Immortal. Thus, willing sacrifice was possible, although it is easy to imagine that in later times the Opfer was not so willing. [To finish] a mature woman (often shown naked and seated upon a pile of skulls) holding up the severed head of the Sacrificed Priest.³⁷

While the opfer explained above first seems to be a willing victim, it later changes. Long once again in another book describes that the ONA members need to

---

35. Riabhaich, *CIRA*, p. 16.
36. Anton Long, *Codex Saerus: The Black Book of Satan III*, ed. Anton Long (Houston Texas: Vindex Press, 1998), p. 4.
37. Long, *The Temple of Satan*, p. 44.

[t]rain several members, and yourself, in the undertaking of the tests relevant to choosing an opfer – a human sacrifice. Select some suitable victims, using Satanic guidelines for so selecting a victim, and undertake the relevant tests on each chosen victim.[38]

The victim here is usually either kidnapped or killed in what could be classified as a random killing or assassination attempt. The importance of the opfer and the reason why a suitable one is required is given below by an unknown author.

> The word 'opfer' generally refers to the sacrifice that occurs – symbolic or otherwise – during certain rituals. There are, generally, two types of opfer: (1) associated with rites to open a nexion (or 'Star Gate'), between Aeons – when such an opfer(s) is considered necessary in terms of the 'energy' required; (2) those associated with traditional beliefs regarding the 'working of the 'cosmos'.[39]

To continue to understand how the opfer applies to the greater argument in this work, another term needs to be introduced. Long again explains that

> [t]o understand the nature of these tasks, it is necessary for the Satanic novice to be familiar, and in agreement with, the secret teachings themselves, particularly as these relate to human sacrifice, or culling.[40]

To further explain how a culling occurs, Long continues that to "undertake a culling by disposing of the victim either during a suitable rite (e.g. The Ceremony of Recalling) or via practical means (e.g. assassination)."[41] So, we can see here that assassination is a form of culling, but there is ironically a few more. Culling's can

> result from events brought about by Satanic ritual and/or planning (such as wars). Voluntary sacrifice results from the traditional Satanist belief that our life on this planet is only a stage: a gateway or nexion to another existence. This other existence is in the acausal realm where the Dark Gods exist. The key to this other existence is not negation, but rather ecstasy.[42]

Again, something very familiar here is starting to come to the front. The ONA, if they need to provide human sacrifices, or opfers, will commence a culling via wars that they planned and got into motion. These

---

38. Anton Long, *A Complete Guide to the 7-Fold Sinister Way* (Houston, Texas: Vindex Press, 1994), p. 6.
39. Author Unknown, "Baphomet and Opfer," *Opfer, Fenrir* Vol. II, no 2 (2009): p. 1.
40. Long, *The Temple of Satan*, p. 116.
41. Long, *7-Fold*, p. 5.
42. Long, *The Temple of Satan*, p. 76.

"culling wars", so to say, would be initiated in order to allow a nexion(s) to open to allow the acausal realm, and the dark gods in that realm, to descend to earth.

Those who are made as opfers and culled cannot just be random individuals, they need to be mundane people that are insignificant to the ONA. Long defines what a mundane person is.

> Satanism is at it is – dark, and dangerous, and full of diabolic ecstasies and diabolic triumphs over the "ordinary", the mundane and those who would keep everyone in servitude and thrall. So it is, so has it been, and so shall it continue to be – to enable evolution, to create what must be created, while the fearful majorities in their sloth, delusions and ignorance continue their morbid, Nazarene-like, subhuman existence.[43]

Not surprisingly, the arguing line about whom the mundane are, again, sounds very familiar. Aside from the familiarity of who the mundane are, Long makes it very clear that Jews, and especially Christians are mundane. The ONA uses the term Homo Hubris to describe them. The Homo Hubris are defined as

> distinguished by their profane lack of numinous balance, by a lack of knowing of and feeling for the numinous; by a personal arrogance, by a lack of manners, and by that lack of respect for anything other than strength/power and/or their own gratification.[44]

In defending why the Homo Hubris need to be culled

> Whatever the actual genesis of natural justice, it was a feeling, an attitude, of only some – not all – humans. This feeling, this attitude, this instinct, this natural justice, was that some things – some types of behaviour and some particular deeds by humans – were distasteful: that is, not wrong or evil in any moralistic, dogmatic, modern manner, but just distasteful, disliked; that such behaviour or such deeds was rotten, and generally unhealthy, that is, not conducive to one's well-being and so something to be avoided.[45]

> Hence, that a type of natural culling was desirable – the rotten were removed when they proved troublesome or became a bad influence, and were seen for what they were: rotten.[46]

> The O9A [ONA] goals are concerned with our evolution, our change into a higher species of human beings, the breeding – by our Dark Arts

---

43. Long, *7-Fold*, p. 5.
44. Rachael Stirling. "Masculous And Muliebral: The Sinister Feminine And Homo Hubris," *o9a Order of Nine Angles*, July 16, 2023, https://www.o9a.org/wp-content/uploads/o9a-development-arete.pdf, p. 1.
45. Anton Long, "The Development Of Arête," *o9a Order of Nine Angles*, July 16, 2023, https://www.o9a.org/wp-content/uploads/o9a-development-arete.pdf, p. 1.
46. Long, *Arête*, p. 3.

> including The Art of Culling – of more and more individuals of noble character, and thus the development of a new aristocracy.[47]
>
> it should be noted that individual culling in traditional O9A nexions was/is regarded as both natural and necessary.[48]
>
> The collective is when a specific method – such as combat, insurrection, revolution – is being used either by one of us as a causal form or within a rôle, or by a nexion (or collocation of nexions) as a means or tactic to implement Aeonic strategy, and which collective type of culling does not target specific, named, individuals, but rather 'the sworn enemy' any of whom are deemed acceptable targets.[49]

As can be see from multiple of Long's quotes, not only do the ONA believe that culling's are necessary, but a good thing that will help to evolve humanity because they are ridding themselves of "the sworn enemy." Note that the ONA are the only ones that are able to determine who is to be culled and who the Homo Hubris are. No one else is allowed to make that classification. Since the ONA have some kind of master ability to determine who are and who are not of the "acausal" reality, they can thus put these people to death either individually, or as entire groups of people. To the ONA, this form of mass murder, is a form of an opfer that will help to open a nexion.

In order to complete the understanding of what the ONA is doing and teaching, there are another two elements to their rituals that was mentioned that are important in order to close the argument of what is going on with this LHP group.

The first was the mention of a "crystal" that was to be the focus of each ritual, whether sexual or a ritual human sacrifice. Long describe the importance of the crystal and its connection to a nexion.

> Thus, for instance, in the Nine Angles Rite, the crystal represents one aspect of the nexion, the Priest and Priestess the other: together (i.e. the bringing together in the ritual) they enable the nexion to be opened.[50]

Supporting this information above, Long also states that "the crystal was the key to the Star Gate."[51] The reason the crystal is so important is according to Long is described in a fictitious-like narrative. Although the narrative is a story, this is a confirmed belief with the ONA.

> She felt her crystal, [...] begin to respond and draw down power from the Abyss beyond. The power came to her, slowly, through the gates

---

47. Long, *Arête*, p. 4.
48. Long, *Arête*, p. 5.
49. Long, *Arête*, p. 5.
50. Long, *Codex*, p. 19.
51. Long, *The Temple of Satan*, p. 26.

> [...] Her consciousness was beginning to transcend to the acausal spaces where her Dark Gods waited and she sensed their longing to return, to fill again the spaces of her causal time. They were there, [...] ready to seep past the gate to feast upon the blood of humans.[52]

Not surprising that there is once again a direct focus on vampirism which is common in LHP groups and was explained above in some Satanist churches of the Prosperity, WoF, and NAR movements. Even with the vampirism, collecting all this information together is particularly disturbing. There are a lot of connections undoubtedly that any reader of this book will have picked up on. I will describe the details below for those that are unsure about what is being said. There is however, one more important point about the acausal and nexions that the ONA believe.

> Our own sentient life [...] is therefore the largest intersection of these two universes. We access more of this specific acausal energy than any other organism we know. In effect, each individual is a nexion – that is, a connection or nexus between the two universes.[...] we possess the latent ability to directly access the acausal.[53]
>
> Causal and Acausal, was the core of his being.[54]

Putting this into layman's terms: you have the demonic power of the acausal in you because you are a portal for that demonic power, and you have ability to access what you do not have already. Again, putting this way, that access to the acausal sounds awfully familiar.

The Neo-Satanist Eschatological Beliefs Revealed

What has been shown about the ONA above is disturbing and frightening. Any reader that has been keeping close attention to all the arguments about what the Satanic church believes, will have noticed certain similar ideas within the Hillsong, Prosperity, WoF, and NAR movements. While this next section may be unneeded to some, I believe it is important to directly show what many of these Satanists truly believe about bringing heaven to earth and how they intend on doing that.

Stating it directly Brian Houston is clear that "we need to take the things of Heaven and apply them to earth, allowing our children to see the testimony of God working in our lives."[55] This is not an inherently evil idea. Even I cannot disagree that teaching your kids

---

52. Long, *The Temple of Satan*, p. 46.
53. Long, *The Temple of Satan*, pp. 45-46.
54. Long, *The Temple of Satan*, p. 26, Footnote 16.
55. Houston, *Maximise*, Location 1134.

the "ways of heaven" is bad. But we need to be taking statements like this with the rest of Houston's theology about heaven. When speaking about your "purpose", Houston comments in a different book that "[y]ou were born for a cause that embraces humanity but resonates from heaven. It is a cause that bridges history and alters eternity."[56] That quote from Houston is now problematic. Your "purpose" does not have the power to alter "eternity". It is not difficult to see that this purpose that Houston is speaking about can be identified in the same way as the ONA and their acausal energy that can be used to open nexions/portals to the acausal, or in Houston's terms "heaven", and bring the acausal to earth, which in the Satanist church would constitute "bridging history and altering eternity."

Trying to use a Satanic form of Jesus, Houston continues by saying that

> Jesus himself taught us to seek first the kingdom of God. The kingdom is not a mystical place in the heavens; it is everything in the realm of Christ. Having kingdom purpose involves bringing the will of heaven to earth. Kingdom purpose is a revelation that will change your life and has the power to impact the life of everyone you encounter.[57]

Houston here has really used a lot of Christian phrases and terms to mask the true intentions of what he believes about his eschatology. I have no issue in saying that heaven is truly a literal place that does exist somewhere. However, while we can argue that our lives, lived in a Christian way, will impact the lives of those around us, biblically that change happens through the work of the Holy Spirit in our lives. These changes and "impacts" are not caused by us alone. Houston, in claiming that "kingdom purpose involves bringing the will of heaven to earth [...] that will change your life and [...] impact the life of everyone" is again a plea for the demonic acausal within and not the Holy Spirit that the Bible gives credit for such change. In order to support this thinking, Houston continues to say that "Kingdom spirit means you have a vision that is bigger than you – you will always be devising generous strategies or plans to bless others."[58] Again, this Christian way of talking "sounds good", however you may have noticed something in these quotes. There is something missing in what Houston is saying. Looking back, I hope that you have noticed that there is no scripture, at all, that Houston is using to back up his ludicrous ideology. The reason that Houston is not quoting the Bible to back up what he is saying, is because what he is saying is not scriptural at all and is

---

56. Houston, *Born*, Location 76.
57. Houston, *Born*, Location 81–82.
58. Houston, *Maximise*, Location 537.

not where Houston got the idea from. Houston got the idea about the acausal changing people from somewhere else.

Bobbie Houston in her book *Heaven is in this House* makes a very alarming claim that when speaking on Isaiah 42:8 that "His awesome glory is reserved for those that who can humbly spread His fame abroad and not become seduced in the process."[59] On the page previous, Houston says that, "God's glory in the coming days will attach itself to such spirited people and thus we will witness more and more as we venture the Church into her future."[60] I mentioned earlier how no person, even a Christian, would be able to enter into God's glory without God's holiness striking the person dead. Bobbie Houston here is saying that we will, and even are, carrying that same glory right now.

To see how horridly wrong Houston is here, we need to look at the context of that verse.

> I am the LORD; I have called you in righteousness; I will take you by the hand and keep you; I will give you as a covenant for the people, a light for the nations, to open the eyes that are blind, to bring out the prisoners from the dungeon, from the prison those who sit in darkness. I am the LORD; that is my name; my glory I give to no other, nor my praise to carved idols. Behold, the former things have come to pass, and new things I now declare; before they spring forth I tell you of them. (Isaiah 42:6–9 ESV)

Bobbie Houston's use of this verse is a big perversion of what is being said. When Yahweh states that he will not share his glory with another it is because he will not bear to have his praise given to idols. In also stating that Yahweh will not share his glory, it is because it is to be shared with the "light for the nations", which is not the church, or even Israel, in this passage. The light for the nations was the coming Christ, Jesus. John N. Oswalt shows us that "The glory of God is his essential reality, which is *his alone*." (italics mine)[61] In saying that believers, or the false gospel believers that her husband Brian, is saying is the "true gospel", not only will bear the glory of God but are able to bear the glory of God, Bobbie Houston, just like Brian, has declared that they are not only "gods" but directly equal to the biblical God himself. But since, both Houston's are preaching a Satanist ideology, this glory that Bobbie Houston is speaking of is really some kind of demonic power, or acausal energy like the ONA argue, that they will spread across the

---

59. Bobbie Houston, *Heaven is in this House* (Castle Hill, New South Wales, Australia: Leadership Ministries Inc., 2001), p. 134.

60. Houston, *House*, p. 132.

61. John N. Oswalt, *The Book of Isaiah Chapters 40–66* (Grand Rapids, Michigan: Wm. B. Eerdmans Publishing Company, 1998), p. 119.

earth. Remember Long above in footnote 30 quoting that "there is only a working with the acausal energies or forces or 'entities' as those things are: a becoming-like the Devil." Both Houston's are pushing the same Satanic ideology. Since they are the ones that preach the "true gospel", only they will be able to determine who the mundane Homo Hubris are in the Christian church.

Going back to Long's comment above in footnote 33,

> it is possible for an individual to journey into the other realms where the Dark Gods are waiting just as it is feasible – if the psychic Gates are opened – for those dreaded and negative entities who are seldom named to manifest on our level. Such travels are manifestly only feasible when a nexion is about to be opened.

See what Brian Houston is saying here, "an eternal or cause-driven focus enables you to see things from heaven's perspective—from above the sun rather than under it."[62] Again, there is no scripture given to support this. Houston tries to use the verse "I hated all my toil in which I toil under the sun, seeing that I must leave it to the man who will come after me," (Ecclesiastes 2:18 ESV) as the basis of his argument, but this is again an example of pulling scripture out of context. This whole section is speaking about the futility of existence when separated from God. Ecclesiastes 2:18 has nothing to do with driving us to look down on earth as if we are in heaven, "above the sun". As the quote from Long shows, the idea that we can be able to look down on the earth "like heaven", is not from the Bible at all. There is no reference point for being able to look down from heaven like that. We can see the world in the same "metaphorical" way that God does, a world full of sin that is in need of a saviour, but to take the way that Houston is using Ecclesiastes 2:18 to push the doctrine that he is, is again rooted in the Satanic about being able to ascend into the acausal.

Next, Brian Houston brings Jesus into the picture. Houston comments that

> Jesus taught us to pray, "Your will be done on earth as it is in heaven" (Matt. 6:10). You can live in such a way that you are completely occupied by a commitment to see the will of heaven accomplished on earth, [...] Bringing the will of God and his blessing into people's lives.[63]

Jumping across the Pacific Ocean, we have Bethel in Redding, California saying the same type of thing and that their book is

> like blasts of a trumpet calling the royal army to take its place on the

---

62. Houston, *Born*, pp. 90-91, Location 865.
63. Houston, *Born*, p. 91.

battlefield. The Son of Man appeared for this purpose—to destroy the works of the devil. [...] We have been anointed and equipped to destroy giants and extend the borders of the Kingdom, causing Heaven to collide with earth!⁶⁴

Like with Brian Houston, Vallotton, and Johnson are saying that, like Jesus, we are responsible for literally bringing heaven to earth. Again, this is not biblical in anyway. While not needing to restate all the evidence above, this is the same ideology that the ONA uses for calling the acausal to the material realm. See what Darlene Zschech has to say about how worshipping Jesus brings heaven to earth. Zschech says that

> [w]hen we worship Jesus, we declare His kingdom and announce His presence. [...] When we worship, kingdom dominion is established in our lives.⁶⁵

By attributing this to Jesus, Zschech believes that

> [a]long with the woman at the well who received living water and ran to share it with others, we too become witnesses to God's goodness. We are experiencing His kingdom come on earth, as it is in heaven, and so we go and share this good news with all who will listen.⁶⁶

Later in the book, with that miracle as an early example, Zschech claims that the "Father wants to give you the very kingdom itself."⁶⁷ Despite how good this sounds to those of us that believe what Hillsong and the Satanist churches are saying, this statement by Zschech is in fact heresy. Psalm 2:6 states that "[a]s for me, I have set my King on Zion, my holy hill." (ESV) This is in reference to Jesus. Then in 1 Corinthians 15:24–26,

> Then comes the end, when he delivers the kingdom to God the Father after destroying every rule and every authority and power. For he must reign until he has put all his enemies under his feet. The last enemy to be destroyed is death. (ESV)

Jesus has been given the kingdom as Matthew 28:18 says that "[a]ll authority in heaven and on earth has been given to me." (ESV) That authority gets transferred to the Father, and to the Father alone. Luke's statement in Luke 12:32, "Fear not, little flock, for it is your Father's good pleasure to give you the kingdom," (ESV) is not that we will be given the kingdom to rule. Joel B. Green comments on this verse that

---

64. Vallotton, *Supernatural*, Logos Edition.
65. Zschech, *Everything*, Location 129–132.
66. Zschech, *Everything*, p. 21, Location 448.
67. Zschech, *Everything*, p. 136, Location 221.

> [i]f vv 29–31 constitute the climax of Jesus' argument, these verses comprise its denouement. Here we encounter both the foundation and the resolution of his message on faithfulness regarding possessions. Fear, in this instance, refers to the anxiety and misgivings associated with the uncertainty of life, modeled so well by the wealthy farmer-landholder in Jesus' parable (vv 16–20). Jesus' disciples, referred to in language that recalls God's care for his people as a shepherd for the flock, need experience no such dread. This is because God's pleasure (or will) is manifest in his gift of the kingdom. It is likely that we are to understand the kingdom as having already been given—undoubtedly, then, a reference to the ministry of Jesus among them.[68]

While Zschech in her book is commenting on not worrying about possessions in that section, the way she is arguing to not be worried about possessions is because we will be given rulership of God's kingdom. That belief by Zschech is heresy.

Zschech however does not end there, in Zschech's belief worship is key.

> What a prayer. His kingdom on earth. His kingdom. The sound of heaven is worship, the currency of heaven is people, the presence of heaven is God's glory, majesty, and reign. The more we shine God's light over this earth, the greater impact we will have—His kingdom, heaven's reign, will be felt across the earth.[69]

Despite the arguing point in her book, Zschech's, Hillsong's, as well as the entire Satanist churches beliefs, including Tomlin's, have shown that they literally believe music is what brings "heaven" or the acausal to earth. Their music is being used as a "ritual" to try and bring the most horrendous demonic powers, via nexions/portals, down to earth. At the conclusion of this chapter, I will comment more on the reality of whether that is even possible.

To end off what Zschech believes about the acausal, or heaven, coming to earth, Zschech believes that the demonic reality is already here. Zschech says that "I believe that heaven starts here on earth, as we bring His Kingdom reign to wherever we find ourselves."[70] Remember how the ONA believe that the acausal is already in us. While we are representatives of the kingdom, the kingdom is not everywhere that we are. If we walk into a room, the kingdom does not automatically follow. That line of belief is in line with the ONA and the acausal within their adherents.

Going back to Bethel church in Redding, California, we can see from that churches writings that perverting the kingdom narrative is a

---

68. Green, *Luke*, pp. 494–495.
69. Zschech, *Everything*, p. 217, Location 3458–3461.
70. Zschech, *Everything*, p. 235, Location 3728–3729.

key part of their doctrine. Look what Johnson and Mike Seth say about Jesus' statement about the kingdom.

> When Jesus said, "The Kingdom of Heaven is at hand" (read Matt. 4:17), these people were ready for the party! They knew Jesus wasn't just some poor baby born in a barn. He brought the Kingdom of Heaven with Him![71]

This is a wrong statement by both Seth and Johnson. The Jews of 1st century Judea were not celebrating that the Messiah had come to bring the kingdom. Look at Matthew 13:57, "And they took offense at him. But Jesus said to them, 'A prophet is not without honor except in his hometown and in his own household.'" (ESV) This does not sound like the people were excited to meet him at all. The crucifixion trial before Pilate clearly shows that the people did not accept Jesus as the one to bring any kingdom. Again, these Satanist churches need to pervert the narrative in order to justify their doctrine from the LHP, and possibly the ONA, about the acausal. People giving recommendations to this book have said, "Bethel Church—an 'open heaven' where advancing the Kingdom is not just an idea, but a reality."[72] That is a very dangerous statement.

Johnson and Seth continue that you "need courage to complete your royal mission as an ambassador, bringing Heaven to earth and defeating satan. It takes courage to change the world!"[73] To put this quote in a proper rebuke: we are not the ones who defeat Satan, Christ alone is. We have no power over the devil and the works of the demonic,[74] however, since the entire Satanist church are devoted to bringing the acausal to earth, they need us to believe that they can literally defeat demonic powers. As was shown in the chapter where Wagner justified mass murder as strategic-level spiritual warfare, this is an intentional perversion to push a different gospel.

What is the "vehicle" of this acausal power? Johnson goes on to use Christian terminology. "Whole cities and even countries can turn to God as people begin to see with faith."[75] To them, the acausal, what Bethel and other Satanist church call "faith", is enough to change the world, much in the same way the ONA believes their acausal energy

---

71. Bill Johnson and Mike Seth, *When Heaven Invades Earth for Teens: Your Guide to God's Supernatural Power* (Shippensburg, PA: Destiny Image, 2014), Logos Edition.

72. Johnson, *Heaven*, Logos Edition.

73. Johnson, *Heaven*, Logos Edition.

74. I show this in the appendix of my book *Biblical Demonology: Their Origins and Unwilling Role in Sanctification* (Ingersoll, Ontario, Canada: Devoted Publishing, 2022), pp. xiii-xviii.

75. Johnson, *Heaven*, Logos Edition.

will.

By using this "acausal" energy Johnson continues that you will,

> [b]ring Heaven to earth. Your royal mission is to change the world! What did Jesus need for that kind of job? God's power. You Can Have Both! [...] When you obey and pray for them, the Holy Spirit does two things. [...] He will leak out of you and do the miracle.[76]

That is a highly disturbing quote. Understanding what Johnson, and the Satanist churches, are arguing for, they are pushing their demonic acausal energy on the rest of the world. Johnson continues to push this in is his book *The Mind of God*, "My assignment is to bring heaven to earth through my prayers and acts of radical obedience."[77] Considering what we have been looking at and seeing, the idea of "radical obedience" seems like a disturbing war cry, and the evidence above shows that it is.

Going back to Houston, when talking about faith, Brian Houston claims that, "[p]urpose will shape the way you speak about your future, what you believe about God and yourself, and what you have faith for."[78] To support his claim, Houston once again quotes scripture out of context in Deuteronomy 30:14. In chapter six I pointed out how the idea that words being used in the way that Houston is explaining them here, are from the occult. The Kabbalistic concept of the words of creation are an idea that many, not just Houston, distinctly rely on to make their claims legitimate. Since the LHP claim to not want much to do with Judeo-Christian thought, members of the LHP still have an abundance of Kabbalistic thought in their practices. Because of the LHP connection to the Kabbalah, and the Satanist church's connection to the LHP, it should not be surprising that Houston and his allies are using similar ideology.

Another disturbing quote from Houston says that within

> our changing society, church growth experts have noted that certain sectors of the church are declining. [...] they want their faith to be channeled into making a positive difference to others. It is no coincidence then that churches that are truly exalting Jesus Christ and bringing the power of the gospel to people in a relatable way are increasing and growing.[79]

The last line of the above quote is a commonly held misunderstanding by many "Christians". The idea that the church is growing, so it must

---

76. Johnson, *Heaven*, Logos Edition.
77. Johnson, *Mind*, Logos Edition.
78. Houston, *Born*, p. 102, Location 949–953.
79. Houston, *Born*, p. 19, Location 233–241.

be doing something right, is inherently flawed. Many of the suddenly growing churches are either steeped in Satanic doctrine, or soon show their true colours in their arrogance about their own ability to grow that church.

Houston in all his books continues to emphasize the point that his version of faith, or acausal energy, will bring you what you want in your life. In speaking about how God can give you what you want/need, Houston states that

> [h]ow can we actualize the dream God has for our glorious future if we don't have the resources, the degree, the property, the capital, or the supporters? All I can say is that we have a perspective limited by what we see on earth, which keeps us from recognizing the invisible, unlimited resources of our Father in Heaven.[80]

Houston also states that if you "[l]ive, love, and lead like Jesus and your life on earth and in Heaven will reflect the ongoing glory of God—in all things!"[81] Houston lastly emphasizes the key way to get all these benefits and the reality of heaven itself here on earth: faith.

> Having a faith perspective on life, love, and leadership isn't about playing down the difficulties of life—it's about being certain that God is bringing new life, both in the now and not yet of his kingdom.[82]

At this point, this should not be surprising. Faith for Houston, or the acausal, can get you whatever you want. By making claims about the "not yet of his kingdom", Houston has already shown what that implies. This "not yet" state for Houston is speaking about a demonic kingdom here on earth.

Vallotton and Johnson quote with even more certainty about the power of their faith and acausal power. The two men claim that

> when we have a revelation of the nature of God as the "Sun of Righteousness," who arises "with healing in His wings," (Prov. 13:22) and we see that Jesus healed every person who came to Him without exception, our faith will operate in a larger space. A person with the first belief probably doesn't pray for the sick, or if they do, they pray for perseverance. A person with revelation takes authority over the sickness and commands the sick person's body to be healed "on earth as it is in heaven."[83]

This special "revelation" that allows faith, or the acausal, to take authority over material things apparently comes to special Satanists be-

---

80. Houston, *Lead*, pp. 227–228.
81. Houston, *Lead*, p. 255.
82. Houston, *Lead*, p. 254.
83. Vallotton, *Supernatural*, Logos Edition.

cause they inherit it, or gain it, from the Kingdom or acausal realm. Vallotton and Johnson once again try to claim that

> revelation is meant to be the inheritance of the Kingdom, [...] The fruit of revelation is personal transformation and supernatural demonstrations of the nature of God. Therefore, the inheritance of revelation is the inheritance of models, heroes who became a revelation of God's nature.[84]

And again

> [w]hen this is realized, our identity changes and our faith embraces the purpose of our salvation. At some point we must go beyond being simply "sinners saved by grace." As we learn to live out of our position in Christ we will bring forth the greatest exploits of all time.[85]

Once more, we see here that Vallotton and Johnson, like Brian Houston, are using faith as equivalent to the acausal. According to Vallotton and Johnson

> agreeing with God empowers us. It frees us from the power of a lie and enables us to live according to the will of God. This [...] is empowerment because of God.[86]

If the truth of what these men are saying is the reality of our world, then there is something deeply troubling coming from the demonic. These Satanist churches will argue that it is the promised kingdom of God.

Johnson and Seth in their combined book claim that the ability to use acausal energy to bring heaven to earth is confirmed again and that being

> a son or daughter of God, you have been given a powerful gift—the gift of faith. With this power, you will be able to see different worlds and different kingdoms that can't be seen with physical sight. Faith gives you spiritual eyes. With these eyes you can see what is invisible to everyone else. [...] anybody can have it.[87]

This power according to Johnson comes to use because

> [w]hen Jesus came to earth, [...] After His death, He rose from the dead and appeared to the disciples, announcing that He now had all authority in heaven and on earth: And Jesus came and spoke to them, saying, "All authority has been given to Me in heaven and on earth. Go therefore and

---

84. Vallotton, *Supernatural*, Logos Edition.
85. Vallotton, *Supernatural*, Logos Edition.
86. Vallotton, *Supernatural*, Logos Edition.
87. Johnson, *Heaven*, Logos Edition.

make disciples of all the nations, baptizing them in the name of the Father and of the Son and of the Holy Spirit, teaching them to observe all things that I have commanded you."[88]

The key to understanding the Satanist churches argument is in who they believe Jesus was on earth. This is important to understand to get why these Satanist churches believe that they can do like Jesus and call heaven/the acausal to earth.

In misinterpreting John 5:19, Johnson says that

> That means He didn't bring any special powers with Him when He came to earth. Even though Jesus was 100 percent God, He chose to live on earth as a regular person just like you. Why would He do that? Because He loves you. Jesus did many miracles, and He did them as a person, [...] If Jesus did all those miracles as God, then you couldn't do them, because you're human. But because Jesus healed the sick, raised the dead, and cast out demons as a person—you can too![89]

Another NAR apostle, Kimberly Daniels in her book *Clean House, Strong House: A Practical Guide to Understanding Spiritual Warfare, Demonic Strongholds and Deliverance* claims that

> Jesus came to set the captives free. He could have sat in heaven and loosed fire on the devil's head, but He came down as a man and wupped up on some devils. He came as an example to us that we, in our fleshly nature, can resist and attack demonic forces in victory. Jesus did not walk the earth as God! He took on our fleshly nature so that we could take on His spiritual nature.[90]

This is often described as a variation of the kenotic heresy that says that Jesus was only a human on earth. The variation is that many of these NAR apostles will say that Jesus still had the fullness of God while on earth but chose not to use his godhood to do the miracles but relied on the Holy Spirit. In either way, the Satanist churches use this argument to try and justify their miracles, really magic, because "Jesus could do them, therefore so can I."

There is unfortunately another problem with their claim about Jesus. To find that out and how it relates the Satanism taught by Hillsong, Prosperity, WoF, and NAR churches, we need to turn to the Kabbalah and who the Kabbalists believe that Metatron was and is.

---

88. Johnson, *Mind*, Logos Edition.
89. Johnson, *Heaven*, Logos Edition.
90. Kimberly Daniels, *Clean House, Strong House: A Practical Guide to Understanding Spiritual Warfare, Demonic Strongholds and Deliverance* (Lake Mary, Florida: Charisma House, 2013), Logos Edition.

The Kabbalah, Metatron, and Jesus

While many people will understand who Metatron is supposed to be, it will be important for the sake of this chapter to explain fully who Metatron is and his significance to the argument at hand.

One of the easiest ways to explain who Metatron is, is to go back to the Hekhalot texts from Merkavah Mysticism explained in chapter three. When a fictional character by the name of Rabbi Ishmael is brought up to heaven, he notes that "[a]t once the Holy One, blessed be he, summoned to my aid his servant, the angel Meṭaṭron, Prince of the Divine Presence."[91] The "Holy One" here indicated Yahweh, or Yhvh. When Ishmael asks who this Metatron really is he states that "I am Enoch, the son of Jared."[92] Surprised by this, Ishmael asks how the lowly Enoch from Genesis 5 became such a powerful being. In response Metatron/Enoch says that

> the Holy One, blessed be he, brought me up in their lifetime, before their very eyes, to the heavenly height, to be a witness against them to future generations. And the Holy One, blessed be he, appointed me in the height as a prince and a ruler among the ministering angels.[93]

Yet, this is not all. In addition to this high glory, Metatron says that

> the Holy One, [...] made for me throne like the throne of glory, [...] the herald went out into every heaven and announced concerning me: "I have appointed Meṭaṭron my servant as a prince and a ruler over all the denizens of the heights, apart from the eight great, honored, and terrible princes who are called Yhwh by the name of their King. Any angel and any prince who has anything to say in my presence should go before him and speak to him. Whatever he says to you in my name you must observe and do, because I have committed to him the Prince of Wisdom and the Prince of Understanding, to teach him the wisdom of those above and of those below, the wisdom of this world and of the world to come. [...] From that time onward I looked and beheld deep secrets and wonderful mysteries. Before a man thinks in secret, I see his thought; before he acts, I see his act. There is nothing in heaven above or deep within the earth concealed from me.[94]

If that was not enough, Yahweh also goes and proceeds to have "called me, 'The lesser Yhwh' in the presence of his whole household in the

---

91. P. Alexander, "3 (Hebrew Apocalypse of) Enoch (Fifth–Sixth Centurty A.D.) A New Translation and Introduction," in *The Old Testament Pseudepigrapha Volume 1*, ed. James H. Charlesworth (New York, New York: Yale University Press, 1983), p. 237, Logos Edition.
92. Alexander, *3 Enoch*, p. 258.
93. Alexander, *3 Enoch*, p. 258.
94. Alexander, *3 Enoch*, p. 263–264.

height, as it is written, 'My name is in him.'"[95] It does not take much to see the Christological overtones here. Metatron is being likened to the biblical Jesus, not as Jesus, but as a replacement for Jesus. Noticing this great honour, some of the angel's protest, but Yahweh responds that "What right have you to interrupt me? I have chosen this one in preference to all of you, to be a prince and a ruler over you in the heavenly heights."[96] The fact that a human has been promoted to being like God himself is not to be questioned. This is most likely looking very familiar to you in what the Satanist churches are claiming about their own "apostles" and King James "divine authority".

Within the Sefar haZohar, one of the key collection of texts when it comes to Kabbalistic thought, we find that the idea of Yahweh with a son, is also present.

> *Aleph* symbolizes the Father, and when it ascends and descends, the *Mem* unites itself with it, producing *em*, which signifies Mother; the *resh* is the Head (*rosh* =head), signifying Son. When these three unite the result is they form "Word", "Speech". Thus the Father, the Mother and first born Son radiate one within the other in one union. (italics in original)[97]

Seeing this, the connection of Metatron as a lesser YHWH and so being equal, thus a "son" of the Father is not a stretch to make. The academic world has also been making these connections for a number of years.

> This is a struggle over the messianic character of Joseph, using a homily on the mystery of the soul of Adam-Enoch-Metatron and its reincarnation in Joseph, who becomes the symbol of the "righteous" Messiah, saving Israel through his struggle against the Christian Messiah—a struggle that is apparently also reflected in the messianic self-consciousness of the authors of the Zohar.[98]

Benarroch finishes his argument by saying that

> [t]he main goal of this article is to show how the combined depictions printed at the end of Tikkun 70 make up yet another example of the complex linkage between Metatron and Jesus and of the hidden Zoharic polemics against Christianity, as a discourse that both borrows from and

---

95. Alexander, *3 Enoch*, p. 265.
96. Alexander, *3 Enoch*, p. 265.
97. Harry Sperling, Maurice Simon, and Dr. Paul P. Levertoff, *The Zohar: An English Translation Volume Three* (New York, New York: The Socino Press, 1984), p. 391.
98. Jonathan M. Benarroch, "'The Mystery of (Re)incarnation and the Fallen Angels': The Reincarnations of Adam, Enoch, Metatron, (Jesus), and Joseph—An Anti-Christian Polemic in the Zohar," *Journal of Medieval Religious Cultures*. Volume 44, No. 2 (2018): p. 134.

refutes its Christian opponents.[99]

Gedaliahu G. Stroumsa notes that the

> hymn adds that Christ was given by God "the Name which is above every name" (vs 9), in other words, the divine Name. This formula is strikingly similar to the tradition about Yahoel-Metatron, according to which he received his Master's name.[100]

In other words, the connection in esoteric and Kabbalistic circles to Metatron being Jesus has been made. Although theologically, this is a heretical view of Christ, and Enoch, esotericism is not so worried about being theologically correct. In Kabbalism they try to note that "Metatron, who is reviving the dead, is also the Messiah."[101]

Robin Main, a practicing New Age advocate, who claims to be Christian, is part of a group called *Sapphire Throne Ministries* confirms the thinking that within esotericism

> Metatron is the 100-percent fullness of the Heavenly One New Man in Christ. The Metatron Matrix consists of Messiah Yeshua (Jesus Christ), which is the Head of the Body of Christ, and those individuals in the Body of Christ who have matured into the exact same image as Jesus Christ.[102]

Main further explains in her book *Understand the Order of Melchizedek: Complete Series* that the

> culmination of holding fast to the Head to the utmost is what I call the undifferentiated state of the Messiah in which the Messiah's Head and His Body are indistinguishable, because they are one. This is the oneness matrix of Messiah Yeshua. I like to call it the Oneness Metatron Matrix; because the white-haired fully mature Head of the Messiah and His fully mature Body is in a word, Metatron; or in other words, Metatron Messiah.[103]

---

99. Benarroch, *Metatron*, p. 140.

100. Gedaliahu G. Stroumsa, "Form(s) of God: Some Notes on Metatron and Christ," *Harvard Theological Journal* 76:3 (1983), p. 283.

101. Matthias Däumer, "Eschatological Relativity. On the Scriptural Undermining of Apocalypses in Jewish Second Temple, Late Antique and Medieval Receptions of the Book of Watchers," in Cultures of Eschatology: Volume 1: Empires and Scriptural Authorities in Medieval Christian, Islamic and Buddhist Communities. Volume 2: Time, Death and Afterlife in Medieval Christian, Islamic and Buddhist Communities. Edited by Veronika Wieser, Vincent Eltschinger and Johann Heiss (Berlin, Germany: De Gruyter, 2020), p. 214.

102. Robin Main, "Metatron – Oneness of the Messiah Yeshua," *Sapphire Throne Ministries*, July 15, 2023, https://sapphirethroneministries.wordpress.com/2017/07/01/metatron-oneness-of-the-messiah-yeshua/.

103. Robin Main, *Understanding the Order of Melchizedek: Complete Series* (Masonville, Colorado: Sapphire Throne Ministries, 2017), pp. 489-490.

Walter Martin, in his posthumous book, *The Kingdom of the Occult*, states that

> Christian Cabala differed from Judaic Kabbalah in its analysis of the Tree of Life and the nature of God. Cabalists taught that Jesus Christ, by His atonement and resurrection, replaced the Ten Sefirot as a means of reaching the [...] immanent deity.[104]

To show how this is all possible.

> The letter Tau advanced in front and pleaded: May it please Thee, O Lord of the world, to place me first in the creation of the world, seeing that I am the concluding letter of EMeTh (Truth) which is engraved upon Thy seal, and seeing that Thou art called by this very name of EMeTh, it is most appropriate for the King to begin with the final letter of EMeTh and to create with me the world. The Holy One, blessed be He, said to her: Thou art worthy and deserving, but it is not proper that I begin with thee the creation of the world, since thou art destined to serve as a mark on the foreheads of the faithful ones (vide Ezek. IX, 4) who have kept the Law from Aleph to Tau, and through the absence of this mark the rest will be killed; and, further, thou formest the conclusion of MaWeTh (death).[105]

In the Talmud we get the following statement:

> And Reish Lakish said: The letter tav is the last letter of the seal of the Holy One, Blessed be He, as Rabbi Ḥanina said: The seal of the Holy One, Blessed be He, is truth [emet], which ends with the letter tav. Rabbi Shmuel bar Naḥmani said: The letter tav teaches that these are people who observed the entire Torah from alef through tav.[106]

Aryeh Kalan in his translation of *The Bahir: Illumination* makes the connection very clear. It is important to remember that "Tav being the last letter of the Hebrew alphabet. Since Malkhut-Kingship is the last of the Sephirot, it is represented by the letter Tav."[107] That being said note that

> [t]he Alef is the first Sephirah, which is the Keter-Crown. This is totally hidden and only serves to receive from God, holding back his light so that it does not overwhelm creation. The Alef is therefor open in the back. Even Keter-Crown must receive its existence from the Infinite

---

104. Walter Martin, Jill Martin Rische, Kurt Van Gorden, *The Kingdom of the Occult* (Nashville, Tennessee: Thomas Nelson, 2008), p. 147.

105. Harry Sperling, Maurice Simon, Dr. Paul P. Levertoff, *The Zohar: An English Translation Volume One* (New York, New York: The Socino Press, 1984), p. 9.

106. Sefaria, "Shabbat 55a," *The William Davidson Talmud*, July 18, 2023, https://www.sefaria.org/Shabbat.55a.12?lang=bi.

107. Aryeh Kaplan, *The Bahir: Illumination* (York Beach, Maine: Samuel Weiser, Inc. 1989), p. 90.

Being which is infinitely higher than this Sefirah.[108]

Remember in Revelation 1:8 Jesus tells us that "'I am the Alpha and the Omega,' says the Lord God, 'who is and who was and who is to come, the Almighty.'" (Revelation 1:8 ESV) With the Kabbalah using Alef and Tav as the first and last letters of the alphabet to indicate the highest of the Sefirot (Sefirah) and Tav as the lowest of the Sephirot, the way that Kabbalists, and Christian Cabalists have claimed that Jesus, being the Alpha (the first letter of the Greek alphabet) and the Omega (the last letter of the Greek alphabet), is the "bridge" that can get them to "heaven" or even to call heaven down to earth.

The occultic use of Jesus, via the Kabbalah, by Hillsong and the other Satanist churches is now clear. Jesus is just a tool for these Satanists to use to get to the acausal, or what they are calling "heaven." Just in the same way that the ONA claim that the use of the crystal allows them to access and open the nexion to the acausal, the Satanist church try to use Metatron/Jesus to access the acausal instead.

Another author that has come to be popular in WoF and NAR circles in the last few years is Zen Garcia. Garcia on his website has a very strange obsession with Enochian prophecies and Enochian calendars as a legitimate source of information and truth.[109] Having read through his introduction to the book *Yahushua Christ: Infancy Childhood and Lost Years* there is some very telling information as to why.

> May you be blessed by the Holy Trinity, the Father, Yahaveh, the Mother, the Ruach HaKodesh, and the son, Yahushua Christ when studying these teachings. I pray that through them you come to know and be in deeper relating with the Godhead.[110]

Three problems here: 1) the three names given to the three persons of the Godhead are never given in that fashion in the Bible. Even the name of Jesus in Hebrew, Yeshua, is never given to us in the entirety of the Old Testament. No name was ever given for the coming Messiah in any Old Testament book, chapter or verse, especially Yahushua. 2) the Holy Spirit is not "the Mother." The Holy Spirit as "the Mother" is a gnostic, and as has been shown above, a Kabbalistic teaching. While his Hebrew name for the Holy Spirit given there does mean "Spirit/Wind of the Holy", that Hebrew term is never used for the Spirit of God in the entire Old Testament. 3) the texts given in this

---

108. Kaplan, *Bahir*, p. 99.
109. Zen Garcia, *Sacred Word Publishing*, July 20, 2023, https://sacredwordpublishing.com/.
110. Zen Garcia, *Yahushua Christ: Infancy Childhood and Lost Years* (Atlanta, Georgia: Sacred Word Publishing, 2017), p. 9.

book are all distinctively Gnostic texts. By praying that you will come into "deeper relating with the Godhead", Garcia is hoping that an occultic esoteric experience will happen with you through heretical/occult books. Since the term "esotericism" is used as a legitimate source of truth many times on his website, it saddens me the number of WoF/Satanist deceived young people that are taking Garcia's writings as legitimate and truthful. Garcia is an all-out Kabbalist and needs to be recognized for the demonic teachings, like the other Satanist churches, he is putting in his books.

If anyone doubts the fact that Garcia is a Kabbalist, in the following quotes from his book The Collected Works of Enoch the Prophet which reprints a plethora of Enochian literature, Garcia first says that

> [t]he Most High God declares in the Scriptures that at the end of days, the Spirit of truth would be poured out upon all flesh and that those things which had been lost, forgotten, hidden, and forbidden to the masses so that all that had been known and treasured previously with regard to the sanctity of the Scriptures would be restored to those seeking them.[111]

Although the Bible never says that hidden writings that were purposely "hidden, and forbidden" would be brought forward again as "Scripture", Garcia believes that all these heretical texts, as I have shown earlier, are scripture. First, Garcia says that "[l]ike the many other Scriptures and books of wisdom published by Sacred Word Publishing,"[112] which shows that what is in the book under discussion, he believes these texts are as authoritative as the Bible. When talking about 3 (Hebrew) Enoch specifically, Garcia says that "[m]odern scholars describe the book as Merkabah literature, a pseudepigrapha written by Rabbi Ishmael who became a 'high priest' after ascending to Heaven."[113] So, Garcia admits that 3 (Hebrew) Enoch is in fact a Merkabah (Merkavah) text, and the introduction (page 4–5 in his book) by Garcia states that it is scripture. Since 3 (Hebrew) Enoch is a text that is included not only in Merkavah Mysticism but the Kabbalistic literature, the fact that Garcia believes it is as authoritative as the Bible itself, is not only blasphemous, but heresy. Again, Garcia is a Kabbalist posing as a Christian. Since so many of the Satanist churches are teaching Kabbalistic beliefs in their churches, it is no wonder that the people that follow these Satanists, are also being deceived by outright Kab-

---

111. Zen Garcia, *The Collected Works of Enoch the Prophet* (Atlanta, Georgia: Sacred Word Publishing, 2017), p. 4.
112. Garcia, *Enoch*, p. 5.
113. Garcia, *Enoch*, p. 331.

balists, like Garcia, that falsely claim to be Christians.

Back to the Statements of the Satanist Churches

Up to this point, the evidence has shown that Hillsong and the other Satanist churches along with them, are indeed attempting to take their Satanic gospel and to use their power, and their false Jesus to try and pull the demonic acausal, or what these churches refer to as "heaven" to earth. Earlier in this book when I showed that these Satanist churches do believe that any means of growing the church, even violently, is acceptable, I left the argument open as to how much these fake apostles really believe this. This question now needs to be answered.

In an earlier chapter I showed how Brian Houston believes that the prosperity gospel is the true gospel and that is the gospel that Houston believes will take over the world. The quote from Johnson's book *When Heaven Invades Earth for Teens: Your Guide to God's Supernatural Power* also shows that Johnson, Bethel, and other WoF and NAR churches believe in a different gospel as well. Johnson argues that the

> name Jesus Christ means "Jesus, the anointed one." It was this anointing that helped Jesus do what He saw His Father doing in Heaven. It was this anointing that caused all of those powerful miracles. [...] That's what they wanted. That's why they left everything behind to follow Him. This anointing terrifies the devil and wrecks his kingdom of darkness. He will do anything he can to kill the anointing. He tried when Jesus was on earth, and that's why the religious leaders had Jesus put to death.[114]

Again, we need to note here that Johnson provides no scriptural basis that states directly, that Satan had any hand whatsoever in the death of Jesus. The reason that Johnson cannot provide such a reference is because the Bible never says, or even hints at, the fact that Satan killed Jesus, even via the Jewish people. This may shock some people, but the Bible never says Satan was involved. The reason it does not say that Satan killed Jesus is because if Satan was the one that killed Jesus, even by a mediator in the Jewish people, then the satisfaction of the law in the Torah could not be made. In order for the law to be fulfilled, the sacrifice had to be made by the high priest. Who was this high priest? The book of Hebrews tells us who that high priest was.

> But when Christ appeared as a high priest of the good things that have come, then through the greater and more perfect tent (not made with hands, that is, not of this creation) he entered once for all into the holy places, not by means of the blood of goats and calves but by means of

---

114. Johnson, *Heaven*, Logos Edition.

his own blood, thus securing an eternal redemption. (Hebrews 9:11–12 ESV)

The high priest that offered the sacrifice for the fulfillment of the Torah law was Jesus. Jesus testifies to this fact before his death.

> For this reason the Father loves me, because I lay down my life that I may take it up again. No one takes it from me, but I lay it down of my own accord. I have authority to lay it down, and I have authority to take it up again. This charge I have received from my Father." (John 10:17–18 ESV)

Satan had absolutely nothing to do with the death of Christ. Johnson saying that Satan was the one that killed Jesus, and thus would be the "high priest" that offered Christ as the atoning and Torah fulfilling sacrifice, would give the demonic as a whole, much more power than we could possibly imagine. If Satan could kill Jesus, it would introduce a system of dualism that is common in Gnostic though. This is a completely false gospel given to us by Johnson and his church, Bethel.

Johnson does not only make this heretical statement about the death of Christ either. Johnson claims that it was the anointing that people followed Jesus for, and that Satan killed Jesus for. Again, this is a false gospel. People in the time when Jesus was on earth, some did follow him, however most wanted him dead. Christ however, since he is the one that had the only authority to lay down his life, could not be harmed by the people.

> Some of the people of Jerusalem therefore said, "Is not this the man whom they seek to kill? [...] So they were seeking to arrest him, but no one laid a hand on him, because his hour had not yet come. (John 7:25, 30 ESV)

Those that did follow him as Peter says in Matthew 16:15–16 "He said to them, 'But who do you say that I am?' Simon Peter replied, 'You are the Christ, the Son of the living God.'" (ESV) Here the apostles, and other people, were not following Jesus for his anointing, the people were following him because he was the promised Messiah, God on earth. Johnson has turned the gospel into a pursuit of occultic, acausal, and Satanic power to deify yourself.

Johnson continues on with his gospel spreading across the earth by saying to

> repent actually means to change the way you think about things—things like who God is and what He wants to do here on earth. [...] You will get a look at things in God's world, stuff straight out of Heaven—[...] These worldly things don't last a minute compared to Heaven and the

love of God![115]

Again, Johnson here is perverting the gospel. To Johnson, repentance means to change the way you think into the way that God does. In that way, you will receive your own divinity. Hodge shows us what repentance truly is

> our Lord said, "I am not come to call the righteous, but sinners to repentance." (Matt. 9:13.) This external call includes, (1.) A declaration of the plan of salvation. (2.) The promise of God to save all who accede to the terms of that plan. (3.) Command, exhortation, and invitation to all to accept of the offered mercy. (4.) An exhibition of the reasons which should constrain men to repent and believe, and thus escape from the wrath to come. All this is included in the gospel. For the gospel is a revelation of God's plan of saving sinners.[116]

This biblical gospel of "repent and believe," even by Jesus' own words about calling sinners to repent, has nothing to do with "change the way you think about things [...] like who God is and what he wants to do here on earth." Johnson is pushing a false gospel and is wanting his Satanism and acausal energy to overtake the earth. The fact that Johnson is teaching a form of Satanism is also shown below. Because to Johnson it was not just the faith of the woman who was bleeding for twelve years that healed her. To Johnson it was necromancy because

> faith got the Holy Spirit to leak out of Him and break the chains [...] You have the same Holy Spirit anointing and power that Jesus had. Listen and He will tell you when you can pour out God's presence. Just let the Holy Spirit do what He wants to do, and miracles will happen. Let God smear you with Himself![117]

This faith that Johnson speaks of is the power that he believes will change the "atmosphere" of their immediate community and also change the culture around his church. Johnson claims that the changes he is pushing for, in bringing the acausal to earth, is what everyone wants. As a result, Johnson says that it

> is not that we don't want people to attend our fellowship of believers. [...] We just changed the way we measure our success as a church. Our measure changed from increased attendance on Sunday to the transformed attitude and value system of our city. In biblical terms, such a measure would demonstrate the reality of heaven affecting earth [...] Kingdom culture works outside our congregational services quite well,

---

115. Johnson, *Heaven*, Logos Edition.
116. Hodge, *Theology*, p. 468.
117. Johnson, *Heaven*, Logos Edition.

and it is essentially what everyone longs for.[118]

When commenting about the civil war in Guatemala, and the use of Wagner's strategic-level spiritual warfare as a justification to mass murder entire villages of innocent people, Wagner stated that the kingdom needs to grow and that the "ends always justify the means." The reason the dictatorial military was using this type of warfare was because the tyrant in control of Guatemala at the time named the pagan Mayan's "demons" and therefore, they needed to die. Johnson starts to hint along the same line.

> Establishing a Kingdom culture is vital because in most cities people do not realize that the demonic realms that were given permission to influence that city are often influencing their thinking. What a Kingdom atmosphere does is give people permission to think for themselves—to think clearly, [...] Influencing the atmosphere in a place helps set the stage in such a way that people are much more likely to respond to the profound invitation given in the good news of the Kingdom.[119]

Johnson wants us to realize this because we

> were placed in the middle of a war, with an assignment to see the Kingdom come "on earth as it is in heaven." When Jesus said there would be wars and rumors of war, He was not giving us a promise. He was revealing the conditions into which He was sending His last days' army.[120]

Even from a basic level of spiritual warfare understanding, there is no doubt that we can correctly say that there is a spiritual battle happening in our world right now. The problem that Johnson, Houston, and the other Satanist churches have said is that this spiritual war needs to spill out into the physical world by getting rid of the "demons." The quote with footnote 115 is evidence that anyone that opposes Johnson's gospel and the spread of his Satanist church, falls under the definition of "demonic."

Johnson needs this idea of "[e]stablishing a Kingdom culture" to justify his Satanist and acausal thinking. While true biblical gospel teachings are useful in every part of society, Johnson argues that it is his true "Kingdom experiences and values are transferable to every part of society."[121] Johnson believes this because as the true church with the true gospel, to him they "live as people with access to heavenly solutions for earthly problems. We were created to create."[122]

---

118. Johnson, *Mind*, Logos Edition.
119. Johnson, *Mind*, Logos Edition.
120. Johnson, *Mind*, Logos Edition.
121. Johnson, *Mind*, Logos Edition.
122. Johnson, *Mind*, Logos Edition.

Humanity was not "created to create." The Westminster Shorter Catechism of Faith states that

> Q. 1. What is the chief end of man?
> A. Man's chief end is to glorify God, [a] and to enjoy him for ever. [b]
> [a]. Ps. 86:9; Isa. 60:21; Rom. 11:36; 1 Cor. 6:20; 10:31; Rev. 4:11
> [b]. Ps. 16:5-11; 144:15; Isa. 12:2; Luke 2:10; Phil. 4:4; Rev. 21:3-4[123]

There is nothing in that statement or the scriptural proofs provided that humans were "created to create." That statement by Johnson, is founded in occult, ONA and even LHP ideology.

And while Johnson's mission of bringing the acausal to earth may seem dangerous and unattainable to us as a wider body of believers, Johnson asserts that "while that may seem impractical to some, it has become intensely practical to me. 'On earth as it is in heaven' is the mandate of the Church."[124] Johnson fully intends to bring the acausal to earth in any way that he can.

Showing how far Johnson wants his followers to go in one instance, as shown again by Hardy,

> [i]nstead of taking no for an answer, they blocked her wheelchair with their feet underneath one of her wheels so that she couldn't move, and they subjected her to it. She was humiliated to the point of tears. [...] We've had problems with them here in town at both hospitals, [...] They push their ways into there and go beyond medical staff to do the healing and prayers. I've seen patients who made a special request [that] no one from Bethel is allowed to come into the room, because they'd become that disruptive.[125]

Taking what Johnson has said that sounds loving and good, the reality is that within the community of Redding, California, many consider the entire church of Bethel, and the *Bethel School of Supernatural Ministry* as a public menace. How long will the world be allowed to continue to resist Johnson, Bethel, Hillsong and the other Satanist churches before these Satanists turn around and say, "enough is enough."

Kabbalistic Children by Sexual Rites

This is a very serious accusation and needs to be backed up properly. To start with where this accusation comes from, I once again quote from Bobbie Houston's book Heaven is in this House. When commenting on how the kingdom can grow through natural families, Bob-

---

123. Assembly at Edinburg, "The Westminster Shorter Catechism," *A Puritan's Mind*, July 18, 2023, https://www.apuritansmind.com/westminster-standards/shorter-catechism/.
124. Johnson, *Mind*, Logos Edition.
125. Hardy, *Beyond*, p. 159.

bie Houston says

> when two individuals come together (as we did), and when they choose to reproduce in their marriage the *nature of God's divine family* (i.e. endeavour to live according to his principles) then I believe *an anointing from above will rest upon that natural family and the fruit will be supernatural*. In other words, the children that emerge from that household will not be average, run-of-the-mill kids. Oh, they'll be kids in every sense of the word, but they'll have a supernatural something about them that will separate them from those who choose to live outside God's way. (italics in original)[126]

Once again, like most claims like this in these Satanist's books, there is no scriptural evidence to back it up. The reason being is that there is none, at least for "good" spiritual reproduction.

While this is not the place to get fully into this debate, one of the three possible explanations for the Nephilim of Genesis 6 is that they were the giant offspring of angels (the sons of God) and human women (the daughters of men).[127] Despite whatever the reader may think about this being true or not, if it is true, the paradigm shown here is that mixing spirituality with human reproduction has always led to something evil. This is the only example of spiritual beings involved in human reproduction and the result is that God sends the flood, destroys the world as it was, and restarts humanity through Noah and his family. The incarnation of Jesus was different because God the Son incarnated himself and did not procreate with Mary to give birth to a son.

Outside of the Bible though, we do find occultic and Kabbalistic beliefs in how sex can be used in a magical way to help someone reach divinity. Going back to the section about *The Kabbalah, Metatron, and Jesus* we once again encounter the idea of the "letters" that has led people into believing Metatron is also Jesus. The *Sefer Yetzirah*,

---

126. Houston, *House*, p. 42.

127. There are three general explanations for the origins of the Nephilim. The first is that they are the giant children of fallen angels (sons of God) and human women (daughters of men). This view is supported by the use of "sons of God" as angels in Job 1:6 and 2:1. The other common explanation is that the Nephilim were children of the godly line of Seth (sons of God) and the line of Cain (daughters of men). The third is that the sons of God are ruler/kings and that the daughters of men are peasant women. The last two seem doubtful since when Christians and non-Christians marry, giants are not the resulting children. Same with ruler and peasants. As a modern example, when Prince William Wales and Catherine Middleton got married, their children have not proven to be giants. Therefore, my personal belief is that the Nephilim are the giant offspring of demons and humans. How they survived the flood (Numbers 13:33), I have no explanation. The curse by Yahweh in Genesis 6:3 seems clear that these sexual encounters would no longer result in Nephilim offspring.

another early Kabbalistic text explains that

> Yah, the Lord of hosts, the living God, King of the Universe, Omnipotent, All-Kind and Merciful, Supreme and Extolled, who is Eternal, Sublime and Most-Holy, ordained (formed) and created the Universe in thirty-two mysterious paths of wisdom by three Sepharim, [...] which are in Him one and the same. They consist of a decade out of nothing and of twenty-two fundamental letters. He divided the twenty-two consonants into three divisions.[128]

Again, we see here the divine "letters" now being used in the process of creation. However, the text continues in a couple chapters that the

> three first elements, א״מ״ש are typified by a balance, in one scale the merit and in the other the criminality, which are placed in equilibrium by the tongue. [...] are sealed by six rings, or elementary circles, namely: air, water and fire emanated from them, which gave birth to progenitors, and these progenitors gave birth again to some offspring.[129]

We have here three specific Hebrew letters that are birthing progenitors who then give birth to offspring. This is a direct sexual connection between the divine letters of divinity within us, that allows rebirthing of yet more divine children. You will once again notice that the aleph (א) and mem (מ) are present. Although the tav (ת) is replaced with the shin (ש), the similarities as shown in the section with Metatron and Jesus are eerily similar.

Commenting on this Marla Segol in the book *Kabbalah and Sex Magic: 23 (Magic in History)* says that "as alef brings fire, mem creates water and earth, and shin creates air. In this way, the human being, the cosmos, and time are alike generated by sexual reproduction."[130] Continuing to comment, Segol says that

> [t]ogether, each letter participates in the divine and in the elements the letters are used to create. [...] If symbols are rightly used, they reveal a creative power that comes directly from the divine. [...] They are also intended for human use. The first section of the text describes the function of the gendered, sexualized letters, the second contains a description of the letter-combination ritual, and the third depicts human performance of letter-combination rituals. In this way, the Sefer Yetsirah consistently instructs the reader to replicate the divine creation process made possible by the inherent power of letters and names and their direct relation to both the divine body and the material world.[131]

---

128. Kalisch, *Yezirah*, p. 8.
129. Kalisch, *Yezirah*, p. 14.
130. Marla Segol, *Kabbalah and Sex Magic: 23 (Magic in History)* (University Park, Pennsylvania: Penn State University, 2021), p. 76, Kindle Edition.
131. Segol, *Kabbalah*, pp. 77–78.

The next two Kabbalistic books need some explaining before I show the connection between these divine letters and the ritual sexual procreation of the Kabbalah. Segol mentions two authors that are linked together in the thinking even though it may not seem like it at first.

> Solomon ibn Gabirol's *The Improvement of the Moral Qualities* [...] provides instructions for the transformation of the soul and even the cosmos through the proper use of the senses and emotions. (italics in original) (italics in original)[132]

Solomon ibn Gabirol wrote that

> the inferior substance among them is contained in the superior substance because the latter possesses and knows it. And the universal soul bears the corporeal world in its entirety, imagines and sees all that is in it, as our particular souls possess our bodies, imagine and see all that is in them: and still more the universal intelligence, by reason of its perfection, its faculty to extend, and the nobility of its substance. You will understand thereby how the First Author, sublime and holy, knows all things and how all things exist in his knowledge. And know this: Just as the essence and the form of the corporeal substance correspond to the essence and the form of the spiritual substance, so the envelopment by the spiritual substance corresponds to the envelopment by the corporeal substances, since the inferior is the image of the superior, as you have often heard it said. In these circumstances, it is evident that the envelopment of the corporeal substance by the spiritual substance indicates that the corporeal substance exists in it and that it is contained in it as all bodies exist in the body of heaven and are contained in it: and the turning of the spiritual substance upon itself in eternity and in permanent duration is like the turning of heaven upon itself by displacement and revolution. [...] And I consider that the order of the particular soul imitates the disposition of the universal world.[133]

Reading through this, we can distinctly pick out that ibn Gabirol indicates that our human souls (the inferior substance) are directly related to the divine (spiritual substance), the divine letters, or in New Age/LHP terms the "universal world."

The next Kabbalistic author, Bahya ibn Paquada is where we are able to finally make the connections, Segol first makes that connection that

> Bahya ibn Paquda wrote *Al Hidayah ila Faraid al-hulub* (Guide to the Duties of the Heart), [...] probably five years after ibn Gabirol's *Improvement of the Moral Qualities* [...] Bahya writes that he "wished to fill a great need in Jewish literature," for he believed that neither the

---

132. Segol, *Kabbalah*, p. 89.
133. Solomon Ibn Gabirol, *The Fountain of Life* (Location Unknown: E-Bookarama, 2023), pp. 127–128, Kindle Edition.

rabbis of the Talmud nor subsequent rabbis had adequately brought all the ethical teachings of Judaism into a coherent system. Moreover, he thought that many Jews paid attention only to "the duties to be performed by the parts of the body" (Hovot ha-evarim), without regard to the inner ideas and sentiments that should be embodied in this way of life, [...] Bahya, too, retells the foundational stories of Judaism to remythologize human creation, the meaning of the human body, and the import of its senses. (italics in original)[134]

In making this connection to ibn Gabirol it is easy to see that

Bahya enjoins the reader to meditate on the creation of the human body, beginning with its embryology. As in ibn Gabirol's work, meditation is a ritual practice used to form a mode of perception in which sensing is a meaningful religious act.[135]

Realizing how Bahya intends his work to be as a focus on meditation of the divine within humanity to generate divinity in our children, Bahya says that is

it our duty to study created things or not? We reply that the examination of created things and deducing from them the wisdom of the Creator is a duty which can be demonstrated from Reason, Scripture, and Tradition [the oral torah]. From Reason: For our reason bears witness that a rational creature's superiority over an irrational one consists in the former's superior ability to perceive, understand and acquire knowledge of the marks of wisdom found throughout the universe.[136]

The wise an intelligent man will choose from the world for study its fine and spiritual elements; use them as a ladder by which to obtain proofs of the existence of the Creator of all, to Whose service he will then cling to according to his heartfelt recognition of the greatness and exaltedness of the Creator, and his realization of the Almighty's gracious benevolence to all of His creations and that G-d has graciously bestowed abundant benefits to him, and has elevated him (above the animals, etc.] while had done nothing nor possessed any moral quality that would entitle him to deserve any divine reward.[137]

The womb [in a woman] servers to preserve and develop the seed. And so, it is with the rest of the bodily organs. They all of their specific functions, of which more are unknown than are known to us. So too, one who reflects on these on these matters will take notice of the natural processes by which the nourishment received by the body is appointed

---

134. Segol, *Kabbalah*, p. 93.
135. Segol, *Kabbalah*, p. 94.
136. Rabeinu Bahya, *Duties of the Heart: Chovot HaLevovot: Chapter Two Second Treatise on Examination*, trans. Rabbi Yosef Sebag (Niagara Falls, New York: Simchat Chaim, 2020), p. 67, Kindle Edition.
137. Bahya, *Heart*, pp. 72–73.

to every one of its parts. These marks of wisdom observed by him will stir him to thank His Creator and praise Him for them.[138]

Bahya focuses on the concept of meditating on the body to develop the seed in a woman's womb. The connection between the letters of creation, that also created offspring, through ibn Gabirol about uniting the physical with the cosmos, down to Bahya telling readers to meditate on their own inner divinity, via the scriptures, to bring nourishment to all parts, thus infusing the child with divinity also.

Houston's Kabbalistic beliefs, which was shown earlier to be embedded in the LHP as well, make her believe that the gods of her Hillsong, and other Prosperity, WoF, and NAR churches, can produce more gods that help them to spread their demonic acausal kingdom all over the earth.

Bringing this Entire Chapter Together

The realization that the biblical Christian church is engaged in battle with the demonic forces of one of the biggest Satanist organizations in the world, that being the Hillsong, Prosperity, WoF, and NAR churches, is no longer in question. The problem is how far do we let it progress, how far are these Satanists willing to go, and how can we stop something so traumatic from happening?

To address the issue first about magic and the attempt to bring the acausal to earth, magic is something that is powerless before the triune-God and also really has no existence outside the spiritual forces in our world. Despite Jonathan Cahn's claim in his book *Return of the Gods* that "as the spirits had been cast out of the house, they could only return by casting out that by which they had themselves been cast out, the Spirit of God,"[139] the Spirit of God cannot be "forced" out by any force, by any means whatsoever. For Cahn to hold to a view of God like that, Cahn believes in a heretical view of God that is dualistic in the means that he believes the demonic can overpower God and force the Holy Spirit out of an area, a nation, even a continent. Theologically, the demonic overpowering the Holy Spirit is nonsense.

At the same time, Christ does warn us that "false christs and false prophets will arise and perform great signs and wonders, so as to lead astray, if possible, even the elect." (Matthew 24:24 ESV) So these false signs and miracles can happen, but as Christ has told us, these are to test the Christian church to make sure we do not fall away. There have been accounts of occultic power working in some way, why God

---

138. Bahya, *Heart*, p. 89.
139. Jonathan Cahn, *The Return of the Gods* (Lake Mary, Florida: Charisma House, 2022), p. 199, Kindle Edition.

allows this is hard to say, but going back to Matthew 24:24, it is most likely so that God is warning those with "eyes to see" what these false powers really are.

With political groups like Klaus Schwab's WEF that wants to commit mass murder to make us gods, the likely links from the WEF to Brian Houston and Hillsong, to the belief of these Satanist churches, like Hillsong in chapter six, what will happen when their magic spell does not work. It is not hard to imagine that starting Sunday at 0000 hours at the International Date Line, that there is a 24 hour, and more, long ritual going on in churches in every time zone that are singing occult music designed to try and draw the acausal, or "heaven", to earth. Despite every argument given in defense of the music, the connection to these Satanist churches, the ONA and the acausal, the ritual purposes of their music, and what the end goals in their eschatology are, what will happen when these churches get tired of their weekly ritual that goes for over 24 hours around the world, constantly not working?

In Chapter 11 of her book *Beyond Belief*, Hardy shows some groups that are worshipping the military of Israel, some even in the area of Palestine that are running war drills for when the time comes to "fight for the kingdom."[140] This may be funny to some, but the reality is that there are "religious military" groups that are training for literal war. Likewise, Sanctuary Church, a Trump-loving church from Newfoundland, Pennsylvania is a church that is also preparing for war.[141] The pastor of the church Reverand Hyung Jin Moon is known for preaching from his pulpit with a firearm. There are churches, not just across the oceans, but in North America that are ready for a bloody conflict. These same churches are worshippers and fully committed to the men, like Trump, that are connected directly to the higher echelons of the Satanist churches that are being exposed in this book.

As I said already in this section, when the weekly ritual fails, and the acausal fails to come, what will Houston, Johnson, Meyer, Tomlin, and their other associates decide to do? Are we ready to have armed militia of these Satanist pastors invade our churches? The hope of the Satanist churches of bringing the acausal to earth is also embedded in Russo's idea about the New Atlantis. If Russo is correct, and the mixing of the political and religious in the United States suggests that he is, will the starting point be right here in North America? What will you say when they hold a gun to your head and ask: "Are you a Christian?" obviously, you will say, "yes." When these militiamen

---

140. Hardy, *Beyond*, pp. 259–260.
141. *Sanctuary Church*, July 19, 2023, https://www.sanctuary-pa.org/.

ask the second question: "What is the gospel?" are you ready to take a bullet in your head if you do not say either, "the prosperity gospel" or that "I am a god"? Remember that just like Guatemala, when the main head apostle of this movement C. Peter Wagner said that in expanding the church "the ends always justify the means," eventually these Satanists, using the defense of strategic-level spiritual warfare, will use the excuse that they are getting rid of "demons", not "people", in order to come after the biblical church founded on the true gospel of Christ.

This bloodshed can be stopped in its tracks before it goes too far. The solution is to stop playing their music in our churches every Sunday. The Proclaim program offered through Faithlife is one of many musical permissions distributors available to churches. With the Proclaim user agreement, if you put the copyright information, otherwise known as CCLI, at the bottom of the first screen of the song you are using, then the money that is paid to that service every month, a share of that will only go to that artist. However, there is another option, where you do not have to disclose the CCLI information, but in that case, the money you are paying Proclaim will go to these Satanist churches regardless of whether you play their songs or not. With their bloody intentions to spread their church with "the ends always justify the means", are you as pastors, laypersons, music leaders comfortable sending money each week that will one day be used to persecute and execute the very members of your church? As leaders we are called to protect the sheep from wolves, however, the very wolves we are to be protecting the sheep from are being paid every week and month money that will lead our sheep to needless slaughter. Looking at how deep these Satanist churches infrastructures are across the world, without that weekly income from royalties, their churches will not survive long at all.

Are you as leaders of a "biblical" church okay with this? If you as a leader, are morally ambiguous, or are completely in agreement, towards funding a Satanist war machine, you should not be in ministry.

Chapter X: The Flawed Argument of the "Doctrinal Smell Test"

Some of you might not be aware of the "doctrinal smell test" terminology. When a group of church leaders claim that: "we have gone over the words and find them okay/acceptable and that there is no problem with them", this is what is meant by the "doctrinal smell test".

Anyone that has had true experience with or has extensive knowledge about the occult will inherently find this argument flawed. I will show why this argument is flawed below. The reason the New Age movements, and particularly esotericism is so tricky and deceptive in the evangelical church, is because of how close the language and terms are that are used both in evangelicalism and esoteric practice. The Satanist church has also adopted this language to get their music past a church's "smell test". This has undoubtedly shocked many of you when you first read this, but you will see a whole new side of deception with this that proves that the doctrinal smell test is a flawed argument. And since, the evidence will show that the doctrinal smell test is a flawed argument, what does that leave as an argument for using it?

To be honest, the doctrinal smell test argument is nothing more but a rephrased excuse for emotional manipulation. Again, if this statement angers you, be prepared to have your conscience challenged. Realize that when emotional manipulation is involved, there is no room for theological facts and realities. The reason why facts do not matter is because the occult has used that same emotional manipulation to convince these leaders to use Satanism as regulative in church liturgy.

Do These Pass the Doctrinal Smell Test?

At this point I am going to quote three sources. Before I tell you what these sources are, I want you to think through what is being said, and what is being "praised" in these verses. Those that have experience with the occult will probably pick these up right away for what they are.

> Here is the first:
> God, YHWH, God of Israel
> Blessed are you YHWH, great God in might
> Who is like you in heaven and on earth?
> Holy in heaven and holy on earth?
> He is the holy King
> He is the blessed King
> His is the magnificent King over the whole chariot
> You have stretched our heaven
> You have founded Your throne
> And Your great name is ornamented over the throne of your glory
> You spread out earth and You founded on it a throne as Your footstool
> Your glory fills the world
> Your great name is an all might
> And there is no number to your acts of understandings
> You know the mysteries of the world
> You know the mysteries of the world
> And search out wise things and ways of things made secret
> Who is comparable to You
> Who tests hearts and searches out the inner affections
> And understands thoughts?
> There is nothing at all hidden from You
> And nothing is made secret from before your eyes
> All the living and dead
> Blessings and curses
> The good and the evil are give into Your hand
> And Your name is magnificent in heaven and on earth
> Great of vigor in heaven and on earth
> Blessed in heaven and on earth
> Glorified in heaven and on earth
> Merciful in heaven and on earth
> Holy in heaven and on earth
> Zeal for the invocation of Your name I forever and ever and ever until the end of all generations
> This is Your name forever
> And this Your invocation from generation to generation
> Merciful and gracious is Your name
> Your mercies are mighty upon the uppermost ones and the lowermost ones
> Your words are good upon lovers of Your Torah

Your pronouncements are pure upon those who declare Your name
>holy
Your way is on the sea
And Your road on the waters
You founded Your throne with vigor and might
Song and melody
Clouds of fire
Zealous ones of awe
Captains of fear
A thousand thousands of thousands
And myriads of myriads of myriads
The praise and laud to Your great, might and fearsome name
Before Your stand all the mighty ones who are magnificent
In praise and in melody
In chambers of Torah
And in treasures of blessing
From Heaven they praise
And from the firmament they bless
On one side is blessing
And on the other praise
Who is God like you[1]

The theology in here seems perfectly okay. Here is the second one:

[Title] Your Kingdom Comes
Let your kingdom's glory be revealed
Over a poor and wandering people
And reign, Lord who has ruled forever
Before the reign of any King.

Ransom the nation that longs for your presence
Lord who dwells in the heights of heaven
Over all gods you have dominion-
Who won't fear you, O my King?

A living Lord, you surround me with favor;
My songs of praise have given you pleasure.
Into your city gather the scattered,
For the people's greatness is the glory of the King.

I hope for the time of your redemption,
And wait with patience for your salvation.
If it tarries, Lord, in our absence,
I will look for no other King.

Without believing the good would appear,
In no time at all, I would wither.
May my bud of deliverance be watered-

---

1. James R. Davila, *Hekhalot Literature in Translation: Major Texts of Merkavah Mysticism* (Leiden, Netherlands: Brill, 2013), pp. 256–258.

O my Living Lord and King.

Strengthen the bars of my gates and doors
As you raise up the flock that remains.
Set my footsteps toward Sion's mountain;
Let me walk by the light of my King.

Bring my people back to you There,
And I will rejoice around your altar.
With a new song, I will offer
Thanks to you, my Lord and King.[2]

Once again, there really seems to be no problem here doctrinally. Here is the third and last example:

> Oh you [who] dwell are mighty in the Parts of the Earth, and execute judgement of the Highest. To you it is said, Behold the face of your God, the beginning of comfort; whose eyes are the brightest of the heavens; which provided you for the government of the earth and [its] unspeakable variety; furnishing you with a power (of) understanding to dispose all things according to the providence of Him that sitteth upon the Holy Throne.[3]

This last one I will admit there is some "odd" wording in it. This one is quoted and has one word in each square bracket changed to make a point that I will reveal below after I show where each of these "poems" or "hymns" come from. Even the one above with footnote 3, compared to some of the songs that pass the "doctrinal smell test", this last poems' theology is not as bad as some songs that have worse theology that is sung every Sunday morning. So again, this "poem" proves a point.

The first, seems good, and the words seem joyful and triumphant about the person of Yhwh. Well, it is not. This in fact a Merkavah Mysticism hymn from the Hekhalot texts of the first millennium. I described what Merkavah Mysticism was in chapter three.

As well, the Merkavah Mysticism texts, and this quoted hymn in particular, is a necromantic hymn that is designed to call on angels and to be given authority to command them. So, what is the reality of this hymn that passes the "doctrinal smell test"? It is a hymn designed for necromantic purposes, that being the calling of and commanding of angels. The reality of this "hymn" should trouble you. Since most of you read through it seeing no issue with it, again, it shows the "doctrinal smell test" is a flawed argument.

---

2. Peter Cole, *The Poetry of Kabbalah: Mystical Verse from the Jewish Tradition* (London, England: Yale University Press, 2012), pp. 166–167.

3. Leitch, *Angelical*, p. 164.

The second poem is from a text you by now will be quite familiar with. The second poem is a Kabbalistic poem. Again, this poem passes the "doctrinal smell test". What anyone that does not know where this poem comes from has just done, is allowed a poem, designed to draw esoteric power to yourself, into your Sunday morning liturgy.

The third one was a bit manipulated by me for a very specific purpose. With the square bracketed changes, it really is not that bad. Strange in a way, but doctrinally not a problem. Just seems like a strange way to acknowledge Christ. This is not a poem or a hymn in any way. This text comes from a text written by John Dee. John Dee is the one that brought in the idea of "Angel Magic" the "angelic language" and also the idea that a language called "Enochian" was used by Adam and his descendants until the time of the flood.

This should shock all of you. By altering two words, a flat-out necromantic call, that is used to divine secrets from magic tables and angels, is now being used as praiseworthy in your Sunday morning liturgy. This "changing of words" is the same thing that the Satanist churches have done in taking the acausal teaching and changing the words to make it sound "Christian".

The point should be clear here. The "doctrinal smell test" is flawed in every way. Many churches are happy to admit that churches like Hillsong, the other Satanist churches and even some of Tomlin's actions are in stark error and even steeped in the occult. However, these "biblical" churches insistence on using this music is in clear error and forbidden by the Bible.

If the songs coming out of those churches that are steeped in occultic and Satanic doctrine are acceptable for use in your church, then songs that are praising, and even calling on necromantic spirits are being used in your church. There is no "two-tiered" level here. The Bible does not offer areas of grey when it comes to the occult. From the first stroke of the law to the final chapter of Revelation, any and all use of the occult and spirits/necromancy is forbidden and will leave people that use this stuff outside the kingdom. I am not saying that if you are using this music in your churches that God will declare you apostate, what I am saying is that you are involved in occultic activity and are pushing it on your fellow church members and congregants by supporting the use of these occultic songs and hymns. The comparison is made. The "doctrinal smell test" argument is stamped out and does not work. To argue that is to contradict yourself.

To church leaders: if you do not believe this all, read the evidence above again. You have allowed yourself to have been led away and to lead others away to false teachers that Christ warned us about.

> Then if anyone says to you, "Look, here is the Christ!" or "There he is!" do not believe it. For false christs and false prophets will arise and perform great signs and wonders, so as to lead astray, if possible, even the elect. See, I have told you beforehand. So, if they say to you, "Look, he is in the wilderness," do not go out. If they say, 'Look, he is in the inner rooms,' do not believe it. (Matthew 24:23–26 ESV)

By bringing this Satanism, and LHP doctrine, into your church, and using it as regulative worship, like Christ warned, the elect have been deceived. Using this Satanism, and LHP music, as regulative worship, you have told the very people in your church, "here is the Christ!", "he is in the wilderness," and most shockingly "he is in the inner rooms" (our church sanctuaries/chapels/gathering rooms etc.), even though Christ has said, "do not believe it." However, because of you as a church leader bringing this Satanism, and LHP deception, into your church, you have in fact done the very things Christ warned us not to do, or to be fooled by.

Why Do Churches Use This Stuff Then?

In the introduction I suggested that the reason that church leaders will allow this music because they have deemed it okay to be nothing more than emotional manipulation. What do I mean by that?

Let us look at a quote by a well-known NAR Satanist:

> Music bypasses all of the intellectual barriers, and when the anointing of God is on a song, people will begin to believe things they wouldn't believe through teaching. —The 'apostle' Bill Johnson.[4]

Read that again if you are in shock. Bill Johnson is not wrong in this quote. Music has often been used historically as a brainwashing agent. Music has also been used in many circumstances to purposely emotionally manipulate you even in the grocery store and movie theatre. Music that has certain tempos or certain lyrics can put us into moods and mental states that will make us more likely to purchase items or even believe things we normally would not. Johnson is aware of the manipulative power of music. And since Johnson is aware of this manipulative power, the music that passes the "doctrinal smell test" is

---

4. Bill Johnson as quoted by Holly Pivec and R. Douglas Geivett, *Counterfeit Kingdom* (Nashville, Tennessee: B&H Publishing Group, 2022), p. 139, Kindle Edition. In an endnote about this quote the authors note that "This quote by Bill Johnson was posted to the WorshipU Facebook page on September 24, 2019. WorshipU is the online worship school of Bethel Redding. The original WorshipU Facebook page can no longer be found, but a screen capture of the post quoting Johnson was posted to the *Bethel Church and Christianity* Facebook page, September 24, 2019, accessed October 12, 2021, https://www.facebook.com/BethelChurchandChristianity/photos/a.604267139610313/2363002987070044." (p. 249), Kindle Edition.

part of this emotional manipulation to get "biblically literate" church leaders to allow occultic music that is not designed to praise the God of heaven into regular Sunday morning liturgy. Let me be plain here: the church leaders that are allowing this music into your church using the "doctrinal smell test" have been emotionally manipulated into getting not just this book's definition of Satanism, but the LHP into your church. This manipulation has been done on purpose. Because they have been emotionally manipulated, they are passing that emotional manipulation to their own church members and congregants making it a breeding ground of Satanist doctrine.

What is worse, is that because churches like Hillsong, the other Satanist churches, including Chris Tomlin have admitted to occultic purposes for their music, these "biblical" churches are allowing magical rituals, or "chants", that are changing the minds, convictions, and beliefs of the very flock they are supposed to be shepherding. A flock that may well turn into a Satanist church that will have no problem turning other believers over to the sacrificial sweep that is due to come when the Satanist churches fail to bring the acausal down to earth.

When using this music, it inevitably draws people that are supporting these Satanists to your church. Having interacted with some of these individuals, they admitted that they would go home and turn on Satanist churches YouTube sermons for "deeper truth" when that pastor that Sunday is not saying the things they want to agree with. Although pastors will claim that their preaching should change people's minds, the fact is that it does not. The claim is also often made that the people in the church should know better that what music from the Satanist churches is good or not. This assumption that people should know better is again flawed. It is a subvert emotional manipulation technique where the leaders of the church are passing the blame to the congregants if they get caught in the Satanist trap. The leaders of the church will do as Pontius Pilate did and "wash their hands of it" and claim this was the congregants' fault and not their own.

Conclusion

I do not usually use analogous stories to make a point, but this may be a point at which one is useful.

A person, wishing to open a bar is a big fan of the band *The Cure*. So, he opens a bar and dedicates two nights to his favourite band where on those two nights only *The Cure* is being played.

After a few months, the bar owner notices that on these two nights, there is a larger and larger goth crowd coming and becoming regular patrons of his bar. The owner does not even like goth subculture and finds it weird and creepy. He tries to make it clear that this is not a goth bar and to get the goth kids to go somewhere else.

Instead, on the nights the bar is not playing *The Cure*, the goth kids start showing up then as well. The goth attendees of the bar continue to increase throughout the week. The bar owner is wondering what is going on.

Calling another bar that is not connected to his in any way that is on the other side of the city, the bar owner asks that owner if he has ever heard of this first owner's bar.

The other bar owner that was called says that "oh, that's that new goth bar on the other side of town, right?"

Dismayed, the bar owner does not know what to do. If he stops playing *The Cure* like he is, he will be bankrupt in a matter of days. The bar now has that reputation, and anyone that knows the bar and club scene knows that once a bar has a reputation of being a goth bar, it never goes away and pushes away a lot of potential customers.

In case you were not aware: *The Cure* is a pioneer goth band. If you talk to the goth community and ask them about *The Cure*, all of them will tell you that band is a goth band.

To quote a well-known movie as well, "if you build it, they will come."

What is my point here? This music from the Satanist churches is derived from the occult. The occultic poems, hymns and calls I gave show that even the most devious of occultic material can pass the doctrinal smell test. Using this Satanist music will draw the wrong "Christians" to your church. Just because something is claiming to be "Christian", even though the elders and church leaders are aware of the dangers of the Satanist churches and their Satanist beliefs, does not allow permissive use of this music in any way.

The only reason the "doctrinal smell test" argument is used, is because Bill Johnson, in the quote I provided from him, has succeeded in doing what he intended to do all along, emotionally manipulated your church leaders, via the occult, to get his Satanic music into your church. Hillsong is no different as was shown in previous chapters.

If your church is playing this music and justifying it "because the words are good", show them those poems, hymns, and calls I provided, ask them if they are "okay". If the churches leaders say these are okay, those leaders need to be called to account.

Another defense that has been attempted is the example of the Christmas Tree being "redeemed." There are two problems with this argument. The first problem is that it is not guaranteed by historical evidence that the Christmas Tree was originally a pagan item. There is evidence from the earliest church fathers that suggests the Christmas Tree was in use already then. Second, the Christmas Tree was never an active ritual item, but rather a festive one. The songs and hymns given in this chapter are active ritual spell chants, just like the songs from Hillsong and other Satanist churches. To put occult music and a festive tree under the same label is a huge category error.

Therefore, just as no hymns, poems, or chants from the occult, no matter how "theologically correct" they are, have ever been "redeemed" from the occult, the songs from the Satanist churches cannot be redeemed either. To put it simply: you cannot redeem the occult. The reason they cannot be redeemed is that they are intended as active occult practices that are intending to cause occultic things to happen. Trying to redeem the occult is again due to being emotionally manipulated by the occult to bring Satanim into your church.

Conclusion: Call Your Leaders to Repent

I get it. This entire book, and what it shows is disturbing. The problem is that the facts are the facts and too many people want to brush them aside for the sake of their own emotional preferences and the emotional manipulation of others in their churches. Enough is enough.

One thing that I am not saying is: I could not care less what you listen to in the privacy of your own home or while singing a Grammy winning performance in your car. If you want to listen to Hillsong in your own time, go right ahead. The problem has become when churches are normalizing this music as regulative worship. For instance, no one in a church would care if you were playing the Backstreet Boys at home. Would that music be appropriate for Sunday morning worship liturgy? No, but at home, no one, even myself, would care that you like to listen to Backstreet Boys at home.

However, the question does need to be answered, after seeing all the information above, is your conscience okay with playing any of these Satanists music in the privacy of your own home? If the answer is "yes", then I have no issue with it, but do not force it on other people such as Romans 14 commands you not to. If it does bother you however, in the privacy of someone else's home, it is not your place to tell them not to listen to Hillsong, Bethel, Elevation, Chris Tomlin etc. This was the problem in the church that asked me not to come back. They accused me of committing a greater sin of "neglecting the fellowship" for not wanting to be involved in the music program at all because of their convictions with this music on Sunday mornings. I told the leadership that as Jesus says, "a little yeast goes through the whole bread," but they maintained that I was neglecting the fellowship, completely not just for the music by leaving and coming back when the music was done. Doing that, to them I was committing a greater sin than violating my conscience. This is where the accusation of spiritual abuse from the elders came from. Anyone reading that can see that the accusation is justified. Apparently, since I did not want to participate in Satanism, I was committing a greater sin by stepping out for the music, then being a part of it. I will leave that for you, the reader, to think about yourself.

Personal insults, and ad hominemn, are also not beyond their pervue. When challenged about my convictions, an elder, who runs a prominent street ministry in my country of origin, as well that as received money for his independent ministry from the elders board he sits on, felt it necessary to call me "immature" for refusing to be a part of Satanism being practiced in that church almost every Sunday and properly showing the spiritual abuse for what it was. An elder, who runs a street ministry that accepts Satanism as regulative for Sunday mornings. Again, I will leave that for you to think about.

This is how far those people that want to justify using Satanism in their churches on Sunday mornings will go. When they cannot give a good theological reason to say why this music *theologically* is okay, they will instead twist and pull scripture to try to find a way around the issue entirely and accuse of you something else, which is a red herring fallacy.

As can be seen, however, with the claim to divine right like King James proclaimed to tell his people that he had the right to do "whatever" he wished, the Satanic apostles in these movements do as well. Then an analysis was done that showed that the leaders of Hillsong, Prosperity, WoF and NAR movements do truly believe that we are our own "gods", that there is a problem. The next chapter defined what esotericism from the Right-Hand Path is and how that enables these movements to use biblical language to infiltrate the biblical church. Chapter four defined very directly what the Left-Hand Path is and clearly showed that the Satanist churches, of Hillsong, Prosperity, WoF, and NAR all fit appropriately under that occult movement. Chapter five revealed how far these Satanists will at one time go to push what this chapter shows, through Brian Houston, to be the "true" gospel, and not the real gospel of penal substitutionary atonement. In chapter six the evidence is undeniably given about how Hillsong, and Chris Tomlin, are intending their music for occultic purposes. Chapter seven gives the facts about the belief in many churches about "praying for angels to protect us" and how that entire belief falls under what the Bible condemns as necromancy, and how the church leaders in chapter six directly intended their music for necromantic purposes. Chapter eight is where the conversation became more serious and the reality of Lilith, the LHP, and the involvement of the demonic Assyrian-Lilith in the Satanist churches was laid out clearly. Then, the most disturbing chapter of all, where the intentions, beliefs, and eschatology of Hillsong, Prosperity, WoF, and NAR churches falls line for line the same as one of the most dangerous groups of LHP Satanists in the world, the Order of Nine Angles. A lot of disturbing information was given in that long chapter, but it clearly showed that these Satanist movements are preaching and teaching the world things from the Bible that are not biblical but are rooted in one of the most extreme forms of the LHP we could ever imagine. Lastly, chapter ten shows that when using the "Doctrinal Smell Test" argument that churches are just trying to emotionally manipulate you with the occult just like they were. The argument does not work. When these church leaders are playing the music from these Satanist churches and telling you that you can "meet Jesus" here, that they are doing exactly as Jesus warned about false teachers in Matthew 24:23-26.

At this point can church leaders really look anyone in the face after reading this and say that they can justify sending money to churches that promote and encourage murder? Remember that Wagner said this, and these churches are all promoting him and pushing his teaching as a new gospel.

The influence that these leaders have on United States politics already is showing that these churches are moving to most likely seize control of one of the most powerful nations via a proxy in Trump or mostly likely, someone else. When this happens, since these men and women have all shown, and admitted just how far they are willing to go, can we continue to justify sending them money and using their music? Are you as church leaders comfortable funding a future war machine against your own flock? The evidence points in that direction in every way, and it cannot be denied.

Leaders, pastors, music teams that have all pushed this music on people who have been resistant to it and have even enacted church discipline on the resisters up to and including excommunication, over music that is funding a war effort against their own people, need to be confronted. These same leaders need to stand up in front of their churches, admit to what the facts are about what these churches are doing, promoting, and intending and repent for it and to repent to the people they have spiritually abused in order to be claiming "ignorance" on the issue.

Going back to *The Matrix*, how many Cypher's are in our churches that are willing to do whatever they need to, in order to remain "ignorant"? As I said, in Romans 1, ignorance is not an excuse in any way. God will not accept ignorance as an excuse. God's wrath will come to these churches that are claiming wilful ignorance on the issue.

Emotionalism cannot be involved here. "The words are okay" cannot be an excuse anymore.

Like in *The Matrix* after Cypher was about to kill the main character Neo, another character in the protagonist team that Cypher thought he had killed, Tank, stood up and shot Cypher dead. I am not encouraging that we take these leaders out and do the same, but these leaders need to stand and have the church discipline them for what they have done to their own people and to victims that they have metaphorically, "thrown out the door".

When it comes to God's truth and his church: keep fighting, even if you are no longer able to stand, keep fighting. Never willingly let the demonic win.

If you are a church leader that is unwilling to repent of the use of this music because you are unwilling to accept the facts, then you are not qualified to be in ministry.

BIBLIOGRAPHY

Alexander, P. "3 (Hebrew Apocalypse of) Enoch (Fifth–Sixth Centurty A.D.) A New Translation and Introduction." In *The Old Testament Pseudepigrapha Volume 1*. Edited by James H. Charlesworth, pp. 223–315. New York, New York: Yale University Press, 1983.

Apologia Studies. "Debate With LGBT Theologian Brandan Robertson." *YouTube*. July 15, 2023. https://www.youtube.com/watch?v=ti0FzdOHW_8.

Assembly at Edinburg. "The Westminster Shorter Catechism." *A Puritan's Mind*. July 18, 2023. https://www.apuritansmind.com/westminster-standards/shorter-catechism/.

Author Unknown. "Baphomet and Opfer." *Opfer, Fenrir* Vol. II, no 2 (2009): p. 1.

Bahya, Rabeinu. *Duties of the Heart: Chovot HaLevovot: Chapter Two Second Treatise on Examination*. Translated by Rabbi Yosef Sebag. Niagara Falls, New York: Simchat Chaim, 2020. Kindle Edition.

BattleDungeon. "Joyce Meyer – Little Gods." *YouTube*. July 12, 2023. https://www.youtube.com/watch?v=9–hsd7MTq24.

Benarroch, Jonathan M. "'The Mystery of (Re)incarnation and the Fallen Angels': The Reincarnations of Adam, Enoch, Metatron, (Jesus), and Joseph—An Anti-Christian Polemic in the Zohar." *Journal of Medieval Religious Cultures*. Volume 44, No. 2 (2018): pp. 117-147.

Bethel Church and Christianity Facebook page, September 24, 2019, accessed October 12, 2021, https://www.facebook.com/BethelChurchandChristianity/photos/a.604267139610313/2363002987070044." In *Counterfeit Kingdom* by Holly Pivec and R. Douglas Geivett, p. 249. Nashville, Tennessee: B&H Publishing Group, 2022. Kindle Edition. Kindle Edition.

Brown, Francis, Samuel Rolles Driver, and Charles Augustus Briggs. *Enhanced Brown-Driver-Briggs Hebrew and English Lexicon*. Oxford, England: Clarendon Press, 1977. Logos Editioin.

Bullard, Roger A., "The Hypostasis of the Archons (II, 4)." In *The Nag Hammadi Library in English*. Edited by James M. Robinson. Translater by Bentley Layton, 4th rev. ed. (Leiden, Netherlands: Brill, 1996).

Burket, Walter. *Greek Religion*. Malden, Massachusetts: Blackwell Publishing, 1985.

Cahn, Jonathan. *The Return of the Gods*. Lake Mary, Florida: Charisma House, 2022. Kindle Edition.

Callahan, Wesley. "Satyrs, Liliths & Lunatics." In *The Forgotten Heavens*. Edited by Douglas Wilson, pp. 115–124. Moscow, Idaho: Canon Press, 2010.

Carboni, Romina. "Between Astarte, Isis and Aphrodite/Venus. Cultural Dynamics in the Coastal Cities of Sardinia in the Roman Age: The Case Study of Nora." In *Naming and Mapping the Gods in the Ancient Mediterranean*. Edited by Thomas Galoppin, Elodie Guillon, Max Luaces, Asuman Lätzer-Lasar, Sylvain Lebreton, Fabio Porzia, Jörg Rüpke, Emiliano Rubens Urciuoli and Corinne Bonnet, pp. 561–576. Berlin, Germany: De Gruyter, 2022.

Carsten, June. *Blood Work*: *Life and Labratories In Penang*. London, England: Duke University Press, 2019.

Cavendish, Richard. *The Black Arts*: *An Absorbing Account of Witchcraft, Demonology, Astrology, and other Mystical Practices Throughout the Ages*. New York, New York: TarcherPerigee, 2017.

Chapell, Bryan. *Ephesians*. Edited by Richard D. Phillips, Philip Graham Ryken, and Daniel M. Doriani. Reformed Expository Commentary. Phillipsburg, New Jersey: P&R Publishing, 2009. Logos Edition.

Cole, Peter. The Poetry of Kabbalah: Mystical Verse from the Jewish Tradition. London, England: Yale University Press, 2012.

Conway, David. Magic: An Occult Primer. Newport, Rhode Island: The Witches' Almanac, 2019.

Daniels, Kimberly. Clean House, Strong House: A Practical Guide to Understanding Spiritual Warfare, Demonic Strongholds and Deliverance. Lake Mary, Florida: Charisma House, 2013. Logos Edition.

Däumer, Matthias. "Eschatological Relativity. On the Scriptural Undermining of Apocalypses in Jewish Second Temple, Late Antique and Medieval Receptions of the Book of Watchers" In Cultures of Eschatology: Volume 1: Empires and Scriptural Authorities in Medieval Christian, Islamic and Buddhist Communities. Volume 2: Time, Death and Afterlife in Medieval Christian, Islamic and Buddhist Communities. Edited by Veronika Wieser, Vincent Eltschinger and Johann Heiss, pp. 254–274. Berlin, Boston: De Gruyter Oldenbourg, 2020.

Davila, James R. Hekhalot Literature in Translation: Major Texts of Merkavah Mysticism. Leiden, Netherlands: Brill, 2013.

Denton, Andrew. Kingdom Builders. Castle Hill, New South Wales, Australia: Shout! Publishing, 2020. Kindle Edition.

Douglas, J. D. "Lilith." In New Bible Dictionary. Edited by D. R. W. Wood et al., p. 691. Downers Grove, Illinois: InterVarsity Press, 1996. Logos Edition.

Easton, M. G. Illustrated Bible Dictionary and Treasury of Biblical History, Biography, Geography, Doctrine, and Literature, New York: Harper & Brothers, 1893. Logos Edition.

Eckhart, John. Deliverance and Spiritual Warfare Manual. Lake Mary, Florida: Charisma House, 2014.

Edward, Pauline. *Aquarius: The Age of Revelation, Choice and Transformation*. Montreal, Quebec, Canada: Desert Lily Publications, 2021. Kindle Edition.

Eldridge, Lori. "Benny Hinn's False Teachings About God Exposed," Endtime Prophets, July 22, 2023, https://www.endtime–prophets.com/hinn.html.

Elwell, Walter A., and Barry J. Beitzel, "Necromancer, Necromancy." Baker Encyclopedia of the Bible, p. 1535. Grand Rapids, Michigan: Baker Book House, 1988. Logos Edition.

Fischer, Lars. "The Legacy of Anti–Judaism in Bach's Sacred Cantatas." In *Jews and Protestants*. Edited by Irene Aue–Ben–David, Aya Elyada, Moshe Sluhovsky and Christian Wiese, pp. 79–96. Ingersoll, Ontario, Canada: Devoted Publishing, 2023.

Flowers Ph.D., Stephen E. *Lords of the Left–Hand Path: Forbidden Practices and Spiritual Heresies*. Toronto, Ontario, Canada: Inner Traditions/Bear & Company, 2012. Kindle Edition.

Ford, Michael W. *The Bible of the Adversary: 10th Anniversary Edition* (Houston, Texas: Succubus Productions, 2017. Kindle Edition.

France, R. T. *The Gospel of Matthew, The New International Commentary on the New Testament*. Grand Rapids, Michigan: Wm. B. Eerdmans Publication Co., 2007. Logos Edition.

Garcia, Zen. *The Collected Works of Enoch the Prophet*. Atlanta, Georgia: Sacred Word Publishing, 2017.

---. *Sacred Word Publishing*. July 20, 2023. https://sacredwordpublishing.com/.

---. *Yahushua Christ: Infancy Childhood and Lost Years*. Atlanta, Georgia: Sacred Word Publishing, 2017.

Gesenius, Wilhelm, and Samuel Prideaux Tregelles. *Gesenius' Hebrew and Chaldee Lexicon to the Old Testament Scriptures*. Bellingham, Washington: Logos Bible Software, 2003. Logos Edition.

Geivett, R. Douglas, Holly Pivec. *A New Apostolic Reformation?: A Biblical Response to a Worldwide Movement*. Bellingham, Washington: Lexham Press, 2014. Logos Edition.

Goll, James W. *Angelic Encounters: Engaging Help from Heaven.* Lake Mary, Florida: Charisma House, 2013. Logos Edition.

Granholm, Kennet. *Embracing the Dark: The Magic Order of the Dragon Rouge – Its Practice in Dark Magic and Meaning Making.* Sarrijärvi, Suomi: Åbo Akademi University Press, 2005.

Green, Joel B. *The Gospel of Luke, The New International Commentary on the New Testament.* Grand Rapids, Michigan: Wm. B. Eerdmans Publishing Co., 1997. Logos Edition.

Guthrie, Donald. *Pastoral Epistles: An Introduction and Commentary, vol. 14, Tyndale New Testament Commentaries.* Downers Grove, Illinois: InterVarsity Press, 1990. Logos Edition.

Haggart, G. P. *Screech Owl: The Lie Behind Lilith.* Morrisville, North Carolina: Lulu Press, Inc., 2009. Kindle Edition.

Hardy, Elle. *Beyond Belief: How Pentecostal Christianity Is Taking Over the World.* London, England: C. Hurst & Company, 2021. Kindle Edition.

Harris, Kevin A., Kate M. Panzica, and Ruth A. Crocker. "Paganism and Counseling: The Development of a Clinical Resource." *Open Theology*, vol. 2, no. 1, (2016): pp. 857–875.

Hart, David. *The Age of Aquarius: The Golden Age of Mankind.* London, England: Austin Macauley Publishers Ltd., 2018. Kindle Edition.

Hartley, John E. *Leviticus, vol. 4, Word Biblical Commentary.* Dallas, Texas: Word, Incorporated, 1992.

Heiser, Michael S. *Reversing Hermon: Enoch, The Watchers & The Forgotten Mission of Jesus Christ.* Bellingham, Washington: Lexham Press, 2017. Logos Edition.

Hendriksen, William, and Simon J. Kistemaker. *Exposition of Ephesians, vol. 7, New Testament Commentary.* Grand Rapids, Michigan: Baker Book House, 1953–2001. Logos Edition.,

Hodge, Charles. *Hodge's Systematic Theology Volume II – Anthropology* (Ingersoll, Ontario, Canada: Devoted Publishing, 2019.

Holladay, William Lee, and Ludwig Köhler. *A Concise Hebrew and Aramaic Lexicon of the Old Testament.* Leiden, Netherlands: Brill, 2000. Logos Edition.

Houston, Bobbie. *Heaven is in this House.* Castle Hill, New South Wales, Australia: Leadership Ministries Inc., 2001.

---. *The Sisterhood.* New York, New York: FaithWords, 2016. Kindle Edition.

Houston, Brian. *For This I Was Born.* Nashville, Tennessee: Thomas Nelson, 2018. Kindle Edition.

---. *How To Maximise Your Life.* Sydney, Australia: Hillsong Music Australia. Kindle Edition.

---. *Live Love Lead.* New York, New York: Faithwords, 2015. Kindle Edition.

---. *There is More.* New York, New York: Waterbrook, 2018. Kindle Edition.

Hutter, M. "Lilith." In *Dictionary of Deities and Demons in the Bible.* Edited by Karel van der Toorn, Bob Becking, and Pieter W. van der Horst, pp. 520–521. Leiden; Netherlands: Brill, 1999.

Ibn Gabirol, Solomon. *The Fountain of Life*, Location Unknown: E-Bookarama, 2023. Kindle Edition.

Introvigne, Massimo. *Satanism: A Social History.* Leiden, Netherlands: Brill, 2016.

Irenæus, *Against Heresies.* Ingersoll, Ontario, Canada: Devoted Publishing, 2020.

Isenberg, Wesley W. "The Gospel of Philip (II, 3)." In *The Nag Hammadi Library in English.* Edited by James M. Robinson. Translated by Søren Giversen. 4th rev. ed. Leiden; Netherlands: Brill, 1996. Logos Edition.

Johnson, Bill. *The Mind of God: How His Wisdom Can Transform Our World.* Grand Rapids, Michigan: Chosen, 2020. Logos Edition.

Johnson, Bill, and Mike Seth, *When Heaven Invades Earth for Teens: Your Guide to God's Supernatural Power.* Shippensburg, PA: Destiny Image, 2014. Logos Edition.

Johnson, Bill, as quoted by Holly Pivec and R. Douglas Geivett, *Counterfeit Kingdom*. Nashville, Tennessee: B&H Publishing Group, 2022. Kindle Edition.

Kalisch, Rev. Dr. Isidor. יצירה *Sepher Yezirah: A Book on Creation; or, The Jewish Metaphysics of Remote Antiquity*. Ingersoll, Ontario, Canada: Devoted Publishing, 2020.

Kaplan, Aryeh. *The Bahir: Illumination*. York Beach, Maine: Samuel Weiser, Inc. 1989.

Kidner, Derek. *Psalms 73–150: An Introduction and Commentary*, vol. 16, Tyndale Old Testament Commentaries. Downers Grove, Illinois: InterVarsity Press, 1975. Logos Edition.

Kruse, Colin G. *John: An Introduction and Commentary*. Edited by Eckhard J. Schnabel. Second edition., vol. 4, Tyndale New Testament Commentaries. London, England: InterVarsity Press, 2017. Logos Edition.

LaVey, Anton Szandor. *The Satanic Bible: Central Religious Text of LaVeyan Satanism*. New York, New York: William Morrow, 2022. Kindle Edition.

Lawrence, Abel. *The Books of Forbidden Knowledge: Witchcraft, The Satanic Bible and Necronomicon: Black Arts, Practical Magick, Demonology and Other Mystical Practices*. Independently Published, 2021. Kindle Edition.

Leitch, Aaron. *The Angelical Language Volume I*. Woodbury, Minnesota: Llewellyn Publications, 2010.

Levin, Tanya. *People in Glass Houses*. Collingwood, Victoria, Australia: Schwartz Publishing Pty. Inc., 2015. Kindle Edition.

Lewis, Charlton T. *An Elementary Latin Dictionary*. Medford, Massachusetts: American Book Company, 1890. Logos Edition.

Liddell, Henry George, et al. *A Greek–English Lexicon*. Oxford, England: Clarendon Press, 1996. Logos Edition.

Long, Anton. *Codex Saerus: The Black Book of Satan III*, Houston, Texas: Vindex Press, 1998.

Long, Anton. *A Complete Guide to the 7–Fold Sinister Way*. Houston, Texas: Vindex Press, 1994.

---. "H. P. Lovecraft & The Dark Gods." In *Codex Saerus: The Black Book of Satan III*, pp. 112–114. Edited by Anton Long. Houston, Texas: Vindex Press, 1998.

---. "The Development Of Arête." *o9a Order of Nine Angles*. July 16, 2023, https://www.o9a.org/wp-content/uploads/o9a-development-arete.pdf, p. 1.

---. *The Temple of Satan—A Symphonic Allegory*. Gent, Belgium: Skull Press, 2003.

LongforTruth1. "8 Reasons You Should Stop Listening to Andrew Wommack." *YouTube*. July 12, 2023, https://www.youtube.com/watch?v=B8wQasfaYto.

Main, Robin. "Metatron – Oneness of the Messiah Yeshua." *Sapphire Throne Ministries*. July 15, 2023. https://sapphirethroneministries.wordpress.com/2017/07/01/metatron–oneness–of–the–messiah–yeshua/.

---. *Understanding the Order of Melchizedek: Complete Series*. Masonville, Colorado: Sapphire Throne Ministries, 2017.

Marie, Hope. "Luciferianism & Our Origins." In *Wisdom of Eosphoros*. Edited by Michael Ford. Houston, Texas: Succubus Productions, 2015.

Martin, Walter, Jill Martin Rische, and Kurt Van Gorden. *The Kingdom of the Occult*. Nashville, Tennessee: Thomas Nelson, 2008.

Merrill, Eugene H. *Deuteronomy, vol. 4, The New American Commentary* (Nashville: Broadman & Holman Publishers, 1994. Logos Edition.

Morales, L. Michael. *Who Shall Ascend the Mountain of the Lord?: A Biblical Theology of the Book of Leviticus*. Edited by D. A. Carson. Vol. 37, New Studies in Biblical Theology. Downers Grove, Illinois: Apollos; InterVarsity Press, 2015. Logos Edition.

Morris, Leon. *Luke: An Introduction and Commentary, vol. 3, Tyndale New Testament Commentaries*. Downers Grove, Illinois: InterVarsity Press, 1988. Logos Edition.

Mounce, William D. *Basics of Biblical Greek Grammar*. Edited by Verlyn D. Verbrugge and Christopher A. Beetham, Fourth Edition. Grand Rapids, Michigan: Zondervan, 2019. Logos Edition.

Moyer, J. Alec. *Isaiah*. Downers Grove, Illinois: IVP Academic, 1999.

NBC News. "Christian Leaders Pray Over Trump During Launch Of Evangelicals For Trump Coalition | NBC News." *YouTube*. July 21, 2023. https://www.youtube.com/watch?v=HrBvMFJ_drs.

Oswalt, John N. *The Book of Isaiah Chapters 1–39*. Grand Rapids, Michigan: Wm. B. Eerdmans Publishing Company, 1986.

---. *The Book of Isaiah Chapters 40–66*. Grand Rapids, Michigan: Wm. B. Eerdmans Publishing Company, 1998.

Parke, Caleb "Pastors, worship leaders pray for Trump in Oval Office amid impeachment fight." *Fox News*. July 21, 2023. https://www.foxnews.com/politics/pastors–worship–leaders–pray–for–trump–in–oval–office–amid–impeachment–fight.

Pearson, Birger A. "The Testimony of Truth (IX, 3)," in *The Nag Hammadi Library in English*. Edited by James M. Robinson. 4th rev. ed. Leiden, Netherlands: Brill, 1996. Logos Edition.

Peterson, Joseph H. *Elucidation of Necromancy*. Lake Worth, Florida: Ibis Press, 2021.

---. *Secrets of Solomon*: *A Witch's Handbook from the trial records of the Venetian Inquisition*. Kasson, Minnesota: Twilit Grotto Press, 2018.

Pitterson, Ryan. *Judgment of the Nephilim*. New York, New York: Day of Noe Publishing, 2017.

Polite Leader. "Kenneth Copeland 'Adam Was God.'" *YouTube*. July 12, 2023. https://www.youtube.com/watch?v=J0PokWF4ees.

Plaskow, Judith. *The Coming of Lilith*: *A Feminist Theology*. Boston, Massachusetts: Beacon Press, 2005.

Psychology Today Staff. "Gaslighting." *Psychology Today*. July 20, 2023. https://www.psychologytoday.com/us/basics/gaslighting.

Redfern, Nic. *Secret Societies*: *The Complete Guide to Histories, Rites and Rituals*. Canton, Michigan: Visible Ink Press, 2017.

RevAlexMeadows. "Kenneth Copeland Prays For Trump (Latrobe, PA)." *YouTube*. July 21, 2023. https://www.youtube.com/watch?v=uw40kns811c.

Revealing Truth. "Kenneth Copeland Takes Creepy to a Whole New Level." *YouTube*. July 13, 2023. https://www.youtube.com/watch?v=–At56s393Ko.

Riabhaich, Coire. "CIRA: A Satanic Guide to Future Magick." In *Codex Saerus*: *The Black Book of Satan III*. Edited by Anton Long, pp. 93–111. Houston, Texas: Vindex Press, 1998.

Robinson, James McConkey, and Richard Smith. "Coptic Gnostic Library Project, On." In *The Nag Hammadi Library in English*. Edited by James M. Robinson. Translated by Søren Giversen. 4th rev. ed. Leiden; Netherlands: Brill, 1996. Logos Edition.

Rooker, Mark F. *Leviticus, vol. 3A, The New American Commentary*. Nashville, Tennessee: Broadman & Holman Publishers, 2000. Logos Edition.

Roy, Julie. "Leading Evangelicals Embrace Joyce Meyer at 40th Anniversarty Event." *The Roys Report*. July 13, 2023. https://julieroys.com/leading-evangelicals-embrace-joyce-meyer-at-40th-anniversary-event/.

Russo, Ed. *Lilith*: *The Power of the Woman's Spirit in the Age of Aquarius*. Morrisville, North Carolina: Lulu Press, Inc., 2014. Kindle Edition.

Salt and Light. "Bill Johnson teaches 'little god' heresy – 'You are the one'." *YouTube*. July 12, 2023. https://www.youtube.com/watch?v=o1nkAq00aBo.

Sanctuary Church. July 19, 2023. https://www.sanctuary–pa.org/.

Scholem, Gershom. *The Early Kabbalah*. Mahwah, New Jersey: Paulist Press, 1986.

Schwab, Klaus, and Thierry Malleret, *COVID–19*: *The Great Reset*. Geneva, Switzerland: Forum Publishing, 2020. Kindle Edition.

Sefaria. "Shabbat 55a." *The William Davidson Talmud*. July 18, 2023. https://www.sefaria.org/Shabbat.55a.12?lang=bi.

Segol, Marla. *Kabbalah and Sex Magic*: *23* (*Magic in History*). University Park, Pennsylvania: Penn State University, 2021. Kindle Edition.

Shaked, Shaul, James Nathan Ford, and Siam Bhayro. *Aramaic Bowl Spells*. Leiden, Netherlands: Brill, 2013.

Sperling, Harry, Maurice Simon, and Dr. Paul P. Levertoff. *The Zohar: An English Translation Volume One*. New York, New York: The Socino Press, 1984.

---. *The Zohar: An English Translation Volume Three*. New York, New York: The Socino Press, 1984.

Stirling, Rachael. "Masculous And Muliebral: The Sinister Feminine And Homo Hubris." *o9a Order of Nine Angles*. July 16, 2023. https://www.o9a.org/wp–content/, p. 1.

Storck, Thomas. *The Prosperity Gospel: How Greed and Bad Philosophy Distorted Christ's Teachings*. Ashland, Ohio: TAN Books, 2023. Logos Edition.

Storm, Tara. "Facebook Reply Post." *Facebook*. July 12, 2023. https://www.facebook.com/anthony.uyl/.

Stratton-Kent, Jake. *Geosophia: I*. London, England: Scarlet Imprint, 2010.

Stroumsa, Gedaliahu G. "Form(s) of God: Some Notes on Metatron and Christ." *Harvard Theological Journal* 76:3 (1983): pp. 269–288.

Stuckey, Allie Beth. "Pro-Life Christian vs Pro-Choice Leftist on Roe & Abortion | Guest: Brandan Robertson | Ep 612." *YouTube*. July 13, 2023. https://www.youtube.com/watch?v=HbxF6SRxJyk.

Swanson, James. *Dictionary of Biblical Languages with Semantic Domains: Hebrew (Old Testament)*. Oak Harbor, Washington: Logos Research Systems, Inc., 1997. Logos Edition.

Tanner, Beth. "Book Three of the Psalter: Psalms 73–89." *In The Book of Psalms*. Edited by E. J. Young, R. K. Harrison, and Robert L. Hubbard Jr. The New International Commentary on the Old Testament. Grand Rapids, Michigan: William B. Eerdmans Publishing Company, 2014. Logos Edition.

Thielman, Frank. *Ephesians, Baker Exegetical Commentary on the New Testament*. Grand Rapids, Michigan: Baker Academic, 2010. Logos Edition.

Thompson, J. A. *Deuteronomy: An Introduction and Commentary*, vol. 5, Tyndale Old Testament Commentaries. Downers Grove, Illinois: InterVarsity Press, 1974. Logos Edition.

Tomlin, Chris. "Wonderful night at the 40th anniversary of the Joyce Meyer conference...grateful to be part of the celebration." *Instagram*. July 13, 2023. https://www.instagram.com/p/Ci8pb2C-gFuA/.

Tomlin, Chris, and Darren Whitehead. *Holy Roar*. Nashville, Tennessee: Thomas Nelson, 2017. Kindle Edition.

Trismegistus, Hermes. *The Emerald Tablet of Hermes*. The Emerald Tablet of Hermes. Unknown Location: iap, 2009. Kindle Edition.

Trites, Allison A., and William J. Larkin. *Cornerstone Biblical Commentary, Vol 12: The Gospel of Luke and Acts*. Carol Stream, Illinois: Tyndale House Publishers, 2006. Logos Edition.

Twitchell, James B. *The Living Dead: A Study of the Vampire in Romantic Literature*. Durham, North Carolina: Duke University Press, 1997.

Uyl, Anthony. *Biblical Demonology: Their Origins and Unwilling Role in Sanctification*. Ingersoll, Ontario, Canada: Devoted Publishing, 2022.

Vallotton, Kris, and Bill Johnson. *The Supernatural Ways of Royalty: Discovering Your Rights and Privileges of Being a Son or Daughter of God*. Shippensburg, PA: Destiny Image, 2006. Logos Edition.

Venneman, Theo Vennemann gen. Nierfeld. *Germania Semitica*. Berlin, Germany: De Gruyter, 2013.

Wagner, C. Peter. *The Book of Acts: A Commentary*. Ventura, California: Regal, 2008. Logos Edition.

---. *Your Church Can Grow: Seven Vital Signs of a Healthy Church*. Eugene, Oregon; Wipf & Stock Publishers, 1998.

Wallnau, Lance, Bill Johnson, Alan Vincent, C. Peter Wagner, Ché Ahn, Patricia King, *Invading Babylon: The 7 Mountain Mandate*. Shippensburg, Pennsylvania: Destiny Image, 2013. Logos Edition.

Whitaker, William. *Dictionary of Latin Forms*. Bellingham, Washington: Logos Bible Software, 2012. Logos Edition.

Wommack, Andrew. *Discover the Keys to Staying Full of God*. Shippensburg: Pennsylvania: Harrison House Publishers, 2008. Kindle Edition.

---. *Spirit, Soul and Body*. Colorado Springs, Colorado: Andrew Wommack Ministries, 2005. Kindle Edition.

Wyatt, N. "Astarte." In *Dictionary of Deities and Demons in the Bible*. Edited by Karel van der Toorn, Bob Becking, and Pieter W. van der Horst, pp. 109–114. Leiden, Netherlands: Brill, 1999.

Your Weekend Show. "'We will become gods…' Yuval Noah Harari–WEF Advisor." *YouTube*. July 16, 2023. https://www.youtube.com/watch?v=XmS5rEKI3eQ&t=9s.

Zen Harvey, Warren. "Foreword: A Maimonidean Kabbalist." In *Abraham Abulafia's Esotericism*, pp. xi-xviii. Berlin: German: De Gruyter, 2020.

Zschech, Darlene, and Brian Houston. *Extravagant Worship: Holy, Holy, Holy Is the Lord God Almighty Who Was and Is, and Is to Come…*. Grand Rapids, Michigan: Bethany House, 2004. Logos Edition.

---. *Worship Changes Everything*. Ada, Michigan: Baker Publishing Group, 2015. Kindle Edition.

www.ingramcontent.com/pod-product-compliance
Lightning Source LLC
Chambersburg PA
CBHW072007070526
44583CB00015B/1371